Out of the Rain

For Doreen,
my wife and best friend,
and for our son, Stephen,
and our daughter, Sydney.

Out of the Rain

A prairie boy's struggle for a new life
in coastal British Columbia
1939 – 1949

Paul Jones

hancock house

ISBN 0-88839-541-8

Cataloging in Publication in Data

Jones, Paul, 1921–
    Out of the rain : a prairie boy's struggle for a new life in
coastal British Columbia, 1939–1949 / Paul Jones.

Includes index.
ISBN 0-88839-541-8

    1. Jones, Paul, 1921–. 2. Ocean Falls (B.C.)—Biography. 3.
Pacific Coast (B.C.)—Biography. 4. Canada. Royal Canadian
Navy—Biography. 5. World War, 1939–1945—Personal narratives,
Canadian. I. Title.

FC3849.O28Z49 2005   971.1'103'092   C2004-904887-2

Editor: Nancy Miller
Production: Mia Hancock
Cover Design: Rick Groenheyde

Front cover: Ocean Falls paper mill.
Back cover: *(From top)* Ocean Falls as seen from a boat entering the harbor; the wooden
streets and appartment buildings of Ocean Falls; Cecil and Kay Morrow, Dick Green and
author on Link Lake; Ocean Falls, looking past the booming grounds to the harbor exit.

We acknowledge the financial support of the Government of Canada through the
Book Publishing Industry Development Program (BPIDP) for our publishing activities.

Published simultaneously in Canada and the United States by

HANCOCK HOUSE PUBLISHERS LTD.
19313 Zero Avenue, Surrey, B.C. V3S 9R9
(604) 538-1114 Fax (604) 538-2262

HANCOCK HOUSE PUBLISHERS
1431 Harrison Avenue, Blaine, WA 98230-5005
(604) 538-1114 Fax (604) 538-2262
Web Site: www.hancockhouse.com *email:* sales@hancockhouse.com

Contents

Preface

The events described in this book are true. They occurred over the ten-year period 1939 to 1949. I wanted to write about them because, not only were they instrumental in shaping my life, but they occurred during a unique time in Canadian history: the winding down of the Great Depression, World War II and the immediate post-war recovery. However, when I finally got around to doing so, much had changed. The areas of Vancouver that I had frequented in 1938 and 1939 had altered dramatically. Ocean Falls, the pulp and paper town where I held my first full-time job and that all during the war I thought of as home, had all but ceased to exist, as had many of the people who dwelt there during my time. I found there was little left to refer to. As a consequence, I have had to rely heavily on memories, some of which are etched deeply, and exploring them was an emotional trip back in time.

Many of the people I encountered along the way occupy a special place in my heart. They have remained lifelong friends and by generously sharing their recollections, have helped in reconstructing the events of that period.

My special thanks to Ray and Carol Shorter for their patience, and for their understanding of what I was trying to accomplish. Also, my thanks to Peter and Betty Ward for reading the first draft of the manuscript.

CHAPTER 1

Vancouver

The Worldly Hope men set their Hearts upon
Turns Ashes—or it prospers; and anon,
Like Snow upon the Desert's dusty Face
Lighting a little Hour or two—was gone
— OMAR KHAYYAM

Vancouver, March, 1939. Cool dampness greets me as I open the door and reach for the milk on the porch. The bottle is cold and the cream is a rich yellow at the top. The line where it separates from the blue of the milk is well down on the curved shoulder. I am cheating, I know, and I feel the sharp teeth of guilt gnawing at me as I pour two-thirds of it onto my porridge. Then I replace the cap and invert the bottle to mix what is left. It will be thin milk with most of the cream gone, but nobody will notice—at least I tell myself that. Mother will complain that the dairy is delivering poor quality milk and that perhaps we should change to one of the other four or five whose huge gentle horses regularly clip-clop past the door in the early hours, but that's all that will happen.

I sit at the kitchen table eating. It is seven o'clock.

It is quiet in the house, just the ticking of the clock and the sighing of the kettle on the back of the stove. Even though I was a little careless and rattled the stove lids as I made the fire, no one stirred. Owen, my brother, was still fast asleep when I left our double bed in the basement. My sister, Olwyn's door is tightly closed. Our parent's door is ajar an inch or so, but there is no sign of life.

7

There is little to stimulate activity in our house in the morning.

Rain streaks the windows. It is a cold March rain out of a thick gray ceiling that hangs above the glistening rooftops. It will wet me through my threadbare windbreaker and the collection of sweaters and shirts under it. It will trickle down my neck from my worn cloth cap and shaggy mop of hair. Within a few minutes, before I have walked more than a dozen blocks, I will be wet. I will stay that way for the rest of the day unless the sun comes out—unlikely though it seems at the moment—or I can find somewhere warm to dry out. Perhaps the museum, with its desiccated artifacts, could benefit from some of my unwanted moisture, if it can be coaxed into leaving my soggy clothing. Maybe inside the huge cavern of the Canadian Pacific Steamship waiting room at Pier D it will be warm enough to dry me out a little or the CN railroad station—either one will do.

Today is my birthday. On this day I am eighteen. Nothing will be said about it though; birthdays are not something to celebrate in our house. Mother might remember. If she does she might mention it, but almost ruefully, as though she has failed me and it is her fault that I have grown almost to manhood without amounting to anything. On the one hand she will be right, so far I have amounted to nothing; but on the other hand it is not entirely her fault, or mine for that matter. Try though I might, I can't see where things could have been different...where I missed a turn that would have put me on a route to being something else, something of substance. I won't say anything about my birthday if nobody else does. It matters less to me than it does to Mother and she does not need a feeling of guilt on top of all else.

I leave almost furtively. If Father wakes, he will want me to make tea and bring it to his bedside. It will take time and I have to go to make my daily rounds, fruitless though I expect they will be.

I exit at the back of the house by the kitchen door, closing it carefully so that the glass panel doesn't rattle. It can't be locked from the outside; there are no keys. I go quietly down the wooden steps to the yard and around to the front of the house along the narrow path close to the foundations, then descend to the sidewalk. Nothing stirs on the street except the neighbor's spaniel who is up and about, checking milk bottles. The small tastes that sometimes ooze past the cardboard caps are worth the effort of climbing to each porch—at least he thinks so. He cruises slantwise down the sidewalk and eyes me, guiltily, as we pass. I pay him little attention; I don't want him to follow me. Let him stay home and have his treat. Only he and I will know that his warm velvety tongue has cleansed the top of every milk bottle on the block. I bury my head into my collar and walk quickly past the sleeping houses. The rain is already running down my neck. A hat with a brim is what I need.

Our street is only five blocks long. It cuts across the slope and all the houses on the upper side are high above the pavement and have flights of narrow wooden steps leading to front porches. There is a boring sameness about them: plain, tall, skinny houses on narrow lots. They have the look of hurried mass-production, built from the same set of plans—if indeed they were planned at all. Our house is in the middle of the block.

It is not our house, of course; it is the house we live in. We rent it from a tall cadaverous man named Green. Each month he climbs the front steps, his eyes running suspiciously over the weathered shingled exterior and the peeling white-painted trim. He sees the untended lawn and shrubbery, the fence with a few pickets missing surrounding it. His sour expression, the one he wears to collect the rent, is in place. He is firmly convinced that we are dedicated to the mistreatment of his house and are cleverly concealing the damage until we have gone somewhere else. He raps on the door and Father hands him twenty dollars. He does so hastily, nods and closes the door. He doesn't want Green to linger. He doesn't want to get into conversation with him. Say what has to be said, no more, and let him be gone. There is always the off chance that if given the slightest opening, Green will suggest an increase in rent.

Where the street ends, I turn left, up the hill. I follow the avenue to Main Street and round the corner. I pause under the shelter of the Windsor theater marquee as the rain increases to a downpour. The wind gusts into the entry, swirling gum wrappers, popcorn, cigarette butts and the torn stubs of tickets against the door. *Sweethearts*, starring Jeanette McDonald and Nelson Eddy, is playing. I squandered fifteen cents to see it the day before yesterday, not so much because it attracted me, but because the seats were comfortable. It was a warm, dry place to linger and avoid going home.

I don't know why, but this particular movie keeps running through my mind. It is not a great movie, in fact it is rather schmaltzy, but it has stayed with me far longer than some of the better ones I have seen. It is a fairytale yarn about clean, healthy, happy people living in comfort. No poverty, no illness, another way of life—a life I have not known. For a while, sitting there listening to them sing, I forgot the drabness of my existence. I dreamed, and when I awoke it was with a dread of going home and re-entering my world.

I look at the photographs decorating the entry and recreate the story. Depression wells upward in me. Somehow, I think, there must be a way to break out of the mold I'm in. There has to be more, a world where there is brightness and music. For others there is more. Why not me?

Still thinking about it, I wander back out into the drizzle that has subsided a little. I shiver. The cold fingers of rain have already probed through my layers.

Main Street has a few people. It is still early, but the small markets are open. The flowers are bright masses. There are shoppers huddled under umbrellas. They sort through the produce in boxes in front of the stores, intent on getting the fewest blemishes for their money while creating more with their careless handling. The grocers watch but don't complain; a customer is a customer and not to be found fault with.

I toy with the idea of snatching an apple, but then decide not to. If I can somehow earn enough to buy a bicycle, there is a chance that one of these markets may hire me to deliver groceries. I don't want them to remember me as a thief.

I have walked the length of Main Street, from home to the waterfront, hundreds of times. There is nothing new that takes my eye. I walk with my head down, skirting around the rain-dimpled puddles in the broken pavement. On the street alongside, the morning rush-hour traffic is building. Trams rattle and groan, their foot bells clanging, their motors whining and their trolleys flashing across connections with a frying sound. I pay little attention to the solemn, sleepy-eyed huddles waiting under umbrellas and water-streaked raincoats. They have the six-cent fare or a weekly pass. I have neither. I keep walking.

My destination is Cordova, Powell and Water Streets. The waterfront streets where small industries crowd together, sharing frontage with wholesale houses and cartage companies. I don't have a ready answer for why I go there, more habit than anything. And, I suppose, because by familiarity, I am comfortable there. I have come to know a few of the people who conduct business there, at least by sight, and I am able to predict their reaction as I approach them to inquire about work. By and large, they are sympathetic. I know, though, that I am but one of the hundreds seeking a day's work in the same area that they have to contend with. Nevertheless, I will go there on the off chance there will be someone who'll pay me for doing something...any kind of work. I go because there is nothing else in my life. If I don't go there, where else will I go? How will I use up the day?

I follow Main Street down the hill, past billboards, weedy vacant lots and car dealerships. One has a 1907 Brush touring car, a flimsy but intriguing conveyance. Above it, is a signboard that each day has a different quote or homily hung on its wires, in letters that dance in the wind. Today it explains the relationship between March winds and April showers...I know about both.

Automobiles rumble over the old brick street surfaces, their tires swishing in the wet. Their exhaust fumes hang heavy in the air.

At the CN station, I detour from the street and seek out a corner inside the cavernous building where warm air is issuing from a vent. I discovered this oasis during the winter. There is always warm air flowing from the vent. I am not curious as to where it comes from or why. I accept it. I turn in front of it, letting the warmth blow on all sides. It will take hours to dry off completely, but the loss of even a little moisture will help. The heat feels good, but I can't linger.

"Be there first thing in the morning, when they are opening up. If somebody doesn't show up for work, that's when there is the chance of being hired, even for a day."

I've heard it many times. It is the tenet of those seeking employment. Solid reasoning I suppose, but in this day and age people come to work even if they have to drag themselves there. Illness doesn't stop them. It seems only death keeps them away.

The trouble is, I don't have much to offer. My skills are those of the Alberta farming country: I can drive horses, stook grain, stack hay, but I don't know how to do things that are needed in a coastal city. I know nothing of electricity or plumbing. I know the rudiments of carpentry, but then so do most men, and some are expert carpenters. I can't drive a car or a truck. My frame is slight; I don't look robust enough to swing a pick or wheel a loaded wheelbarrow. Foremen look at me and select someone with more muscle. I have nothing to offer the business community. My education is little more than basic. Working with numbers, for me, is a slow and laborious process. My handwriting is legible, but I can't spell. I can work. Yes, work that doesn't require skill. I can lift and push and carry within the limits of my slight, undernourished frame, but I can't say I am this or that, or that I have command of some special ability. I haven't. If I look at myself objectively, all I see is someone with a willingness to work but little else. It is a tough sell to make a foreman believe that I can be useful if I have to say, "No, I don't know how to do that, but I can learn."

No one has ever shown me how to do anything beyond labor. No matter what the job, I will have to be shown and there are a great many men walking the streets of Vancouver who don't have to be shown. So I make the rounds, knowing that my chances of a job are practically nonexistent.

I leave the station and return to Main Street.

The Ivanhoe Hotel lobby is warm and dry. I ease into one of the leather chairs in a corner by the window, next to the steam radiator. The desk clerk eyes me over his glasses. He knows I'm not one of the patrons, but he doesn't say anything. If he does, I will explain that I am waiting to meet someone. He will know, of course, that I am not, but he will also know I won't be there long. He has seen me before. It is one of my regular stopping places to get out of the rain for a few minutes.

I feel an attachment to the Ivanhoe. It was the first home we had when we arrived in Vancouver almost a year ago.

The Alberta winter with its piercing cold, its unending stoking of fires and its gray boredom was left behind. We had seen the last of it when darkness shut down the view from the train window somewhere in the Rocky Mountains. When again it became light, the lush greenness of the Fraser Valley was rushing past.

As a family we had pulled up stakes and quit the quiet hamlet where my sister and brother and I had had our beginnings and our parents had failed in everything they attempted, until illness and poverty had finally gained the better of them and driven them out. The rumors were easy to believe—rumors that things were better at the coast. Vancouver. Ah, yes, Vancouver…things were better there. There was work there and wages for doing it.

"You won't have any trouble finding something," they had said to Father, "a clerical job or the like. Tell them you are a war veteran. They usually favor war veterans—maybe the post office, jobs like that, not too heavy. And your boys, they should be able to get something real quick…lots of work for guys that want it."

None of them, the people remaining behind, knew. Rumors. That's all they were—distorted half-truths drifting back. We had believed them, because we'd wanted to. Not that it mattered; we had to leave anyway.

Spring, unbelievable soft blossoming spring, met us. I immediately became a believer. If this was any indication, things were better at the coast. Groggy and heavy eyed from having sat for twenty-four hours in the hard seats of the day coach, heads padded with folded jackets and propped against windows, the clickety-clack of wheels ringing in our ears, we emerged squinting from the station into bright sunlight.

Suddenly, we were in a different world. There was warmth—more warmth than I would have thought possible for early March. Too warm for Alberta clothing; my Stanfields knit underwear was itchy, my wool shirt and jacket insufferably confining.

Across the square in front of the station, were splashes of daffodils and tulips, unbelievably bright after the remembered grayness. There were trees and shrubs in full flower, their pastel pinks, soft against acres of green lawn. Sunlight glinted on glass. The thick pungent air was soft with moisture and spiced with wood smoke, automobile exhaust and the unfamiliar breath of the sea, a sea yet concealed behind steel concrete and stone. In my mind's eye the coast had always meant ocean waves lapping at the doorsteps of houses arrayed along a golden beach. There was no sign of an ocean, or a beach, in any direction.

Our suitcases heavy in our hands, we stood slack, trying to bring the unfamiliar into focus. Each of us thinking, "Where are we? What relationship do we have to anything?" There was the train, but that relationship has just been severed, along with the last threads tying us to the life we had always known. We had just walked away from it. We didn't own its seats anymore.

"Where do you think we should go?" Mother asked, dispiritedly. She was exhausted; her face was ashen, almost as gray as her hair and the knitted beret covering it. There was also apprehension showing there, a fear of the unknown.

Weariness drives us to seek the security of home where we can restore ourselves. At that moment we had no home, not one place, anywhere in the world, where we could say we belonged. All that had been, was gone, irretrievably so. We knew there was no going back; that was out of the question. There was only going ahead, but to what? Security, a sense of place, that is what we sought.

"I don't know...a hotel, I guess." Father was no more confident than the rest of us, his face clouded with indecision. "I've never been here before. Yeah, I guess we'd better find a hotel. I don't know how far. Can you walk, Mother?"

"Yes. I'll be all right, but I can't hurry."

"I'll take your suitcase." Olwyn, concern on her face, took it from Mother's unresisting fingers.

We walked slowly toward the street, a busy thoroughfare where automobiles and streetcars hurried purposefully in both directions, with our worldly possessions tugging at our arms.

"That's a hotel, isn't it?" Olwyn pointed to a dull brick building facing the street. A tall vertical sign on its front said Ivanhoe.

"I wonder...it doesn't look very good," said Father. "I don't know what part of town we're in either. For sure, it doesn't look like the best part, but I suppose we could have a look."

Stale mustiness greeted us. The odors of beer, cigars, ammonia and coal smoke had, over the years, impregnated the very fabric of the place. There was dark varnished wainscoting, a backdrop for sagging, leather-covered chairs and bright brass spittoons. An elevator cage groaned. Its door, a simple grating, opened and emptied two men in suits into the lobby. An unbelievably thin man, pale as death and dressed in a blue suit, sat looking out the window. The desk clerk, a seedy little man with wispy hair peered at us suspiciously. Families didn't stay in the Ivanhoe; it was a hotel populated by single men and, occasionally, the women they brought for brief encounters. We didn't know that then, of course.

"Two dollars for double, one dollar for single," the clerk said.

Father looked at Mother. "It will have to be two doubles and one single, then," she said.

He nodded at the clerk. "Two doubles, one for me and the wife, one for the boys and a single for my daughter here. I don't know for how long, a few nights I would guess. We've just arrived on the train from Alberta," he said, unnecessarily, "...until we find a place."

There were brown metal beds covered with threadbare counterpanes, brown painted bureaus with scars on their fronts. Washbasins with black bruises and green corrosion on the brass taps. Alongside hung single, striped, worn and discolored towels. There were no other furnishings.

There was faded wallpaper, soiled tattered curtains and blinds hanging at odd angles. There were single bulbs suspended on twisted cords, from the middle of the ceilings. In the room Owen and I would share, there was a string attaching the pull-chain switch to the head of the bed. Owen tried it. He yanked on the string, turning the light on and off. "Hey! Look, electric light," he said, in wonder. He had never turned a light on before.

"Don't do that," Mother said. "You'll break it and you're wasting the light."

The small grimy window looked out toward the park in front of the station we just left. At the end of the hall was a toilet and beside it a room with a tub with claw feet. The linoleum under it was cracked and pieces were missing.

It was midmorning and we had not eaten since dinnertime yesterday. Next door was a café, the lettering on the window in Chinese. We entered a long thin room, almost like a railway coach, with small oilcloth-covered tables down each side. The food smells were unfamiliar, herbs and spices that were strange to me.

"A Chink dive," Father said suspiciously, sniffing. He had intolerance for anyone not of British ancestry. Orientals, he considered lesser beings, almost joke people.

"We need three tables, John," he said to the waiter who shuffled toward us on slippered feet. (Later I was to learn he always addressed all Chinese as "John.")

Now, a year later, the narrow building is unchanged and the fare is probably not improved. My mouth remembers the taste of the thin, greasy soup.

Alongside, and on up the street, is the same assortment of gray, weathered buildings housing businesses: plumbing shops, second-hand stores spilling their wears onto the sidewalk; junkyards cheek by jowl with Gypsy fortune-telling parlors presided over by big women in colored dresses and head scarves; and gloomy windows behind which might lurk anything. Across the street is a fortresslike building with B.C. Electric inscribed into the stone above the door; from it comes a mysterious low humming. There are no windows through which I can see what goes on inside, but I am curious and uneasy about the eerie sound.

The rain is easing and the north-shore mountains separate from the clouds. The shipper at Malkins shakes his head. He has seen me coming and I'm sure he recognizes me. "No, nothing today." He says it almost guiltily, as though he has plenty of jobs, but doesn't want to hire me. He disappears into his phone-booth size office by the double doors of the warehouse. We have gone through the same routine every morning for weeks with the same result.

Kelly Douglas, farther along the street, is the same. The thin, harried man doesn't speak; he just shakes his head. He has shaken his head at a number of desperate jobseekers before me and will keep shaking it as long as the parade continues.

At Superior Transfer, a trucking firm with one aged truck, a pile of firewood lies on the sidewalk. It is freshly cut fir slab-wood. A big beefy, man with metal driver's license tags armoring the band of his peaked cap, is inside a small warehouse-office, sitting tilted back in his chair behind a scuffed desk on which a thin sheaf of paper is spitted on a vertical spike. There is a black cast-iron heater with a pipe wandering across the ceiling to the outside, but there is not much else in the room. The truck is parked at the curb.

I pause inside the door. "Do you need any help today?" I ask,

16

almost hesitantly. I am so certain that he will say no, that I start to leave before he answers. He looks at me speculatively, measuring my usefulness, my slight figure in rain darkened windbreaker and jeans wet almost up to the knees. He smiles and removes a cigarette from his mouth, throws it on the floor and grinds it with the toe of his boot.

"You a truck driver?"

"No, but I've worked on lots of trucks. I can work," I say, eagerly.

"What kind of trucks? What were you hauling?"

"In Alberta I worked hauling grain and hay. I can shovel grain and I've humped lots of bailed hay."

He thinks for a moment. "Grain and hay is something we sure have a lot of down here on Water Street." He says it sarcastically. "But, you really want a job, 'eh?" He smiles as though he has some wonderful proposition for me.

"Yeah, I do. I'll do anything."

"Yeah? Anything, 'eh? Well. You see that pile of firewood out there? I'll give you fifteen cents to bring it in and pile it against the wall there." He points to a blank wall near the warehouse door.

I eye the pile. "There's a lot of wood there. Maybe, more than a cord, like." I say. "Fifteen cents? How about a quarter?"

"Ha! I knew it. Go on...get out of here! You say you want a job, and when I offer you one you want to dicker the price. You some kind of a union man maybe? Fifteen cents, union man, that's all." Disgust twists his mouth. "And it's gotta be piled so it don't fall down."

"I was wanting a job on a truck," I say.

"Yeah. I know what you was wanting all right. You're like all the rest. You just think you want to ride around in a truck all day. Well. I need that wood piled. You want it or not?"

"Yeah. I'll do it."

The wood is heavy, green fir with the bark on, and it is wet. Slivers, hundreds of fir-bark slivers that I can't see, bristle my hands. It takes me a couple of hours. The truck never moves from the curb.

The big man shakes the pile to see if he can make it fall down. I know it won't; I've piled too much wood to make a rickety pile.

"I said ten cents, didn't I?" he says, looking at me slantwise.

I get a stab in my middle. If he decides to pay me only a dime, or for that matter, nothing at all, what can I do about it?

"You said fifteen cents."

"Why would I say fifteen cents when the job is only worth a dime? Now why would I? Tell me that."

"The job is worth at least a quarter, but you said you'd only give me fifteen cents."

"Yeah? Well...oh, all right. I was only kidding. Here's the fifteen cents, Union Man."

"Thanks. Ah...how about a job on your truck."

"Sure. Check with me sometime. I might have a job. Oh yeah, I forgot. Did you sweep off the sidewalk?" He hands me a broom from a corner.

I look questioningly at him to see if he is joking. He isn't. He means it. A job on his truck may hang in the balance. I sweep the sawdust into the gutter.

The rain has finally ceased and I have fifteen cents in my pocket, fifteen cents that I could easily be relieved of if any one of the dozens of desperate hard-eyed men lounging in the neighborhood suspect that I have it. The day is not a total loss.

I am hungry, but I shy away from the thought of spending money on something to eat. There are more important things. Money is to savor for a few hours. As long as it is in my pocket I can dream. It is for such things as movies, to buy a few hours of fantasy.

I pry a couple of carrots from between the slats of a crate on the back of a flat-deck vegetable truck.

Finding our way, for Owen and me, came in stages, starting at the Ivanhoe. The sunshine didn't last. Rain, soaking drizzling rain, came easing in from an ocean we had yet to see. Unlike the sudden downpours of Alberta that we were used to, where we scurried like chickens for cover until it passed, this was a thick soupy atmosphere to wallow in, wetter by far than any Alberta rain. There was no avoiding it.

At first, they were brief excursions, within a few blocks of the hotel. The newness of everything hemmed us in on all sides:

strange faces, strange tongues, strange sights. For us, having lived our entire lives where there were no mysteries, where we knew every last building inside and out, every last person and all their relatives and who their ancestors were, everything had a mind-shattering strangeness. Find work in this huge teeming metropolis? Where to start?

We discover that there are thousands of young men here, all looking for work. Where are the great rainforests where rumor had it, there was work for lusty young men? They are certainly not here on Main Street. We become bolder. We venture farther afield, all the way to the waterfront where we catch our first glimpse of saltwater—disappointing, it looks little different from a lake. But there is so much of fascination that actually seeking a job is forgotten. Instead, we spend our days wandering from one marvelously new experience to another.

When we arrive back, we are looked at with suspicion. Have we been looking for work? Father doubts it. "Well we'd better get at it. We'd better pull our weight. Money doesn't grow on trees, you know."

We moved from the Ivanhoe, after five days, to a tall narrow house on Eighth Avenue. A musty, woody smell pervades it, and a fine coating of ash overlays the furnishing. We discover it comes from a huge sawdust-burning furnace, with octopuslike pipes reaching in all directions, sulking in the basement. We occupy two floors. The landlord, a lanky, dour man named Sykes, retains a bedroom on the third floor, but also seems to have retained the right to invade any part of the rest of the house, day or night, whenever he is so inclined. We find him in the kitchen making a cup of tea or sitting on the sofa reading the paper. Father has given him a month's rent, so we put up with him. He doesn't say much that isn't a complaint. One complaint, however, turns into a shouting match that disrupts the quiet of a Sunday evening.

To us, electricity was a novelty. Back home, we'd never had anything electrical. Only the garage and one house had electricity. The rest, ours included, used oil lamps. Nobody had electrical appliances. The local general store, however, had a telephone that used batteries—fat, round, cardboard-encased batteries that occasionally ran down and were thrown into the alley behind the store.

Owen had retrieved a clutch of these one day and discovered that there was enough residual life to make a spark by touching a piece of wire to the posts. From making a spark he went to making an electromagnet by wrapping wire around a nail, and then to fashioning a little motor out of bits of tin and wire, the directions for both he'd found in the encyclopedia at school.

The motor had never quite worked but he'd brought it with him, without batteries. Figuring that electricity was electricity, and one source was as good as another, he poked the ends of the wires into a wall outlet in the kitchen. There was a flash, a ripping sound, a quantity of acrid smoke and Owen was thrown halfway across the room. The motor, reduced to a smoking ingot, was occupying a singed spot on the linoleum. The house was suddenly dark and the radio silent.

Footsteps clattered on the stairs. Sykes began hollering before he reached the bottom flight. The upshot was, Father had to fork out twenty-five cents for fuses.

The museum is one of our first major finds. The hub of Hastings and Main, it costs nothing to enter and becomes a place to linger, out of the rain. Owen discovers Louis Riel's rifle lying in a case and is mesmerized by it. It is scratched and worn—we assume by the actual hands of that long dead Metis martyr. Owen is fascinated to the point I leave him there gazing at it. He returns day after day to look at it.

It is the waterfront that draws me. I stand for hours, leaning on the cold, dripping, metal fence rails, looking at watercraft and dreaming.

There are the great Empress Line passenger ships to look at, freighters, towboats and myriad small, scurrying harbor craft. And there are still the remnants of the great days of sail. They are just hulls now, their white ballooning wings clipped, their masts and upper-works gone. Stripped of their glory, they are little more than black beasts of burden loaded with coal and timber and led around by towboats. I feel sadness and shame for them, for their ignominy. Few will last out the decade; they will be claimed by the sea or some mishap will put them on an up-coast shoal where they will quietly rot away. But still, they bear faint traces of the shipbuilders' art. On transoms and horn timbers I see wonderfully carved scrolls and figureheads—their gilding and paint dulled and peeling under layers of coal dust and industrial grime. Once breathtakingly beautiful, these ships trod the sea lanes in splendor, many made famous by "rounding the Horn" in record time competing in the great grain races. Now they wait as the cancerous onslaught of decay writes *finis* to an all but forgotten age.

The romantic streak within me feeds on sights such as these. I drift along the waterfront. At the North Vancouver ferry dock I stop to watch a wood carver at work. He makes wooden spoons and articulating birds that hang suspended from the eaves of the terminal building and fly in the wind, all from packing-box wood. He sells them to the ferry passengers for a few cents. He shows me the tools he uses: old files cleverly bent and sharpened. For awhile I watch him carve. Maybe if I can just find an old file and sharpen it...

I turn up Main Street heading for home. Today has been marginally better than yesterday and the day before. I have fifteen cents in my pocket. I decide not to blow it on a movie. Instead, it will buy me a small measure of approval when I get home.

Williams Concrete is at the end of False Creek. I have passed it each day both coming and going, but have ignored it, mainly because its buildings look gloomy and forbidding, like a penitentiary. I have no idea what they do there. Today something prompts me to investigate and, even though it is at the end of the work day, I go. There is always the off chance that whoever runs the place may need someone tomorrow.

The timber buildings are the gray of cement and the ground surrounding them is awash in a slurry of cement and mud. A man whose clothes are also gray with cement is assembling something from wood under a shelter beside a loading dock.

"Here. Hold this," he says by way of greeting.

There are four pieces that he is trying to fasten together to form a square. I grab on to two of them and hold them together while he bangs in a nail. His tongue curls from the side of his mouth as he concentrates. I haven't yet said anything.

"Shit!" He says, in exasperation as the wood splits. There are several more like pieces on the floor, all split. He throws down his hammer.

"You got anything to do tomorrow?" he asks.

"No. Just looking for work," I say.

"Be here at eight." With that he walks away.

I've got a job without asking.

I am waiting at the door when the man with the cement-impregnated clothing arrives. I have brought lunch—a peanut butter sandwich. I expect to work all day. How much I will be paid, I don't speculate on.

We start where we left off yesterday. Today he is a little more communicative, but not much.

"What am I supposed to call you?" he asks.

"I'm Paul Jones, but just call me Paul."

He chews that over. "Well, look at that, a famous name. Mister Paul Jones, is it. Well, Mister Paul, I hope you can work."

"Yeah, I can work. Just tell me what you want me to do, and, ah, what's your name?"

He looks sideways at me and gets a strange look in his eyes. A sly conspiratorial smile draws at his mouth and he glances around as though checking for eavesdroppers. Then he says, "I am known as the Spider. Yep. That's me, the Spider."

"Oh yeah," I say, inanely. He looks less like a spider than anyone I've ever seen. He has the thick body of a spider, all right, but his legs are far too short for it, making him almost a dwarf. The legs of his bib overalls sag over his boots, even though they are rolled up several times, and even then, the backs are all tattered where they drag on the ground. He has a round moon face overhung by bushy eyebrows. They partly conceal little squinty eyes peering through black-rimmed spectacles held together on his nose by tape. The lenses are spotted with cement. Thick hair sprouts from his ears and hangs like stalactites from his nostrils. Try as I might, I can't visualize him poised in a web ready to pounce. Anyway, his clothing is so brittle with cement it would be impossible to sneak up on anything; it crackles when he moves. His cement-covered hat alone must weigh a couple of pounds.

His smile disappears and he is suddenly serious. "Never mind about that," he says, "we've got work to do. We've got a bunch of forms to make, so you better get started."

I'm standing there, wanting to pitch in, but without the faintest idea of what he wants. He looks at me for a few moments and then it dawns on him he hasn't told me anything. He takes a deep breath of exasperation.

"Here. This is what we gotta do," he says, impatiently.

I get the idea that paving slabs is what he wants to make, eighteen inches square and an inch and a half thick. The forms for these are what he was attempting to make yesterday without much success. Today he has a different approach.

"What you gotta do is fasten these pieces of two-by-two together in a square, like we was trying to do yesterday, only today we're gonna use hinges," He says it triumphantly, as though he's made a major breakthrough in the science of carpentry. "There should be enough wood here to make a dozen or so forms." He points at a pile of ready-cut pieces. "And here's a bag full of hinges and screws. So go ahead. It shouldn't take you long." That said, he goes stumping off, his stubby legs making him roll like a beached sailor, into the gloom of the building.

Right away I know I'm in trouble; the screws are too big and the wood too brittle, but I try. The only tools are a hammer and a screwdriver with a worn tip and chunk missing from the wooden handle. I try tapping a screw into the wood and then turning it. The wood splits with a loud crack. I look around, guiltily. I have ruined a piece of wood. I find a nail and make a starter hole and then try twisting a screw into it. Again it splits.

After awhile I have a pile of split wood on the floor. I'm worried. I want to make these forms. It's a job needing some skill and I want badly to prove, if only to myself, that I can do it. I am sweating a little with effort. No matter what I do, though, the wood just splits.

I'm standing there helpless, trying to figure out what to do, when Spider comes back.

He looks at the pile of split wood.

"Well mister whatever-you-call-yourself Jones, You're not much of a carpenter, are you."

From somewhere within me anger ignites and swirls upwards. He's given me an impossible task and now is criticizing me for not accomplishing it. I almost shout at him.

"There's no way anybody's going to get these great big screws

23

into these little pieces of wood without splitting it."

That startles him. His face clouds and he looks thoughtful.

"Well, there's gotta be a way," he says. "I gotta have some kind of forms that I can take apart, like unwrap them. You got any good ideas then?"

I simmer down. "Maybe if you had some way of making a hole first to put the screws in, maybe the wood wouldn't split," I say.

He ruminates for a moment. "Hey, why not? That's a good idea. Where'd you get an idea like that?"

"I saw a carpenter do it one time. It worked for him. Have you got any kind of a drill or something?"

He gives me that sly conspiratorial look again.

"Maybe I have, just maybe." He scurries away. I see him rummaging in a cupboard to one side of the dock.

In a few moments he comes back carrying a breast-drill, one with huge hand-crank on the side. It's pretty clogged with rust and cement.

"This here oughta do the job," he says, enthusiastically.

"You got any drills to put in it?" I ask.

That stops him. He thinks for a minute.

"Can't you just..."

"How are you going to drill a hole without a drill? Haven't you got any little drill bits to put in it?"

"God dammit! Ain't you ever satisfied, Mister Paul whatever in hell your name is?" He whirls and goes stamping off. I hear him banging around somewhere in back and then he reappears holding a handful of rusty drills.

"Here Mister Jones, whatever. Is there anything else I can get for you? Maybe a cup of tea or something? Now, I better see some production round here, or by golly..." The remote clanging of a telephone from the gloom of the building sends him scurrying.

It isn't the easiest thing in the world to get a bit fastened into the chuck, and the way it is clogged up, it is hard to turn and hold the wood at the same time, but I manage it.

I actually to get a form put together the way I think Spider wants it. I work through the morning by myself. Spider ignores me. I see him occasionally, but he is occupied with other things. Now and then a truck appears and backs against the loading dock and

24

gets loaded up with concrete blocks and such. Spider operates a big overhead crane to load them—he seems to be the only employee—then they grind away to somewhere within the city.

Twelve o'clock and an orchestra of whistles blares from the sawmills along False Creek. I sit munching on my sandwich and eyeing my morning's labor. I decide I haven't yet achieved the skill of a cabinetmaker, but I am pleased with myself. I have used up most of the cut wood and depleted the bag of hinges. Spider comes by, a toothpick hanging from his mouth. He looks at the pile of forms.

"Well, well, Mister Paul, whatever you said your name was..." He sort of trails off. He scuffs his feet as though embarrassed. Then he says, "I hope what I showed you here today will come in handy sometime. You should always listen to guys like me; you can learn a lot." He reaches into his pocket, takes out a dollar bill and hands it to me.

"I won't need you no more. That's all I wanted, stick these few forms together." He doesn't look at me. His eyes wander everywhere else.

It's like he's hit me in my midsection.

"I thought you wanted me to work all day...maybe all the time," I say. "Not just this morning."

"Naw. We don't need nobody all the time. The dollar's for your trouble, and like I said, I hope you learned something."

"Maybe, maybe when you get something else?"

"Yeah. Maybe."

The sun is out and it is too early to go home. I walk along the False Creek waterfront and look at the boats, a feeling of frustration hanging on me. It was a forlorn hope that any job would last, even as long as a day. Tomorrow I will again be making the rounds of the wholesale houses.

But then maybe, like Spider said, I have learned something. I have learned, but not from him. I have called up a forgotten piece of knowledge and I have shown someone how to do something: I have shown Spider how to get a big screw into a small piece of wood. Maybe I do have something to offer.

Anyway, I now have a dollar in my pocket.

25

CHAPTER 2

Carved in Stone

The innermost end of False Creek is buffered from the hustle of Main Street by a barrier of dilapidated buildings that lean, but remain wearily upright, buttressed by their very nearness to one another. They front on the sidewalk, insulated from it by a thin fabric of weeds that find sustenance in the debris between the walls and the paving. Most are faceless, their peeling facades giving little indication of what, if anything, might go on inside them.

One, however, a rancid yellow stucco job, with black glassless windows through which tides of pigeons ebb and flow and whose accumulated droppings have dried into abstract frescos on the walls below, bears a sign that says "E. A. & C. H. McDonald, Stonecutters."

I ease cautiously through the man-door that is inset into the big roll-up that admits trucks from the street. Spring-loaded, it slams shut behind me, sending shock waves ricocheting between the metal trusses high in the shadowy upper reaches.

It is cool and damp inside, and gloomy, lit only by the light filtering in from the high windows and the remote end that is open. Somewhere water runs, its trickling seeming to come from several directions. I cast around, looking for an office. I don't see one right away but then locate it half way down the south wall, hidden behind piles of stone.

There is stone everywhere, a vast confusion of sizes and shapes, but all of the same general color, that of beach sand on a cloudy day. There are gigantic glowering blocks still bearing the rough-hewn faces and concave drill markings of the quarry. Some lie haphazardly under the crane rails that run the length of the building and extend out over False Creek, dumped there when they were unloaded from barges. And some wait on trolleys, to be drawn into gang saws that, at the moment, are silent. There are several of these odd-looking saws, with up to a half-dozen blades in each. Flimsy contraptions, they hover spiderlike on spindly legs over the steel trolley rails, waiting to pounce on the next block offered. To my eye, none of them seem robust enough to perform surgery on these huge monoliths, some of which would dwarf an average moving van. Their blades are rusted and without visible serrations, and I wonder how saws without teeth can cut their way through solid stone. Obviously they can, though; one is stalled part way through a block, as if it had given up and died midstroke. Water runs over it, down through the saw cuts and over the trolley to form small rivulets that wander away toward False Creek.

There are other blocks, finished in neat manageable rectangles, with clean-cut faces, stacked by the door. They are waiting, I suppose, to be transported to somewhere within the city, to become a bank building, or perhaps a part of the new city hall that is now visible, rising above the houses on Twelfth Avenue.

I move tentatively toward the fluorescent-lit office. I may be rebuffed, but then again, there may be some menial task needing unskilled hands. I'm willing to risk being snapped at or sent on my way with barely a headshake.

I suddenly realize that a clattering I've been hearing isn't coming from the street; the noise is coming from inside the building, from somewhere beyond the mountain range of stone. I change direction and make my way toward it through the maze of narrow canyons between the blocks. There are no floors, just a thick carpet of stone chips that crunch underfoot.

The noise comes from a remote corner, lit by shaded hanging lights, where three elderly gnomelike men in leather aprons are working with tiny air-driven chisels, the staccato bark of which echoes sharply in the cavernous space. If they notice me, they don't let on. I move close, but remain in the shadows, just outside the perimeter of light, and settle onto a block of stone to watch them.

I have become an accomplished watcher over these past

months. And I have learned that as long as I don't interfere or get in the way, I will usually be ignored.

Here, there is little need for concern. The three—who could be brothers, even triplets, and all of childlike stature—seem proof to any distraction. To them nothing exists beyond the cones of light that hang tentlike over them. They are carving designs in large stone tablets.

Art in any form intrigues me, but this more than anything I've encountered face to face, fires my imagination. I've never seen anything comparable to it. As I watch, I too become oblivious to my surroundings.

That stone can be carved, and that it has been for thousands of years, is something I have known, but not given much thought to. In fact, how it is done, or by whom, has never really crossed my mind. I know, of course, like anyone who has ever looked at pictures of European cities, that the ancient Greeks and Romans carved great pillars and statues. Now, here, in this cold draughty, morguelike building, devoid of sunlight and inspiration, an ancient art is being practiced, and it fascinates me. These three small men are patiently bringing forth wonderfully intricate designs from the raw stone, the very same cold, lifeless stone as that on which I sit.

There is nothing of the flamboyant artist about them. They are drab little men in drab clothing going about their business in the shadowy underworld of this shabby building, away from the eyes of the public. At the moment, I am their only audience. They don't talk. They don't even glance around. Their attention is devoted entirely to their carving. They move slowly and deliberately, as befits their age, carefully guiding the points of their tiny chattering chisels as they would charcoal sticks or pencils, drawing on the stone. They pause now and then, but only to clear away the debris with jets from their air hoses and to compare their incising with the full-size drawings they are copying from paper. Dust covers their clothing and whitens their faces and beards.

They are carving murals, huge pictures in stone—each man with his own—on massive sawn blocks slanted on stacked timbers. They climb arthritically, and then, amazingly, hang like monkeys from ladders and scaffolds, reaching out from above to work on the upper corners. Their air hoses, like dusty entrails from some mammoth carcass, are a writhing mass on the floor below.

On one, fishermen pull nets heavy with fish, each scale, and each strand of netting beautifully distinct, and each wave highlighted and seeming to flow across the surface of the stone. There is another with forest-covered mountains, and loggers swinging axes and wielding saws, and yet another with miners with upraised picks and laden shovels. All are done in bas-relief, in wondrous minute detail.

My mind, totally immersed, dismisses the glass-enclosed office and inquiring about work from the two men dressed in white shirts and ties whose heads are bent over desks. Instead, I sit on their hard raw merchandise and watch these diminutive elfin artisans work their magic in stone.

For the last month I have frequented the shores of False Creek. I have squirmed between buildings, picked my way through junkyards and walked on boom logs all the way from Main Street to Burrard, and on both sides of the inlet. As the rains of winter gradually gave way to the sunshine of March, I gravitated here, seeking this waterfront as a change from the docks and the jumble of commercial enterprises sandwiched between them and the Canadian Pacific railway tracks, practically all the way from the waters edge to Hastings Street and from Stanley Park into East Vancouver.

I finally realized that seeking employment, playing the squeaky wheel, in the untidy wholesale and factory district crowded along Water, Powell and Cordova Streets was gaining me little more than worn shoe leather. Lately, I have spent most of my days here, along False Creek, even though it has proven no more productive.

It was not just the fruitlessness, the boredom, of searching the skid row environment with its depressing down at the heel atmosphere that propelled me here; I had finally encountered a deviate side of humanity that I was unaware existed. The meaning of what transpired I wasn't actually clear on, but it confused me. It made me insecure, where, until now, I had never felt even the slightest sense of insecurity. It, more than anything, drove me out.

I should have expected it, I suppose, but nothing had prepared me. In my innocence, I had wandered freely in the seediest, most disreputable neighborhoods, unconcerned by those I rubbed shoulders with. I had assumed that the people here in the city were no different to those I had always known in the tiny Alberta hamlet where I was raised. It never occurred to me that among them were some who might behave differently. I guessed—if I thought about it at all—that they were, just ordinary people, hard up, but basically the same as those I'd always known. After all, poverty was not a behavioral characteristic; it was a condition over which few of us had any control. On the streets I usually frequented, it was painfully apparent—the lack of nourishment; downcast eyes devoid of pride or even hope; soiled, tattered, ill-fitting clothing; shaggy hair and beards. I assumed I was not markedly different from any of them beyond the fact that they were there, like me, seeking a day's work. It never occurred to me to delve into personalities or analyze behavior. For one thing, I knew hardly anyone. Nothing had conditioned me to be wary. What was there to be concerned about? I had nothing worth stealing.

He came up behind me. I saw him first only as a reflection in the glass of Harkley and Heywood's window. Then his body came against mine and his arms extended either side of me, his hands against the glass, imprisoning me between them. He crowded me, pushing me against the window. His breath was hot on the back of my neck. I smelled its tobacco taint and his barbershop talcum.

The sudden physical contact surprised me, but for the moment it didn't really alarm me. On the contrary, it flashed through my mind that it was someone I knew, someone just fooling around—a latent thought, a hangover from home. But there was nothing about the face reflected in the glass that I recognized.

Still not alarmed, but with an urge to be free of him, I acted instinctively. I dropped down, turned and squirmed out from between him and the window. I dodged clear and then turned to look at him.

"Hey! What the...," I started to ask. Then, "What...what's going on?" Then I saw he was smiling.

"Sorry," he said. "I didn't mean nothing."

"Oh, yeah," I said, confused. Then, "Okay," and started to walk away, troubled because I didn't know what had prompted this sudden physical contact from a stranger.

"Just a minute," he said. "I been watching you. You seem

maybe like a nice boy. Don't run away." He smiled again. "Where are you going, anyway. If you got any time, why don't we talk...just get to know each other. Just talk...you got nowhere to go, right?"

He spoke quietly, friendly like, a deep voice with just the trace of an accent. He held out his hand as though wanting to shake or keep me from leaving.

He was a big man, clean-shaven, with broad Slavic features. He was better dressed than the usual down here. His clothes were clean and without patches—a checkered shirt, blue jeans and a windbreaker. His gray felt hat looked almost new.

My wariness filtered away. There was really nothing about him to trigger alarm, not his appearance or the way he spoke. But there was something...I didn't know.

"No. I don't have anywhere special to go," I said. "I'm just going to some of these places...looking for work. You know, asking if they're hiring anybody."

"You want a job?" He looked surprised. "What you need a job for? A nice boy like you shouldn't have any trouble finding work. What kind of work you want, something special you want, 'eh?"

"No, nothing special, just work...any kind. But nobody seems to be hiring. Uh...do you have a job?"

"Me? Oh yeah. Sure. I got a job." He smiled, but didn't look at me as he said it.

"Where do you work? What do you do?"

"I work all over. I got all kinda jobs." He gestured vaguely. "Work ain't hard to get."

"Where. I mean...how did you get all these jobs?"

"It's easy. You want a job? I can fix it for you."

"How? You know some place that's hiring?"

"Sure. I got a list. I know lots of places where you could work. I got a pretty good list. It's up in my room. I could show you if you want. I could help. Yeah, a job, that's easy."

I wasn't thinking straight. If he had lots of jobs, why wasn't he at work? I was that desperate that I clutched like a drowning man at a straw at the slightest suggestion of help.

"Yeah. Well...I wouldn't mind having a look at it. Where's your room?"

"Along here." He indicated the street. "Come on. We'll go have a look. It's not far, up on Main."

His room was above a smoke shop, across from the Star Theater on Main Street. We went up a back stairs that creaked. The handrail was broken, partly missing.

It was a small room with one window that looked out on the street. There wasn't much in it—a double bed, a straight-back chair, a dresser, its top cluttered with papers and magazines, and a shelf in the corner with clothing hanging on a rod underneath.

He took off his coat, threw it on the chair and then sat down on the bed.

"Take off your coat," he said. "Sit. Here." He indicated a space beside him. He wanted me to sit close to him.

"Where's the list...the jobs?" I asked. I felt uneasy, something about this beefy man wasn't right. He sat looking at me, smiling, his eyes half closed.

"We'll find it."

I moved to the window and looked out. The bed creaked and he was behind me, his thick arms wrapped around me. I could feel his thick body all the way down and his face, over my shoulder, against mine, his whiskers rough against my cheek. He kissed me.

I panicked. No man, not even my father, had ever put his arms around me and kissed me. I was stifled and desperate to escape. I jammed my boot on his instep and came down hard. He yelled something, like a curse. I twisted and he let go. I made for the door.

He followed me after that for days. He seemed to be wherever I was. I would be looking in a window and he would appear behind me, or I would glance back and he was there. Always he was there.

I explained to Father what had happened, in a stilted fashion, not exactly knowing what I was trying to tell him. We were at the kitchen table playing checkers. He looked around, as though this sparsely furnished room might conceal eavesdroppers. His face flushed with embarrassment.

"God damn it, boy! Don't you know better than to hang around with guys like that?" he said, not looking at me.

"Guys like what?" I asked.

"You know what I'm talking about. Those kind of guys. Stay away from them."

False Creek is a busy place, a brawling untidy collection of raw industries. A place where people work, and where, I have come to believe that there has to be work for me, if I can just once be standing at the right door at the right time.

It is a place with many things to look at as well. And when, after days of fruitless searching, when I am frustrated and depressed by refusals, by my inability to gain admittance, to crack the impervious shell that seems to protect the whole grime-encrusted area from me, I sit, soaking up sunshine, watching, listening and feeling.

There is energy here, in this unique place that is False Creek's waterfront. There is a vibrancy in the rough interleaving of industry and commerce. I feel it pulsing around me. And strangely, there is also an urge, upwelling though ill defined, to somehow capture and keep the images of it, either with paint canvas and brush or with paper and pencil. I have none of these things, of course, and would have only the vaguest idea how to apply them if I had them. So I sit, content to observe, yet, at the same time, frustrated that I cannot become part of it or record any of it.

I am usually hungry. There is little between my breakfast porridge and supper. I am lonely, too. I have to admit, to the point that I am sometimes homesick for the close-knit friendships of the Alberta town that, a year ago, seemed so dreary and without inspiration. Here I have no one that I can say is my friend. Even my brother, Owen, no longer accompanies me. He has long since given up the search. "Who is going to hire a sixteen-year-old?" he says. He is right.

What he does with his time I no longer ask, but there is a growing tension between him and Father. All is not well there, I know.

I have met other young men. All are searching for employment. I am suspicious of them as they are of me. We are fiercely territorial. We each have what we consider to be our own trap lines, the industries that we have marked as our own, that, if we keep at them, appearing often enough at their doors, one day one of them will hire us. So we don't get close to one another. We don't become friends. We pass the time of day, but that is all.

"Do you think there's any chance of anything at any of these places?" asked Andrew, in his quiet British voice a few weeks ago.

33

He was a pinch-faced man in his twenties who wore an over-coat and scarf even on the warmest days. "Nowhere to leave them without them being stolen," he had said.

"Yes." And I told him about the foreman at the shingle mill who had told me that they might hire someone within the next few days. He wished me luck.

The following morning he was there talking to the foreman when I arrived. He wouldn't look at me as we passed.

If the foreman eventually hired anyone, it was neither of us. We encountered each other in the days following, but we didn't speak.

I sit by myself absorbing the sights and sounds of this place, this False Creek that is neither false nor a creek.

There are sawmills with tall, blackened smoke stacks soaring above rough, weathered buildings. There is blue smoke eddying upward from beehive burners and there is the blinding whiteness of fresh-sawn lumber. There are foreshores padded with the residue of years—decaying bark, sawdust and slabs—and with the intriguing skeletal remains of machinery strewn on them, rusting away in the salt air. There are log booms, boat yards, warehouses and wharves. There are forests of masts and trolling poles standing tall over moored fishing boats. There are small tugboats, like terriers, wor-rying booms and barges, herding them for the sake of doing so, seemingly without plan or direction. There are pilings and the cable-bound clusters of dolphins left from long forgotten ventures, on which sea gulls perch, standing one-legged and dozing or gos-siping raucously with those wheeling above.

And, mirrored, on the oil-slick surface of the water are the reflections of the swing spans of the Cambie and Granville Street bridges.

Over the entire area hangs the pungency of industry—wood smoke, freshly cut fir and cedar, coal gas, paint and the oily tang of hot tar. All are blended with the ageless salty smell of the inlet— shellfish cooking in the sun, seaweed and the sour fermentation of the harbor bottom at low tide.

It is here I have spent my days, looking for work, but also just sitting and dreaming. I have watched the agile boom-men in their stagged-off tin pants and high-topped boots bristling with caulks (I would give my eye teeth for a pair of those boots) culling logs from the booms, much like cowboys cutting cattle from a herd. The sun glints from the hand-slicked shafts of their pike poles as they balance themselves and cat-foot across the floating crosshatch of logs—so fast that small sticks don't have time to sink under them. They lean, straining against the points stabbed deeply into the thick bark of the firs, cedars and massive hemlocks, steering them onto the teeth of the clattering jack ladders that claw them, black and glistening, from the water. Chains and bogies groan under their water-soaked weight as they are drawn upward, and inexorably toward the great saws whistling hungrily beyond the dark gaping doors in the ends of the buildings—their last moments identifiable as trees from the forests.

I have listened to the singing of head-saws, the rattling of conveyor chains and the whine of planer blades. I have heard the chug, chug of one-lung engines and watched boats depart down-channel for the open sea, and I have yearned to go with them. I have talked with fishermen sitting in the cockpits of their boats, sipping their morning coffee. They have told me tales of the upper coast, of handlogging in remote inlets, of crab fishing and of salmon trolling in the great rollers of the outer coast—fuel for the fires of my imagination.

And yes, I have worked. I have had a few jobs, not many, but I have earned the odd dollar, enough to provide grudging proof at home that I have not been entirely idle, that I have been looking for work.

For two days I shoveled sawdust. The gods of chance had nodded in my direction, at my habitual perch on the end of a lumber pile, from which vantage I could watch the carriages feeding logs to the head-saws on one side and the comings and goings on the water on the other.

My guts churned and I tasted the salty flavor of blood as I witnessed a skinny man lose part of an ear and most of his scalp on the metal gate of a sawdust hopper. He was the swamper on a truck and he got caught between the bull-board and the hopper gate as the truck lurched backward under it. He was taken hurriedly away to somewhere inside the mill building, by the truck driver, whimpering, his features obliterated by matted hair and blood.

When the truck driver, a gruff, bearded man, returned, he crooked a finger at me and said, "Hey kid. You want to shovel sawdust?"

I didn't ask how much he was paying or what hours I would work. I said, "Yes," and climbed up on the truck. There was blood on the handle of the hopper gate. I jerked it open and scrubbed my hand clean on my pants while the sawdust cascaded into the box.

It was an ancient, rusting truck, of unknown manufacture, with a homemade rough-lumber box that leaked sawdust, adding more soft upholstering to the mill yard as it ground across it. The yellow trail continued, sifting down to the pavement, along Main Street, up the hill and into the labyrinth of homes in South Vancouver.

Fir sawdust worked its way into every seam and fold of my clothing for the next two days. We shoveled, filling basement sawdust bins all over Mount Pleasant.

On the third day, the skinny man was back, his head swathed in bloodstained bandages, ready to go to work. Len, the driver, whose last name I never learned, paid me three dollars and I went back to sitting on lumber piles.

I painted a toolbox for a millwright who paid me a dollar for an afternoon's work.

I had become familiar to him I guess, a nondescript figure lounging in the doorway near the head-rig. Nobody had told me to leave, so like the camel with its head in the tent, I gradually insinuated myself inside. The millwright, a big kindly man with the dirtiest pair of overalls I had ever seen, smiled and nodded at me, giving me courage to ask if there a chance of work.

"Have you ever worked in a sawmill?" he asked.

"No." There was no other answer. I knew I couldn't fake it. I really knew nothing of sawmills other than what I had learned by loitering and watching.

"They're not hiring anybody these days," he said. "God knows I could use some help, but they're squeezing every penny so hard they squeak. What can you do?"

"I can work hard. I've done lots of hard work," I said, arranging my face into the most earnest expression I could muster. "And I can learn quick, if somebody shows me."

He smiled. "I bet you can." He paused and then, "You want a

little job, just a couple of hours. It's a painting job. Do you know how to paint?"

"Sure. I know how to paint. What do you want painted?"

"Come. I'll show you. But I can't pay much, maybe a dollar?"

"That's okay," I said. I would have said okay to half that much.

He motioned and said, "Now be careful. Just follow me. This place can be dangerous if you don't watch what you're doing."

He led me through a narrow passage between the wall and a timbered platform across which conveyor chains rumbled drawing wide fresh-sawn boards toward a battery of whistling circular saws. It was as close as I had ever been to such lethal machinery and I cringed as they screamed their way through the heavy boards. Board or man, I knew, would make little difference to those saws. I stayed close behind the grease-stained figure of the millwright.

His shop was down a flight of stairs, tucked away in a corner without windows. Overhead, line shafts and conveyors rumbled, their shuddering vibrating the very foundations and making the lights on their hanging cords sway and dance.

He paused in front of a low bench on which a large chest rested. It was made of spruce, single wide boards dovetailed together and bound at the corners with copper strapping. He ran his hands over the wood, lovingly. It was finely crafted, and he was justifiably proud of it.

He had to shout over the noise. "I've been meaning to get this tool box painted before the wood dries out and checks, but I just haven't had time. Do you think you can do it?" He opened the lid. "Inside and out. You'll have to take the trays out and do them separately. Okay?"

"Yeah. Sure. I can do it," I shouted back.

"Okay. Here's the paint." He handed me a gallon bucket. "And here's a brush." A whistle blew three short blasts. He hesitated, undecided, and then said, "Go ahead," and hurried away.

The can was half full of gray paint with a thick skin on top; it had not been opened in a long time. I stirred. There were lumps. I stirred more, fishing out as much of the skin as I could. The paint was in desperate need of thinning if I was to brush it on at all evenly. I sorted through the cans and bottles on the shelves, looking for turpentine. There was none. The only thing I could find was a can of kerosene. I needed to paint that toolbox. I needed the dollar I'd been promised. Without thinking too much of the consequences, I dumped some in and stirred.

The millwright smiled ruefully as he handed me a grease-stained dollar from the pocket of his overalls. He could smell kerosene.

"It may dry...someday."

"You need anything else done?" I asked.

"I guess not. Not right away, anyway."

I sit in the cool gloom and watch the stone carvers work.

CHAPTER 3

The Chain Gang

There was first pain—ragged waves, migrating from the base of my skull into a throbbing knot behind my eyes. Then strange rectangular patterns came writhing and slithering across a shimmering background that was too bright to look at. Weird shapes, without substance, they kept changing, drifting away when my eyes tried to follow them then returning when it seemed I'd lost them. Only by keeping one eye closed was I able to focus on them. They gradually solidified into a web of dark rough-sawn timbers framing sections of sunlit blue sky. Knowing that much was somehow reassuring. I let my eyes sag closed. But the pain kept coming, probing at my temples like a live thing trying to get out. Then I became conscious of other hurts scattered over my body—my back, my hip, both elbows and my ankle—all at once everything hurt.

Slowly, full awareness returned. I was lying on my back looking up through the framework of a partially sheathed roof, and something hard was pushing up into my rib cage. I tried to move, to roll away from it, but the effort was too great, I sagged back.

A deep voice with a familiar accent, from somewhere above, said, "By Jesus I think he's waking up."

I forced my eyes open. There were two distorted faces above me. They were looking down at me. I had to think for a moment who they were. Then I remembered. One was Gus, the other, then, must be Gunnar. It was Gus who had spoken. I didn't know why they were both staring at me, but somehow they were making me feel guilty. I decided it wasn't important and closed my eyes.

Then I heard Gunnar's voice, softer than normal, concern taking the ring out of it.

"What do you think, Dad? Do you suppose he's hurt bad, maybe busted something? Maybe we should get a doctor."

There was a pause, and then Gus' voice, tinged with his usual impatience, "Nah, he don't need no doctor. He'll be alright. He's knocked hisself out, that's all. He'll be okay."

I had no idea what they were talking about. Then suddenly I realized, Hey! Was it me that might need a doctor? There was no question that I hurt, but a doctor—that was alarming!

But I couldn't seem to pull it all together, make any sense out of anything. What had happened to me? Why was I lying on the floor? Why did I hurt? I started working down my body. What did broken bones feel like? Were there any ends grating together anywhere, anything sticking out? I guessed not. I felt beat up, though, like the time back home, when the bicycle I was riding collapsed and I took a header on the steep cinder path going down to the river. It felt just like that. I burned, like I had been flayed.

Then the pieces fell into place. I was lying on the rough planking of the floor among shards of tin and ends of lumber, but how I had got there I couldn't remember. I had been on the roof, nailing sheets of corrugated iron to the lattice of timbers. I must have fallen. I guess that was it. I must have fallen from the roof. But why?

"What happened?" I asked.

"Are you okay, Paul?" It was Gunnar's voice. He squatted down beside me. I rolled my head sideways.

"Yeah. I dunno, but I guess so," I mumbled. "What happened? Did I fall or something?"

"Ya." from Gus. He was standing beside Gunnar, with his thumbs hooked in the shoulder straps of his bib-overalls, looking down at me. "You sure did. Yeah...you sure fell. You fell alright...pretty hard." He kind of chuckled. Relieved, I guess, that I hadn't killed myself and that I was awake and able to talk. "Yeah, you sure as hell did fall...that's for sure. Ya. You bloody near got electrocuted too. You don't remember that? You don't remember nothing?"

"No! Electrocuted? How could I get electrocuted? I don't remember anything like that."

40

He looked down at me for a moment more, then his moon face, upholstered in a day's growth of black whiskers, cracked into a genuine smile.

"Ya. Shit, ya. You gonna be alright? Ya. You tell him, Gunnar. Tell him how he got electrocuted." He turned away. "He's gonna be alright. He's tough. He's gonna be all right."

I pushed myself into a sitting position and looked at Gunnar.

"How could I get electrocuted? I don't remember much."

"That last piece of tin," Gunnar said. "The wind must have caught it. I guess it swung it into the crane rail. Must've hit the wires. There was a big flash....you came tumbling down. Jeez, you hit hard. You hit the cross beam on the way down, then bounced off those planks and then that pile of junk. It's a wonder you ain't dead. You been out for maybe ten minutes...must've hit your head. You gonna be okay?"

"I guess so, but I don't remember anything, no flash, no nothing."

"Well, you just take a look at that piece of tin. There's a big burn mark on it...all black. You're lucky. You're sure you didn't bust nothing."

"I don't think so. I'm okay, I guess. But I think I kind of wrecked myself. My head hurts."

I felt the back of my head and my hand came away sticky with blood. I pulled up my sleeve. My arm was scraped from elbow to wrist. My pants leg was ripped and angry red showed through the gap.

A gong was still sounding in my ears and vibrating in my temples, but I hauled myself upright, not too sure I could stay that way, and limped to the ladder. I leaned against it. The room was moving around me like a ship at sea. Any vertical line had a lean to it away over to the left. Closing one eye pulled things back into place. I clung to the ladder, feeling sick to my stomach.

The ache in my head subsided a little, becoming just a dull throb. I decided I could live with it, but not the pain in my ankle; it was really troubling me, like a knife probing right to the bone. I couldn't put any weight on it. I didn't want to think it was broken, just sprained. It couldn't possibly be broken. The feeling of guilt that I had disrupted the work spurred me to get moving.

41

The ladder seemed to reach up a long way to the roof. I hesitated, but there was no alternative; I hauled myself up, grasping the rungs and taking most of the weight on my arms.

Neither Gus nor Gunnar suggested I wait a few minutes. We had work to do. I couldn't stand, but I could nail sheathing, kneeling. It was up to me not to fall again.

Gus and Gunnar Anderson, father and son, entered my life—I should say re-entered it—through the swinging door of McDonald's Stone Works, a week after I discovered it. I had returned almost daily to watch the stone sculptors work, fascinated by their art. All else had taken on secondary importance to watching the three small men with their tiny chisels release the intricate details of the murals from the soft Newcastle-Island stone. I couldn't get there soon enough in the mornings. This day, late afternoon, I was about to go home along Main Street.

I was reaching for the latch in the man-door, inset in the big rollup, when it flew open, nearly bowling me over. Gus came barging through in bulldozer fashion. In that instant, I didn't recognize him as Gus. There was no time. The thought that he might be someone I knew, someone from another life never entered my mind. His massive figure, filling the doorframe, was just a silhouette against the light. I couldn't see him distinctly. I dodged to one side and let him pass. Then Gunnar came through. We saw each other at the same time and both did a double take.

"Well for Christ sakes! Hey, Paul. Is that you? What're you doing here? Hey, Dad! look who's here," he called after Gus.

"Gunnar!" I said. "I'll be go to hell. How come? What are *you* doing here?"

"What? Who. Who's that?" Gus turned, sputtering. "Ya, ya. You're...you're...sure, I know you. You're...? You look skinny. Ya, Paul, ain't it? You're Paul, ya?" He held out a meaty hand the palm of which was like leather. "You working here?"

"No. I wish I was." I shook my head. "I was just here watching...I was watching the carvers in there." I pointed back into the gloom of the building. "You know...watching them carve stone." I suddenly realized that trying to explain my fascination to someone else, particularly this pair, was going to sound pretty inane. I stopped talking...embarrassed. I had been caught doing something that they would think was so utterly without purpose.

Then my mind shifted. What had brought *them* here. "Are you going to work here?" I asked.

That's how it began: a few months of the hardest work I would ever do, there in the back end of that draughty, ramshackle building housing McDonald's Stone Works. It was the spring of 1939.

They were Albertans—at least I thought of them as such—Gus and Gunnar Anderson, from the same gopher capital as me. They had migrated as a family, the same as ours and a great many others had, to the promised land of the coast. I hadn't seen or heard of them since the day, some two years ago, when we had said a brief goodbye, standing on the snow-encrusted station platform, coat collars turned up and backs to the piercing wind.

They had established themselves in Vancouver, in a rented house, and then gone foraging, Gus as a blacksmith and Gunnar as his helper—a team, father and son, wherever there was work. North from Vancouver to Squamish, Williams Lake, Wells, anywhere, generally in mines, where there was steel to sharpen, or where there was a need for any kind of blacksmithing, but never for long; no jobs lasted very long. At the moment, they were not working.

I got all this from Gunnar, in the first few minutes, standing there in the doorway fronting on Main Street. Gus had gone blustering ahead and had disappeared into McDonald's office.

Gus had never stayed long in one place. Seemed he couldn't settle in to become part of a community—no matter where. A lot of people found him hard to get along with. He could do anything with metal, but he was also ham-handed, ready to use his fists on anyone who disagreed with him. Got so nobody wanted to deal with him. He couldn't stand authority, rebelled against any suggestion of it. Years ago, he'd deserted the Swedish army, just walked away from it, couldn't have anyone telling him what to do.

"Ya. I guess they're waiting for me to stick my nose back in the country," he'd said. "Ha! To hell with them; they can wait. They can get somebody else to 'Yes sir, no sir'."

He'd come to Canada and blacksmithed his way from Montreal, west, always working west. He'd finally come the full distance, spanned the continent. Along the way, he'd married and fathered a family, Gunnar and two girls. What had led him to pause in the jerkwater Alberta village where we had encountered each other had never come to light.

Gunnar was older than me by a couple of years. Built like his father—big, muscular and dark. He had been endowed with smooth-skinned good looks and, fortunately, with his mother's temperament. Understandably, girls liked Gunnar, and he liked girls, an arrangement that had resulted in at least one pregnancy—that anyone knew about—and one dose of clap—that anyone knew about—that he was supposedly cured of.

He also liked hockey. A powerful skater, and with the bulk to go with it, he was formidable to us lesser beings. Whether he liked girls or hockey the most was hard to say; he talked about both equally and to the exclusion of just about everything else.

However, when spring winds lifted the ice from the outdoor rink, he had to turn to something else and baseball filled the void. He could pitch. He was good because he devoted hours to practice, never seeming to tire. Seemed he had an iron arm, too. He'd hand me a catcher's mitt, one he kept in the blacksmith shop, so worn and thin it was little more than a piece of cracked leather, and stand me out front in the middle of the road. He'd throw his repertoire of curves and fastballs, until my hand was so swollen I couldn't close it. From him I'd learned most of what little I knew about baseball.

I was always a little bit in awe of Gunnar. I guess because he was good at things and I wasn't, and because he was easy with girls and I wasn't. We were a mismatched pair, and I suspect the only reason he put up with me was because I was willing to go along with whatever took his fancy at any particular moment, that is, as long as it wasn't something to do with girls. He didn't need me for that.

He could work. There was something about exerting himself that was akin to joy. He was strong and big and loved using his muscles, but, like me, he had no clearly defined ambitions. He had never channeled his ability to work in any particular direction. He was a skiff being drawn along in the wake of the battleship that was Gus.

"How come you're here?" I asked. "You going to work here?"

44

"Maybe. He's gone in there to make a deal," Gunnar said, nodding in the direction of McDonald's office where Gus had disappeared. "He's got an idea that they need somebody to do blacksmithing for them. Yeah, and he wants to start a business. He figures they might lease him some space in the back end of the building here. He thinks he might get it for free if he does some blacksmithing for them. There's an old shed back there we could use." He pointed at the open end of the building that hung over the oil-scummed waters of False Creek.

"What kind of a business?"

"Chains. He wants to make chains. He says there's money in boom chains. I dunno. Maybe there is. It might work out."

At the moment, the details of the venture were still pretty hazy, but Gunnar said Gus had it all figured out in his head.

"He seems to know what he's doing, but, as usual, he don't tell me or anybody else."

We moved further into the gloom of the building, where we could see Gus through the glass of the office window, his bulk almost filling the tiny cubicle. He was gesticulating, waving his arms, his head pushed forward pugnaciously, almost into the face of one of the McDonald brothers. Not the stance of amicable deal-making.

"He's liable to be in there for awhile...if he doesn't get into a fight and get thrown out," Gunnar said. "Let's get out of here. Let's go home to my house; it's up on Twelfth Avenue. Should be a streetcar pretty soon...the next number-three. Okay?"

"Yeah. Great," I said. Then I hesitated. "But you go on ahead. I'll see you there. I'll walk."

"Walk! What do you want to walk for?"

Again I hesitated, ashamed of being broke, but then I blurted it out. "I don't have carfare."

"No carfare! Hell. That's okay. I've got carfare. Come on."

Theirs was a big, old, faded yellow three-storied place at Twelfth and Ontario Street, a drop-siding sheathed mansion that had seen better days. A rental house, the family lived on the main floor and sub-leased the upper floors and the basement.

Gunnar's sisters, Elsie and Gerda, had blossomed, particularly Gerda, the younger one, who was younger than me. The way I remembered her, she had been just an ordinary looking kid, somebody to jostle in the school hallway or borrow something from. Since I'd last seen her, she had gained some height and acquired a soft roundness. I couldn't help noticing the front of her blouse. I was suddenly tongue tied and conscious of my down-at-the-heel appearance.

It was easy for me to fall back into the old relationship with Gunnar, willingly following him as I had in the past, letting him influence my thinking and doing without question whatever he wanted. In the first couple of weeks following, instead of my usual trek straight down Main Street to Burrard Inlet, False Creek, or wherever else I was going in my desperate search for employment, I detoured to Anderson's house—the two blocks off Main Street. There was always coffee on the stove and usually something to eat with it. And there was Gerda, a girl to joke and laugh with. I began paying a little more attention to washing and combing my shaggy mop of hair. There was little I could do about my worn and faded clothing, but I did try to wear those with the least holes.

The change, though slight, was noticed at home. "Your suddenly getting awful fussy," Father remarked one morning when I emerged from the bathroom with my hair slicked down. "You got a girl or something?" He meant it facetiously. I doubt it ever crossed his mind that I might actually be interested in a girl. He watched me like a hawk. Any change in my appearance or routine might mean I had secret money or I might be doing something I wasn't telling him about. Mother, on the other hand, approved. "It always pays to keep yourself looking neat and clean," she said. "People notice, you know. It helps, whether you're looking for work or not. The neater you look the more respect you'll get from people."

I hadn't yet got around to telling them about Andersons. I hadn't wanted to tell them about Gunnar, and that I had again become his shadow, and that I was not applying myself as diligently to the business of looking for work as perhaps I should. I was careful about what I mentioned. If Father knew about Gunnar, he would probably start ranting about hockey and baseball again. He'd considered both a waste of time and hated me playing either one. Here in Vancouver he'd know there wouldn't be any hockey, but with summer coming on there just might be baseball.

With Gunnar, there was suddenly pleasure in wandering the downtown streets. He'd come along at a crucial time in my life. Even though I had fallen in love with Vancouver, the truth was, I was an outsider. I had the feeling of being a transient, someone who didn't belong. If there was a way of becoming part of this city I would have welcomed it, but I hadn't discovered it yet. I had all but given up patrolling the warehouse districts as hopeless, and, without transportation, I was limited to where my two feet would carry me. I wasn't ready to tell anybody yet, but I'd begun thinking about getting out of town, riding a freight back to Alberta, to farming country, country I understood. It would be greening up time back there. Meeting Gunnar changed all that.

Gunnar had money, not a lot, but enough for carfare and movies, and he didn't mind sharing it with me. He hadn't made any friends; he'd been to busy trying to keep up with Gus. But right now, until the business in the back end of McDonald's Stone Works got going, there was a lull, time to get away from Gus, time for less serious things. There hadn't been a better time for me to come along.

So we would head downtown, sometimes walking, but mostly on street cars. We didn't pretend we were looking for work; we didn't have to. Gus didn't care; he was busy with his deal making. We went for fun, to loiter, to discover new things. And, above all, to go to movies. Gunnar, like me, was addicted to the fantasy of movies. For sure if it was raining, but even if it wasn't, we would slide into a movie house in the early afternoon. The Star, the Royal, the Colonial or any of the other half dozen that stood shoulder to shoulder with pawn shops, greasy-spoon cafes and run-down rooming houses along lower Granville, Hastings and Main Streets, we would check out any of those that billed vaudeville-type entertainment. Anything with girls beckoned to Gunnar—the more scantily clad the better. There were a lot of choices, affordable ones. For ten cents each, we could see a vaudeville show, a double-feature movie, news reels and cartoons. It was easy to spend an entire afternoon in the musty gloom, our minds far away from the real world.

Since Gunnar was paying, I didn't argue about which shows we would see. I was agreeable; whatever he chose was fine with me. And by following passively along, I was being quietly introduced to the heretofore forbidden territory of the uncovered female. It was exciting. The dime at the box office was a license to stare. The guilt I felt—a product of a puritanical upbringing—at ogling from the darkness was gradually being eroded and replaced by feelings that, until now, I hadn't really experienced, but was beginning to enjoy immensely. Slouched in the worn plush of the theatre seats my own drab world somewhere far away, I watched, absorbed, as across the footlights long, slim legs kicked high revealing tantalizing glimpses of naked female. And beside me there were always Gunnar's sotto comments.

Like, "Hey, see that one there, third from left. Look at the boobs on her, 'eh," or "Boy-oh-boy, lookit those legs, 'eh. I bet they go all the way up to you know where, 'eh. How about we go down front after the show and meet her, and maybe that one there in the middle, and how about that short one? You want to meet her? I bet I could fix it for you. Want to? 'Eh?"

Knowing how Gunnar got on with girls, I had little doubts he could do what he suggested. It was all too new to me though. Any attempt in that direction and I would have been paralyzed or run in panic. Fantasy was one thing, but…

It couldn't last, of course, but those had been the most relaxed enjoyable days I had experienced since arriving in Vancouver.

Gus had, despite his pugnacious approach, been able to make a deal with McDonalds. He would do their blacksmithing, and in return, they would lease him the dilapidated shed at the back end of their building. The way it stood, it was little more than a frame-work, hanging out over False Creek, but it could be fixed.

An idea had come from somewhere and begun festering in his mind that there was money to be made in boom chains. Granted there were thousands of them in use up and down the coast, and they were being lost regularly, but how he would access the market was something he couldn't, or wouldn't, explain. He must have had some sort of a scheme worked out, but he wasn't talking about it.

"Ya sure. We'll sell them. You don't got to worry about that." He was quite emphatic on that score. "They always need chains. All we gotta do is make them."

And make them we would.

Gunnar was expected to pitch in as a matter of course, and

because I was loathe to let go of him, to go back to my lonely, mostly fruitless, wandering, I tagged along.

"Ya, Paul," Gus said. "You wanna work for nothing until we get set up, then I gonna pay you when we start making money. Okay? I gonna pay you a dollar a day, but by Jesus you gonna work. Ya. You gonna work hard. You gonna earn that dollar. Okay?" He was smiling, but there was never any doubt in my mind that he meant exactly what he said. It was an ultimatum, no doubt about that. It was either work or get lost, cut loose from Gunnar.

"Sure," I said. There was really no choice.

I finally had to tell Father what I was doing.

He knew the Andersons of course, the whole family. He had drunk beer with Gus back in Alberta, but now he shied away from any suggestion of renewing an association with him. Didn't even want to meet him or his family. I didn't think about it at the time, but later I came to realize that it was because Gus was venturesome, a driver. Even though he had trouble getting along with people, he at least tried things, he worked when he could. Father had given up completely from the day we arrived in Vancouver. He lived on his war pension. The fifty dollars a month wasn't much for five people to live on, not for rent, light, heat, telephone, food and clothing. It provided only a slimmest livelihood, and he hadn't made any attempt to supplement it. That was up to us, Owen and me. That was the old-country way with the sons providing for the parents. That he had stagnated was evident to anybody looking at him. He knew it, and he knew Gus would see it, so he let on that he didn't want anything to do with Gus. Said Gus was a troublemaker. Didn't want to associate with him. Perhaps there was still a shred of pride left in him.

Gus and Mrs. Anderson had inquired, of course. "How're your folks, you mother? Is her health any better here at the coast?" Mrs. Anderson had asked. "How's that old man of yours?" Gus had asked, that first day. "He working? He get a job someplace?"

I'd had to tell him. I'd tried to make it sound like there'd been things that just didn't work out, but I had a feeling that Gus knew. Neither he nor Mrs. Anderson said anything about getting together.

The shop came first; it had to be renovated, at least to the extent of keeping the rain out. The corrugated sheet-metal, the nails and timber came from next door, from a junkyard labeled Acme Salvage. Everything came from that junkyard, and everything had been used before—even the nails, most of which had to be straightened. The metal sheets and the timbers had holes in them where they had been nailed, screwed or bolted previously.

We worked hard, all three of us. My hurts repaired themselves, scabbing over and becoming less sensitive. My ankle gave me the most trouble; I limped for weeks, but I was determined to pull my weight. Gus acknowledged my suffering to the point of giving me carfare so I wouldn't have to walk the thirty-odd blocks to and from work.

We got the roof on and three of the walls repaired. There would be no fourth wall, and the wind would scour around through the support steel and on wet days, bring gusts of rainwater to sputter and instantly vaporize on the white-hot metal we were forging.

Gus had cut a deal with the proprietor of the junk yard next door, the details of which were pretty loose. We knocked a few boards from the fence that separated the yard from McDonalds and went scavenging.

Schwartz, a huge German with a round face adorned with mutton-chop whiskers and a nose that looked like an afterthought, who ran the place, kept some sort of record on the back of an dirty wrinkled envelope that he fished from his overall's pocket. He used the stub of a flat carpenter's pencil that he carefully licked before studiously writing down what we were taking. He wasn't always around, but that didn't deter us from carting whatever seemed useful through the hole in the fence.

Gus never wrote anything down. I never saw a pencil in his hand; he kept everything in his head. Gus' philosophy was if your tally doesn't agree with my tally, we'll use our fists to settle the difference.

Scavenging in the junkyard was like shopping in an outsized, rusting supermarket. Everything we could possibly need was there, but unearthing it from the tangle and transporting it was what taxed our ingenuity and our muscles. And it was easy to get side-tracked by some wonderfully complex piece of apparatus that we finally had to admit we had no use for, things that tweaked our curiosity and imagination to the point that we sometimes wasted valuable time trying to adapt them.

Gus could build anything, but to do so he first needed a means of heating metal and bending it. In the maze of junk, we found enough parts to assemble a blacksmith's forge. An anvil and tools followed, surfacing from the piles. From then on, Gus hammered and bent, cursed and sweated, and machines took shape. He fabricated a machine for bending raw stock into chain links, a furnace for heating them and tools for finishing them.

Just inside the salvage yard near the hole in the fence was a magnificently powerful metal shear that could slice through a bar as thick as my arm with only a slight metal on metal grunt. Part of the deal with Schwartz was the use of it. Had it not been there, Gus would have had to build one—and I'm sure he could have.

We found just about everything we needed in that yard, including an almost complete air-driven trip-hammer that, although at the time we couldn't foresee it having a lot of use, it was too good to pass up. So, we took it and hooked it up to McDonald's air system without telling them.

In what seemed an amazingly short while, we were ready to start making chains.

The raw stock, like everything else, came from the junkyard. It was primarily the round metal rods that had tied timbered highway bridges together and that had become surplus when the bridges were replaced with steel structures. They were anywhere from a half inch to an inch thick and up to twenty feet long, all twisted— some almost spiraled—and pitted with rust.

It being impossible, or at least impractical, to try to straighten them, they were fed as they were into the bending machine. I, being smaller and lighter, was assigned the motor switch. Gus and Gunnar steered the stuff into the rollers. Despite their combined weight and strength, sometimes the thicker more twisted ones would get away, throwing them both all over the shop and then flailing around destroying everything within reach until I could throw the switch and shut off the motor. The machine had a huge flywheel that took several seconds to wind down and come to a halt.

The chain links came off the spindle in the form of a coil like a flat-sided spring. Gus separated them with the metal shear by simply chopping the spring apart. It was a hazardous operation, one in which the loss of fingers or even a hand could have resulted from a moment of carelessness. Gus wouldn't let either Gunnar or me attempt it.

We preheated the links in a flat-bed furnace tended by either Gunnar or me, and tossed to Gus who caught them in his tongs. Getting the toss right needed practice and we weren't too good at first, but we got better. If the toss wasn't just right, Gus would miss, and then lookout! We would cringe under the whiplash of his temper. From glowing red, Gus heated them to white-hot welding temperature in the forge, slipped them through the preceding link and hammered them shut. The almost liquid metal fused on contact. The weld was finished with a die, held in place by Gus and hammered on by either Gunnar or me. The sledge hammers weighed six pounds and had slick wooden handles. We traded off, one of us hammering while the other tended the furnace.

The work was hard in the beginning, but it became easier. I noticed the muscles of my arms, chest and shoulders becoming more defined when I looked in the mirror—even though there was precious little surplus meat on my bones—and the palms of my hands took on the hard toughness of the material we were working with.

Gus had, as promised, started to pay me a dollar a day, even though he had yet to dispose of any chains. A portion of my earnings went to buy groceries.

Peanut butter is what I ate, I developed a craving for it. I ate gobs of it. It came in bulk from a corner grocery on Main Street. For ten cents I could get a bucket full, ladled out by a motherly woman who usually remarked on how often I was there to buy it.

"More peanut butter? Your family sure must like peanut butter." She didn't know I was eating most of it.

Even though I was eating more, I was still hungry. For every calorie I ate, I expended ten swinging that sledge hammer.

Now that I no longer limped, Gus saw no reason to give me car fare, so I was again walking to and from work. I wanted desperately, though, to be free of a dependency on streetcars or walking. I yearned for a bicycle. In the meantime, until I could save enough to buy one, I walked rather than pay for a streetcar. Each week I spirited a little away.

Tending the furnace was not as demanding physically, but the heat was fierce, barbecuing Gunnar's and my ungloved hands. Leather gloves were expensive and cooked in no time and any other kind caught on fire. Those made from asbestos were hard come by and were more expensive than leather. So we just worked fast, barehanded, burying links as quickly as possible, raking the coals over them and retrieving them glowing red. We'd toss a link to Gus and then seek relief by jamming our hands in a bucket of water.

Neither Gunnar nor I wore shirts and our upper bodies and arms became decorated with burns from flying slag, ranging from raw to scabbed over. The fronts of our pants were riddled with burn holes. Gus wore a leather apron that covered most of his front but his hamhock arms were a mass of burn scars.

Ours was a primitive way of working metal, at least a hundred years behind the times. But even so, we tuned out a credible product, and as time went on, we became better at it. The heap of new chains lying smoking on the stone-chip floor, where the wall ended ten feet above the high-water mark of false creek, grew into a substantial mound. At the end of the first week we had made upwards of eighty chains, each one having twenty links, a big round ring on one end and a flat toggle on the other.

Then Slim showed up. He walked in as though he owned the place. I couldn't believe it at first, but then found out Gus had hired him.

I knew I'd seen him before, but couldn't place him. I kept looking at him. Somewhere...maybe one of the multitude lounging on the waterfront streets. Then it came to me; he was the blue-suited stickman from the lobby of the Ivanhoe Hotel. He was just as skinny and deathly pale as when I had first seen him, that very first day when we had arrived in Vancouver and carried our suitcases from the station. I wondered at his ability to walk, never mind work.

Where and how he and Gus had encountered each other I never found out, or, strangely, why Gus had thought he could do the kind of work we were doing. I couldn't imagine him working at anything. The man was a walking skeleton, a brittle caricature. He was wearing the same ill-fitting, threadbare suit I'd remembered him wearing in the lobby of the Ivanhoe.

That first morning, all enthusiasm, he shed the jacket and tie, rolled up the sleeves of his once-white shirt—the collar and cuffs of which were frayed to the point of being ragged—to reveal the skinniest pair of pale arms I had ever seen. I doubted he could even lift a sledgehammer. I wondered what he could actually do. I soon found out—nothing much. He didn't attempt much either. He puttered around, tidying up and ineffectually sweeping at the section of floor that was planked, accomplishing little. He sat often, rolled innumerable ragged cigarettes, watched us work and gave unsolicited advice on things he obviously he knew little about. During lunch breaks, when the furnace fans were turned off and we could talk in a normal tone of voice, he'd launch into some weird tale of secretive goings on in the Ivanhoe, of people who were after him, of being hunted by all sorts of shady characters who signaled to each other in the small hours of the night by turning the taps on and off and making the pipes hiss. Or he would start off on some controversial subject, fixing Gunnar and me with his bulging codfish eyes, daring us to disagree with him looking only to start an argument. He treated me with utter contempt. If I tried to reason a way through his arguments, he'd leave the subject entirely, resorting to irrational bluster.

"You young punks. You don't know what you're talking about. You don't know nothing."

I got so I just kept quiet.

For reasons I couldn't fathom, Gus put up with him, not saying a word, almost ignoring him. He paid him when he paid Gunnar and me. And as far as I could tell, he got the same amount, a dollar a day, but for doing nothing. There was obviously more between him them than met the eye, but what, there was never a clue. I never found out what his name was either. He was just Slim or "Shlim" the way Gus' thick accent pronounced it.

Shortly afterward, we sold our first chains. A small tow boat came growling up False Creek and slid its stern in under the overhang of the shop floor. Slim, who spent a lot of time hanging over the railing gazing down into the water, watched the maneuver then spoke to the skipper. I couldn't hear what was said, but the skipper shrugged and nodded. Slim turned to Gus. "He wants some chains."

"How many he want?"

"Gimme fifty," the skipper said, loud enough to be heard over the hum of his diesel.

"Ya. Gunnar, Paul, you hand those chains down," Gus said.

We slid them under the railing and dropped them down onto the deck.

The skipper handed a fistful of bills up to Gus who jammed them in his pocket without counting. I hadn't heard a thing about price.

In the weeks that followed we made more and sold more chains. But stock was becoming a problem. Combing through the junk piles in the Acme Salvage yard was time consuming. We were having to dig deeper. At least one day a week was used up finding enough to do us the remaining five days. It was rapidly becoming apparent we would have to look elsewhere for supplies. Gus didn't own a truck, and buying stock from other salvage yards and having it delivered was going to be too expensive.

We worked from Monday to Saturday, eight in the morning to six in the evening, except on Saturdays, when we quit at noon. Then Gus would pay us for the week. In addition, he would hand Gunnar and me an extra quarter to spend on a movie. We washed the most of the grime from our faces and hands in the cooling tank, donned shirts and, still wearing our dirty ragged jeans, head for Hastings Street. A dime for a movie and fifteen cents for something to eat.

As Gus had predicted, we had no trouble selling our product. I still didn't know how he accessed the market, but suspected that Slim had something to do with it. Small towboats regularly appeared at our back door, money changed hands with little being said and less being written down.

On average we maintained our output of twenty chains a day. We could have made more had we had more and better stock.

Then one day, just at quitting time, a small fishing boat, a salmon troller, appeared, easing its stern under the floor overhang. It was a decrepit craft, its gurdies corroded, its paint flaking and its trolling gear a tangle of twisted poles and rusting wire. The skipper matched his boat—a tattered bearded man. On the weathered deck were a dozen or so boom chains, shrouded in black scale and barnacle encrusted. Slim and Gus talked for a few minutes with the fisherman, then Gus turned and motioned to Gunnar and me. The fisherman handed the chains up part way and we hauled them up the rest and laid them beside the furnace. Gus handed down a few bills. The transaction had taken no more than ten minutes. With a swirl of dark water under its counter, the boat eased out from under the overhang and headed down channel.

Gus hit the button and re-started the furnace blower.

"Hey you, Gunnar, Paul. Get those chains in the fire. Get 'em in there and burn 'em a bit. Enough to burn the rust off 'em."

That these chains were traveling in the opposite direction to normal, raised questions in my mind, however, I had learned better than to query Gus. I could see a question in Gunnar's eyes, but like me he knew better than to ask. He just shrugged and grabbed his chain hook.

We heaved them into the furnace, as many at a time as we could, shoveled fresh fuel on top and let them cook. When we hauled them out a few minutes later, they looked more or less like our home-grown product. Gus, seeming hurried, cut the last links and let the toggles drop off. He slipped new toggles into the links and welded them shut. The old toggles—that I discovered had distinctive brands chiseled into them—he threw as far as he could into False Creek. We were finished in less than an hour. The refurbished chains joined the ones we had made that day, on the pile. There was really nothing to distinguish them, at least to a casual observer.

Visits by fishing boats became a regular occurrence during the following weeks. Every few days one would come, not always the same one, chugging up the inlet, and always just before quitting time. Little or nothing was said. The chains were passed up under the railing and a few bills were passed down. We worked furiously for the next hour, the furnace going full blast and Gus replacing toggles. Slim didn't engage in any of this extra work; he just picked up his coat and left as soon as the fishing boat was out of sight down the channel.

The chains were sold, mixed with those we had made, to towboat skippers who asked no questions.

One morning, about the middle of June, Slim didn't appear for work. He never came back. I never saw him again. I didn't care and it didn't matter much as far as the work was concerned, he hadn't done that much. Gus was noncommittal when Gunnar remarked that he hadn't shown up, and there was little reason to probe deeply.

The following day, two large men wearing suits with white shirts and ties, trench coats and felt hats came wandering into the shop. I couldn't help but notice that their shiny shoes were fouled with the almost-white mud they had trekked through, the residue of stone sawing from the aisles between the blocks in McDonalds. Their clean businessmanlike apparel seemed out of place in the grunge of our two-bit chain factory.

They were pleasant, smiling, behaving rather like sight-seers at some tourist attraction. They shook hand all around, oozing friendliness. There was no sign of distaste at grasping our black, scarred and callused fists—theirs were soft and remarkably clean. They wandered around exhibiting a great deal of interest in everything. However, most of their attention seemed to focus on the pile of finished chains. Gus put up with their curiosity for maybe ten minutes.

"What the hell you guys want!" he finally barked. "We got work to do. Tell me what you want or get out of here. You're getting in the way."

"Oh, sorry," said the larger of the pair. He was as big and dark as Gus, but with an oriental cast to his eyes. "We're just interested in your operation here. How many chains can you guys make in a day, anyway? It must be pretty hard work, 'eh."

"Ya. It's hard work," Gus growled. "That all you want to know?"

"We were just curious. Thank you very much. Good day." They took a last look around and then disappeared into the gloom of the stone works.

"Who do you suppose those guys were?" I said to Gus.

"Sonsabitches." He spat, without looking up from the toggle he was punching a hole in.

The next morning they were back. We continued working, but I could see Gus looking at them from under his bushy eyebrows. They stood around for a few minutes, paying an inordinate amount of attention to the pile of chains.The dark man finally spoke up.

"How many chains do you usually make in a day," he asked. "I know you told me yesterday, but I forgot."

Gus' face became darker yet under its layer of grime, a sure sign he was reaching the point of eruption. "You want to buy some chains?" he shouted, his words tripping over each other and spittle flying. "You want to buy some chains, show me some money. You don't want to buy any chains, get to hell out of here or I'm gonna show you how we pound on things around here." He threw down his hammer and started toward them, his huge hands curled into fists.

They looked at each other, turned and retreated.

"Just curious," the dark man said over his shoulder.

The fishing boats stopped coming. Quit, just like that. Then the tow boats became fewer. We didn't have that many chains to sell anyway. Material was becoming too scarce.

One day Gus got into an argument with one of the McDonald brothers. I hadn't thought about it, but I guess he'd done precious little in the way of blacksmithing for them. At least I hadn't seen any drill sharpening or the like. Now they were calling in their markers; they wanted work or rent. There was some serious shouting without much being resolved.

"We got to shut down for a few days," Gus announced, a couple of days later. "I gotta find some more stock. Maybe next week we work again."

We only worked a couple of days after that. Gus just couldn't pull it all together, so he just walked away from it.

It was a blow. A dollar a day wasn't exactly making me wealthy, but it was better than nothing. I would have to start looking again, knowing full well that the employment situation hadn't markedly improved in the last few months. However, I *had* bought a bicycle, a single-speed rebuild with no two parts the same color and all well worn, but it was mine to ride wherever I wanted. More than that I didn't have. I was back to being broke.

Gunnar didn't have much either, not for movies or vaudeville. There was no longer much fun in prowling the town without money. The need to find work was paramount for both of us, so I found myself alone again. I only saw Gunnar a couple of times after that. The last time, he told me they were thinking of moving out of Vancouver. Gus was again on the move.

More out of curiosity than any wish to renew an association that had been tenuous at best, I dropped in to the Ivanhoe Hotel one afternoon. The desk clerk looked blank when I inquired if Slim was still around.

"Slim.? I don't know who you mean. I don't know any Slim.

"I don't know what his real name is. We always just called him Slim." I said. "He's a skinny guy. Wears a blue suit. Used to sit around here in the lobby."

"Oh, that guy. I know who you mean. No. He's gone. What do you want with him?"

"Nothing much. Just thought I'd say hello. I thought he might still be staying here?"

"No. He's not here anymore...not for awhile. I heard he's got himself a new place. He looked at me over the top of his glasses and smiled. "One with bars on the windows. I hear they call it Okalla, out in Westminster."

CHAPTER 4

The Hireling

The telephone's shrill jangling shattered the sunlit quiet of the kitchen, drowning out the ticking of the alarm clock on top of the cupboard and Father's asthmatic breathing. Its clatter, magnified by the thin hollow wall on which it hung, jerked me out of the drowsiness of sheer boredom. A wooden box with two shiny bulbous bells on front that kept up their tinny vibrating in between frantic bursts of the clapper, it hung by the door on the wall between the kitchen and my sister's bedroom. The explosion of sound lifted me half out of my chair. I bumped the table and checkers went skittering off the board.

"Hey! God damn it! Watch what you're doing," Father snapped.

"Sorry," I mumbled and started toward the phone. Whoever the call was for was not my primary concern, throttling the ringer was. That it might actually be a call for me didn't even cross my mind. Anyway, Olwyn beat me to it. Her door squeaked open and the sleep odor of a teenage girl confined in a closed room wafted into the kitchen. Her arm came snaking out of the gloom, knowing from practice where to go, and her hand snatched the bell-shaped receiver from its hook. I slumped back into my chair as the rest of her followed, dark, tousled, sleepy-eyed and clutching her nightgown to her middle. Only the telephone could have roused her from bed with such alacrity. There was, of course, no question in *her* mind who the call was for. Most of the calls in the last few months, ever since she'd discovered a boyfriend, had been for her, so she didn't doubt for a moment that this one would be. She placed the receiver to her ear, holding it daintily by the end, her pinky upraised.

"Hello-o-o," she trilled, her eyes losing some of their vacant sleepiness and lighting with anticipation. The light went out as quickly as it had kindled. She kinked her head sideways at me. "It's for you." She said it as though I was somehow to blame for getting her out of bed. She let the receiver drop, yawned and disappeared back into her room. It hit the end of its cord and swung. I leapt for it and captured it on the second pass.

"Hello." I had to stretch my neck to reach the mouthpiece.

A gruff voice asked, "Paul Jones?"

"Yeah," I replied, cautiously.

"McGrath at Pacific Mills. If you can come by our office this morning, I may have a job for you."

"Uh. Who? What? McGrath? Pacific Mills? Oh yeah...oh yeah." I squeaked inanely, any semblance of coherent thought abandoning me. Maybe this was some kind of a joke? But who? I didn't know anybody who would joke about a job.

I eventually collected my wits.

"Pacific Mills, 'eh? Ah, when...when should I come?"

"Oh, about eleven. Mm, yes, eleven will be fine. Can you make it by then?"

I looked at the clock, which read 9:45.

"Yeah. I guess so. Yeah, uh, where's your office?"

"Cordova. East. It might not be easy to find; it's buried in a lot of other buildings. There's a big sign on it, though." He explained how to locate it.

"Where's the job?"

"Ocean Falls. You'd have to leave tomorrow. Can you do that?"

"Golly...gee...yeah, I guess so. Ocean Falls, 'eh? Yeah. Great. I'll be there."

I hung up, a little stunned, trying to decide whether or not to forget the whole thing. But what the hell, Ocean Falls. It just might not be a hoax, and if it was for real...but how come? How would McGrath know about me, and why would he be offering me a job? Eleven o'clock, 'eh? I wonder...

By going to have a look, what did I have to lose—a day of checker games with Father; dickering at the corner store for a sec-

61

ond-hand magazine; walking over to Ryley Park for no good reason; riding my bike somewhere just to get away from the house. I could at least go and find the office—if such a place existed.

I sorted out the streets in my mind; it was way down in East Vancouver, almost on the waterfront. I was at Twenty-ninth and John Street, a couple of blocks off Main, almost in South Vancouver. Holy smoke! I'd better move it. Get there by eleven o'clock? How? My choices were few: streetcar, bicycle or my own two feet.

"Hey! I've got a chance of a job at Ocean Falls," I yelled, suddenly coming alive, excitement making my voice go up an octave. "I gotta be there at eleven. Can I borrow car fare?"

Father was still straightening the checkers on the board, meticulously placing them where he thought they had been before I sent them flying. He was agitated, his hand shaking, frowning, his mouth a tight line. A little thing, a disrupted checker game, but enough to annoy him beyond reason.

A short, stocky Welshman, his normal ruddy complexion had faded to an unhealthy pastiness, he looked soft and shabby faced, gone to seed. Over the last year, his appearance had come to mean less and less and this morning he hadn't even bothered to put a shirt on. His undershirt, gray from washing with too little soap, was unbuttoned and a gray curly mat peeked through the gap. His sparse hair, almost white now, was sticking up uncombed. He was unshaven.

My excitement was not infectious. He looked sourly at the board and its pieces. "That's all well and good, but how about finishing the game?" He didn't even look up. "Sure...just walk away when you're losing. The least you could do is finish the game. It's not very sportsmanlike to quit just because you're losing."

To him, finishing a game was all-important, even when a job might be at stake. Checkers had taken on a significance out of all proportion, a thing to block out reality. His interest had dwindled and checkers was all he thought about. I was the only one who would play with him.

"But losing's got nothing to do with it," I protested. "I gotta go. This is a real job. I gotta get there by eleven and its almost ten now. Can I borrow car fare? I'll pay you back."

"Pay me back? Out of what?"

He reached for his tobacco tin. There wasn't much in it and most of that was second hand from butts he had torn the paper off and mixed with new stuff. Some of it had been rolled in cigarettes, probably three or four times—a pretty rank smoke. He twisted a thin tube, licked it carefully and fired it with a big wooden match scraped under the chair seat, still without looking directly at me. I stood, impatiently, waiting for an answer.

Smoke writhed in the sunlight. "What's the matter with your bicycle? You spent ten dollars on that bike. Now you want to borrow money. You know what Shakespeare said."

"No. What?"

"'Neither a borrower or a lender be,' or something like that. You'd better ride the bike. Money doesn't grow on trees, you know. Ride the bike." He straightened a piece on the board. "You've got lots of time. If the job is any good, and whoever that was on the phone means you to have it, it'll wait."

I guess he didn't want to believe that this offer would actually be worthwhile. Or maybe he just didn't want to think about it at all. There had been too many leads that didn't pan out.

Mother called from her chair in the living room, her voice a thin reedy tiredness. "Are your clothes clean, Paul? You better change them, you know. Put some clean ones on, make yourself a little bit presentable and comb your hair. After all, if you're going for an interview, you want to make a good impression, don't you?"

"I'm going to be sweating by the time I get there, anyway, if I ride the bike. What's the point? Maybe if I had car fare…"

"I told you to ride the bike," Father growled. "You're pretty anxious to get on it any other morning and go traipsing off to God knows where. You better get on it now."

There would be no streetcar.

In the bathroom, I looked at myself in the mirror and wasn't impressed with what I saw—a freckle faced kid without even the suggestion of a whisker on his chin, one that looked pitifully weak when compared to the rock-hard jaw of Doc Savage or Dick Tracy. I ran a comb through my hair. It did little to improve things; my straw-colored cowlick, jagged where Owen had trimmed it with sewing scissors, immediately fell back down over my right eye.

There wasn't much else I could do, so I hollered a goodbye and headed out the back door and down the steps. Owen was in the yard throwing a ball for the neighbor's spaniel that leapt the fence between our yards whenever any of us came outside.

"You got any money?" I asked.

"Yeah, tons of it. My old man's got piles," he quipped. "What do you need money for?"

"Car fare. I've got a chance of a job." I told him where I needed to go.

He shook his head. "Nope, not a nickel."

My bike, a single-speed rebuild with a carrier on front, was waiting for me, leaning, saggy framed, against the stairs. I loved that bike, such as it was. It was my freedom—a pile of junk that in the few months I'd owned it had worked its metal heart out for me. It and I had delivered groceries for half a dozen stores along Main Street. It had stood quietly while I piled hundreds of pounds of merchandise on it, and then squeaked and groaned, but held together, as I pedaled halfway across town. Our destinations were not all close at hand, some were indeed far flung, all the way over to Dunbar and Kerrisdale, to houses where people had discovered that it was cheaper and more convenient to phone their orders and have their groceries delivered, than pay car fare and carry them themselves.

It was hard work, work that was little appreciated. Never once was there a tip; sometimes, on a hot day, there was an offer of a drink of water, but that was all. Mostly there were complaints and threats to phone the store because I had taken so long. There was never an offer of help to hump a sack of flour up a narrow staircase, but always a suspicious stare, a furtive searching for a bulging pocket that might conceal a packet of cigarettes, a chocolate bar or a handful of raisins.

All for a few cent, the amount depending on distance, had this bike and I labored. And when there was nothing to deliver, it had carried me to the furthest reaches of the city. On it, I had explored everything from the North Shore to the Fraser Delta all the way out to Ladner and White Rock. I had bought it for ten dollars, out of what I had earned sweating in the dirt and smoke of the chain factory. I was on it, day after day, going anywhere to get away from the house, away from the poverty-induced grumbling, the sight of Mother's frailty, the constant reminders of illness that had been with me almost since birth, and away from the never-ending checker games. I had put thousands of miles on it and freighted tons of groceries with it. The hard wear was showing. The chain wheel and sprocket, well worn when I took it home from the bike shop, had since been honed to knife edges. The chain jumped off at the least excuse and the tires were paper thin, but it was all I had—really, my only possession. If it got me to Pacific Mills office in time this morning, and McGrath hired me, I wouldn't ask anything more from it.

It was a short pump up from John Street to Main, then downhill all the way to First Avenue. I knew every bump on that street, so I let it go, dodging pot holes, street-car tracks, sections of cobblestone and horse manure, without having to think about it, hardly conscious of the whisper of bald tires and the plaintive squeaking of the frame. I didn't have a watch and the only clock sticking up was away across town on a building that was too far to see. I *would* make it by eleven, that's all there was to it.

With an uncharacteristic lack of caution, I went barreling through the light at Twelfth Avenue that had just changed to red, narrowly missing tangling the bumper of a fat Studebaker sedan, feeling guilty but exhilarated at having saved a few seconds. Trouble ahead though—a horse-drawn vegetable wagon sandwiched between a street car and a milk wagon angling in toward the curb. There was no getting between them. I headed for the gutter and tried to beat them. My front wheel hit something in the accumulated rubbish—a piece of glass, a nail, I'll never know. There was a hiss, and the rim was suddenly trying to squirm its way out of the tire, the tube, like gray entrails, flopping out the side.

"Oh Jeez! Oh God damn!" I shouted involuntarily as the bike, like a bucking horse, tried to work its way out from under me. Only by sheer determination did I keep it upright. I skidded to a stop and gazed unbelieving at the tire. Then panic set in. Now what? No patching kit, no pump, no money, no time and still a fair way to go.

Stashing the bike behind a billboard and walking was the first thing that came to mind. But I'd never make it on time. I could try to bum car fare...fat chance. Telephone? Just maybe...

I half carried the bike across the street and back a few doors to the Fairmont Grocery, a corner store run by Japanese people. I knew the son and daughter slightly.

"Can I use your phone?" The old grandfather was the only one in the shop. He was short and wide and without any neck. A thick brush, like a newly mowed gray lawn, bristled the top of his head that wasn't much higher than the counter top. He gave me a suspicious stare.

"Please? I need to use a phone. I've got to phone home," I pleaded.

"Pay phone outside. You go outside...pay phone," he hissed through a mouth full of gold teeth. "Cost only five cent."

"I don't have any money. Please let me use your phone. I won't be long. Please?"

The desperation in my voice and written on my face must have touched some soft spot within him.

"Okay, you use phone. You don't take long time and no long distance." He opened the lift-lid in the counter and let me come behind to the wall phone.

"Aw, c'mon, 'eh! Twelfth Avenue? I don't exactly feel like going all the way down there. Can't you fix it?" I could understand Owen's reluctance, but I wasn't about to accept a refusal either. It took all the persuasion I could muster, plus a few reminders of favors he owed me, before he finally agreed. We would swap bikes.

"And hurry, 'eh"

"Yeah, yeah."

He did better than I thought he would. I was considering the sorry mess that was my bike and fretting about the loss of time, sitting outside with my back against the apple boxes arrayed under the grocery-store window, when he angled across the street and jumped his bike over the curb. He got off.

"And don't go wrecking it," he said, as I swung my leg over it.

"No. I won't," I promised. "And thanks."

He examined the front tire. "Jeez, I gotta push this thing all the way home."

I didn't hear the rest of his complaint. I shouted over my shoulder, "Yeah, but I'll pay you once I get this job." It was all I had time to say. I thought I heard him say, "I bet," and then I was gone.

His bike was better and newer than mine. He'd paid more for it—where he'd got the money, he wasn't telling. Its paint was all one color and not flaking off. His tires had tread on them, too. I pumped like a maniac, although, by now, I had given up all hope of finding Pacific Mills' office by eleven o'clock.

The office wasn't exactly where I had been told it would be, but I found it.

McGrath looked at me through thick bushy eyebrows. I was sweating and conscious that I probably smelled pretty high. He smiled a little when I told him why I was late.

"It really wasn't that important. I just said eleven o'clock." He shrugged. "Any time today would have been good enough."

Oh, great! Nice guy, I thought.

I sat on the hard chair in front of his desk, feeling inadequate, nervously clasping and unclasping my hands. He asked me a few questions and I told him what I thought he wanted to hear—without out and out lying. Curiously, he didn't seem very interested in my qualifications—or the lack of—or where I had worked before.

Finally I had to ask, "How did you know about me? How come I get a chance to work for Pacific Mills?"

He sort of harrumphed and cleared his throat. "You know an Irishman by the name of McConaghie?"

"Yeah," the connection escaped me for the moment, though.

"He was in here a few weeks ago, said you were a hard worker. Asked that I give you a chance if something came open. You better not let him down then, 'eh."

So that's how McGrath had heard about me. I hadn't got the job on my own, it had been arranged for me. My reputation as a conscientious worker had not preceded me to McGrath's office, as I imagined it must have. I could just hear Father saying it, "I told you so! It's not what you know, it's who you know."

I guess he was right.

John was an ex-policeman from Belfast, a tall pleasant man with an Irish sense of humor. I'd known him for a long time. And now, I guess I owed him one.

Lured by talk of a better life in Canada, he and his family had traded Belfast for an Alberta farm. They had settled few miles south of the windswept clay-belt village where we had had our beginnings, and many an evening he'd wandered over to sit at our kitchen table to drink tea and talk. Ostensibly interested in Father's political views, it was nevertheless apparent he was more interested in Olwyn, who was then in her early teens. Despite his Irish charm, he hadn't gained much ground. She liked him, as we all did, but that was about it. I guess, his age was against him; he was, at that time, almost twice her age. He had forsaken the farm, left it to his parents and brothers, done some winter freighting with his team of horses and sleigh, and then given up entirely and headed for the coast almost three years ahead of us.

His job search had taken him to Pacific Mills hiring office where he discovered that McGrath had also served on the Belfast police force—a fortunate discovery. At the first opportunity, McGrath had hired him for Ocean Falls. Thereafter, whenever he was in town, he dropped by the office to chat. During his last visit, while he was on holiday in July, he had asked McGrath to give me a break next time he was hiring. He hadn't said anything to me, even though he had spent a few evenings sitting on our front porch at John Street, seemingly still interested in kindling a warmth in Olwyn, but having usually to settle for conversation with Father and Mother. Olwyn, having developed other interests, was usually somewhere else.

I realized, a little deflated, that without John's friendship with McGrath and his putting in a word for me, I wouldn't have had a hope in hell of landing a job with Pacific Mills. There were just too many men, hundreds at least—bigger, stronger, better qualified than me—hungry for a chance at any job anywhere on the coast. Well, I wasn't proud and I would take it, no matter who had arranged it.

McGrath filled out a form and put a little X where I was to sign.

"They're paying 54¢ an hour and they're guaranteeing four days a week, eight hours a day. A room in the bunkhouse is $8 a month and board is a $1.15 a day."

It sounded good to me. Much less would still have sounded good.

He handed me an envelope. "Here's your boat ticket. They'll deduct the fare from your first paycheck. You'll be on the *Catala*. She leaves from the Union Steamships dock at seven tomorrow evening. You better be on her. You'll get off at Bella Bella the day after, that'll be Sunday, and a company boat will pick you up there and take you to the Falls. There'll be a few others." He smiled, wryly. "And you better not ride that bike to get down to the docks; the boat won't wait."

We shook hands. "You'll find it a good place to work. A lot of fine people live there. Good luck. And say Hello to McConaghie." I thanked him and assured him I would. I still had questions, a lot of them, but I supposed they would be answered all in good time.

I don't think I've ever felt so elated as when I left McGrath's office. In less than two hours I had gone from nothing, a state in which I had pretty well resigned myself I would always exist, to being employed. I had an honest to God paying job—54¢ an hour, eight hours a day. I did a quick calculation. That was $4.32 a day. Even after paying room and board I would have money left over. Wow! I was going to be rich.

I folded the envelope, stuck it inside my shirt and buttoned it all the way up. I wasn't going to lose that envelope—not on your life I wasn't.

I pedaled West on Cordova then cut down to the foot of Carrall and the Union Steamship docks, just to check them out. I wanted to know exactly where to go, leave nothing to chance. Not that I didn't know where to go, I had been down there dozens of times just bumming around. I had even applied for a job near there.

A sign on the dock had said a deckhand was wanted for the *Harbour Princess*, a small excursion boat plying Burrard Inlet. I must have looked the part of the hayseed I was. "Oh sure. I'll tell them you're from Stony Plain or Winnipeg. They're bound to want to hire you. They hire all their sailors from there," was the sarcastic response I got from the thin nervous man at the desk when I inquired.

Along Powell Street, the street of wholesalers, I hooked on to the back of one of Malkins flat-deck trucks loaded with farm produce and let it tow me. A couple of carrots, peeking out between the slats of a crate, were too tempting. My stomach was growling, my morning porridge long exhausted, so I hauled them out and stashed them in the cardboard box in my carrier. At the CPR docks, I sat on a piling and munched them.

I rode slowly homeward, past the museum on the corner of Hastings and Main where Owen and I had spent hours looking, while sheltering from the rain. I went through Chinatown, past the Ivanhoe Hotel, and past McDonald's Stone Works, where I had labored for a dollar a day making boom chains. I had an urge to stop in and tell somebody, to say "Hey! Look at me. I have a better job, and at far better pay than I ever got for swinging a sledgehammer and frying myself in front of a blazing furnace." It was an empty thought; the chain factory no longer existed.

I pedaled uphill, not exerting myself, past the billboard that advertised a brand new Packard roadster for $600, and the used car lot at Seventh, past all the little corner stores, of which there were dozens, the bakeries and butcher shops that struggled for survival on Main Street. They were all familiar to me. Main, between Thirtieth Avenue and the waterfront, had become my street. I knew it by heart and, in some ways, I would be sorry to leave it.

I had no idea what I was going to. Ocean Falls was somewhere up the coast, 300 miles north of Vancouver somebody had said. I had just hired on to work in a paper mill, with not the foggiest notion of what a paper mill looked like and even less idea of how paper was made. "You'll work in the finishing room." McGrath had said—whatever that was.

The date was Friday, August 18, 1939, and I was eighteen years old, five-foot-six, one hundred and thirty-five pounds, virtually uneducated and with a singular lack of skills in my war bag. The only thing I had to offer was a willingness to work and a thirst for knowledge.

My ambition was underdeveloped and with little direction. I had never visualized myself as anything in particular. Thoughts of a profession had not progressed beyond the embryonic stage, it being futile to even dream. By necessity I had had to concentrate on the needs of the moment and the immediate future. And by immediate, I mean like tomorrow and the next day. I was desperate to make money, enough to support myself, to buy such luxuries as new clothes, perhaps a watch, and, all important, go to a dentist and have my teeth fixed and be rid of the nagging ache that was in them day after day.

My excitement had built to almost the bursting point when I

arrived home. *By God! I finally had a paying job.*

Father hadn't waited. My bike was on the porch with a for sale sign on it. Somebody, probably Owen, had fixed the tire. At least they had had confidence that McGrath would hire me.

I spent the afternoon and evening playing checkers with Father and assuring everyone that things were bound to be better now that I was going to work full time. I couldn't tell them much about the job or Ocean Falls. I didn't know any more than they did.

I didn't sleep much that night. I lay in bed, in the basement room, beside the sawdust bin, listening to night traffic sounds drifting in through the open windows and to Owen's quiet breathing in the bed beside me. I thought about Ocean Falls, trying to imagine what it looked like and firming up my resolve that no matter what it was like, I would stick it out for a few years anyway.

Next morning, feeling exhausted and tense at the same time, I packed a suitcase, an old brown cardboard affair that wouldn't stay shut without being tied with twine. I didn't have much to put in it. I didn't even have a complete change of clothes. My spare jeans and shirt were clean, but full of burn holes from flying slag, one of the lesser hazards of working in the chain factory. My only jacket was a threadbare, green-checkered, blanket-cloth windbreaker; the sleeves were well skewered and hopelessly matted with barley beards from having worn it in the chill of autumn mornings, stooking in the Alberta grain fields—what seemed an eon ago. I had one pair of scuffed leather boots. My hat was a tattered tweed cap, with a peak in which the cardboard stiffening had disintegrated in the wet.

"Bring me your socks. I'll darn them," Mother said. She didn't stir from her chair for long these days. Standing was too great an effort. She sat, day after day, sometimes reading a thick book on diet by a Doctor McCoy who supposedly had the answers to most ills, but mostly doing nothing, just gazing out the window, her thoughts miles away.

I stripped off my socks and handed them to her. I had become so used to my toes sticking through holes it no longer bothered me. I brought her basket of wool and needles.

"You'll need some new clothes before winter," she said, tiredly. "That's a long way north you're going. You'll have to dress warmly. Buy some underwear...be sure to..." Her voice trailed off. She knew the futility of piling instructions on me. The truth was, I was going to have think for myself. All responsibility for my upkeep was, from here on, squarely on my shoulders. I would have to make my own decisions. The money I made would be mine to spend on whatever I chose. Mother wouldn't be there to advise me.

Over the last year, she had noticeably run out of energy and the will to worry about everyday things like cooking meals and dressing a family. Mind-destroying poverty and illness had sapped her. Olwyn had assumed most of the household duties. My going would be a relief for everybody, one less to worry about.

It was a long day waiting until boat time. I had no friends to say goodbye to, only a few acquaintances and they wouldn't miss me, so I stayed home and talked. I played innumerable checker games with Father, but my mind was elsewhere and he beat me easily.

"You're not paying attention," he complained.

He was right; I wasn't. I had too many other things on my mind.

How I was going to get to the boat wasn't an issue. I had decided to walk. It seemed the best and surest way. If I left home at about five, I could make the docks in plenty of time.

We ate supper early, sitting at the kitchen table, nobody saying much. By that time we were talked out. Nobody wanted to hear anything more about Ocean Falls. And we all knew, without saying so, that this was the breakup of the family. We had stayed together through economic necessity, it being more practical to remain as a family unit, with each of us contributing our meager earnings to the pot. With what we earned and Father's war pension, we had at least eaten regularly, plain fare, but enough to nourish us—except that Owen and I, in our final stages of growth, were perpetually hungry. None of us would have been able to survive on our own; our earnings were too lean. The competition for the few available jobs was fierce and the pay a pittance. Ours had been a hand-to-mouth existence for most of the last year. Hopefully, that was about to change.

So, I was to be the first to leave the nest for good. I knew I wouldn't be back—not to stay, anyway. Olwyn would probably be next; she was showing signs of wanting to get married and probably would have done so already if her fiancé—as she had lately started referring to him—had a job. That left Owen, and at sixteen he was pretty restless. He and Father were bound to lock horns seriously one of these days. For one thing, he flatly refused to play checkers. And he was close mouthed about his comings and goings—a worry for Mother.

I said my goodbyes. Mother's lips quivered a little, making a lump come up in my throat. Father stuck out his hand. I hardly knew what to do with it. Then he said, "Be a good boy." I should have known he would say that. "And I expect you'll send us something each month. About fifteen dollars would be about right. You'll be earning pretty big money." He nodded. "Yeah, pretty big money. You should be able to spare that much."

I said, "Yeah," and at that moment, I really believed I would. They were so desperately poor and had so little to look forward to.

Mother gave me a hug. I felt her slip something small and hard into my hand. I didn't say anything or look until I was a block away. It was a five-dollar bill folded into a tight square—grocery money for a week. I felt guilty taking it, but I didn't go back.

CHAPTER 5

A Steerage Berth

So I was leaving Vancouver, alone. I was having latent pangs about leaving my family, and indeed about leaving at all, for despite everything, I had come to love this city.

For more than a year, I had wandered throughout its length and breadth, footloose and mostly alone. The days I had worked had been few, the longest period lasting only a few months. Days and weeks when there was nothing else to keep me occupied, I had prowled, mostly in the industrial and commercial districts, wherever I thought there might be a few hours of work. But I also went places where there was no other reason for being there but for their sheer beauty, beauty that was absolutely free to be absorbed for as long as I wanted—the parks, the beaches and even up to the slopes of the mountains. But it was the waterfront and its activity that drew me more than anything else.

Even in these hard times there was always something going on there, something different to see. I never tired of looking. I had spent hours, even with rain leaking down my collar and shivering in the cold, hanging around the docks watching and dreaming, wishing myself onto a ship. I wasn't particular, any ship would have done, and there were many to choose from.

There were the great, haughty passenger ships like the *Empress of Canada*, *Empress of Britain* and *Empress of Asia*, ocean-going cities in themselves. They appeared, lingered a few days and left— aloof entities that plied the seas of the world seemingly dependent on none. And there were cruise ships, the excursion boats to the gulf islands and coastwise passenger ships. They all came and went, night and day and in all weather, their mournful whistles vying with the fog horns at Point Atkinson, Prospect Point and Point Grey announcing their passage through the First Narrows and echoing against the mountains, smoke from their funnels soiling the snow-capped panorama of the North Shore. There were also the grubby little coast freighters scurrying among the inlets ferrying groceries and mail to the pulp towns, to the fishing communities, canneries and lonely logging camps. To me, it wouldn't have mattered, the ship or its destination, as long as it was going somewhere. It was easy to imagine myself as a sailor on any of them.

My personal wheel of fortune, which seemed to have been stuck in one position for most of my life, had finally turned and taken on at least a semblance of vitality. What I had dreamed of was about to happen. I was going somewhere aboard a ship, not as a sailor but, the next best thing, as a passenger to be carried to a paying job. I felt for my ticket for the umpteenth time.

Catala, flagship of the Union Steamship Company, was no leviathan. She was a tea cup when compared to the Empress liners. She did, however, bulk large along side the squat, gray, ramshackle buildings of the dock and her sister ship, the *Cardena*. Somehow I had doubted she would actually be there. I was still not fully convinced this whole scenario wasn't a dream.

She *was* there though, her twin funnels exhaling blue heat-devils over the roof tops, their red paint—the hallmark of all Union steamships—reflecting the evening sunlight and her port holes, a line of dark buttons fastening the white blouse of her upper works to the black skirt of her hull. Yes. She was there, readying herself for the northern out-ports, the mantis arms of her derricks waving load after sling-load of freight to her foredeck. I paused for a moment to look at her through the fence, where I had stood innumerable times to watch the movement of water traffic. But now I had this delicious excitement bubbling inside me. This time I wouldn't turn away to plod on down the street to the CN or the CP docks; I would go through the gate to the waiting room and then I would go on board. I would actually walk up that gangplank that extended like a tongue from the forward section to lick at the rough timbers of the dock. I had a right to. I had a ticket.

The uniformed agent looked questioningly at me when I shoved my ticket through the slot in the barred window. "Is there something wrong?"

"No. I just thought...I thought I was supposed to show my ticket."

"Ah, yes. But not here, when you go aboard. You'll show it at the gangway. Okay?"

"Yeah." Flustered. "I guess. Uh...when can I go aboard?"

He glanced at the clock. "Pretty soon now."

"How will I know?"

He smiled. "You'll know."

Relieved that my ticket was actually valid and my boarding would not be in question, I slumped onto the end of a bench. I had need to take a load from my feet. They were complaining at having just carried me the thirty-odd blocks from home in my broken down ill-fitting boots. I tucked my suitcase between them and relaxed. There were only two benches, the other one occupied by an elderly couple and their bundles. The waiting room was gradually filling. Through the window, I watched them arrive. A steady trickle. The doors banged and the volume of conversation swelled.

A cab drew up in front. The wings of its doors unfurled, batlike, and what was obviously a family emerged. The mother, a portly matron, hair carefully coifed, the ample shelf of her bosom supporting a string of large white beads that lay in a broad toothy grin against the navy blue of her suit, led the way. Two teenaged daughters followed her. She swept into the waiting room as though she owned it.

The tall, skinny father, a harried-looking man, also blue suited, paid the driver, loaded himself with suitcases and struggled along behind them, bumping awkwardly through the door that nobody thought to hold open for him. He stacked the suitcases against the wall then looked around as though there was something else to which he should attend.

"I suppose we can't board yet. I told you we were too early," the mother complained loudly.

"Oh, come," the father protested. He glanced at the clock on the wall and then fished a watch from his vest pocket. It was anchored by a heavy gold chain that drooped across his middle. He consulted it, then compared to the clock. "It'll only be a few minutes. We're not all that early. Nothing to get upset about." He patted himself, absentmindedly searching for something, then withdrew tobacco pouch and a long-stemmed briar from his pocket and went about the business of stuffing it. "Sit down and relax, why don't you? It won't be long."

"I don't want to relax. I want to go aboard. I can relax better when I can sit on something clean. This place is filthy." She rummaged in her purse, found a lace-bordered hanky and wiped the oaken slats at the other end of the bench on which I was sitting. I guessed there wouldn't be room if they all decided to sit, so I half smiled and nodded, indicating I would relinquish my seat in their favor. I stood up. She scarcely glanced at me. My vacating was expected and not worth acknowledging. She eased herself down, like a fussy hen over a clutch of eggs, attempting to put as little of her expensive skirt as possible in contact with the wood. "Emily. Barbara. Come. Sit over here," she clucked.

The shorter of the two, maybe twelve years, with a ribbon in her blonde hair, white dress, bobby socks and black patent shoes, slid onto the bench beside her mother, her face a study of sullen boredom, that is, until she caught sight of me. She inspected me, unashamedly, from top to bottom and then snickered. She put both hands over her mouth and giggled behind them. I felt blood pumping into my face, on up, until even my scalp felt hot.

I tried to keep my expression blank, as though whatever she was giggling at had nothing to do with me, but I couldn't quite pull it off. I couldn't stare her down and had to turn away.

The taller girl chose to disregard the command.

"Barbara. Come sit here," her mother insisted.

"Oh, Mother. I don't want to sit." She turned her back, deliberately exerting her independence. She looked right at me, but, unlike her sister, she never cracked a smile. Her gaze went right through me. I didn't exist. I picked up my suitcase and moved to a far corner, hot, sweat running from my armpits. I wanted to hide. I realized what I must look like to this obviously well-heeled family. My worn shirt, jeans full of holes, run-over boots, my rat-chewed haircut—I was a nonentity.

Suddenly, out of a wilderness of self-detestation, came determination. Sometime, somehow, I would be someone to notice. I *too* would dress decently. From somewhere, confidence would come and people would take notice, not to giggle at, but because I was *somebody*. There would be a time; just you wait.

Right now though, I felt like an alien in this room. Its occupants—all who seemed to know each other, all with an air of confidence that bespoke, if not prosperity, at least substance—were gathered in knots,. They stood like trees in a forest, their conversation a steady drone, the Vesuvian outpouring of pipe and cigarette smoke from their mouths and nostrils hanging in a noxious cloud above them.

I glanced furtively between the figures. Barbara, sixteen or seventeen, her long blonde hair cut like Veronica Lake's, over one eye, the front of her white blouse straining, the straight lines of her skirt swelling over well-developed thighs, calves rounded, no longer the spindly legs of a child. Cool and confident. To me, at that moment, she was beautiful, not just her features but the whole picture she presented, because she was so clean and well groomed, her clothing expensive. Would I ever have the nerve to speak to someone like her? And would someone like her ever smile at me, inviting me to speak? She caught me looking. My eyes fled, seeking sanctuary across the room, as though having merely paused en route to an intensely interesting piece of graphic art—a large fly-specked poster of a red-funneled ship in some northern fjord, tacked to the wall.

I leaned against the wall, waiting.

At some secret signal, I hadn't heard any announcement but somehow these seasoned coastwise travelers knew, there was a sudden alertness, a shifting and a rustling as suitcases and parcels were retrieved. Coats were thrown over arms. Feet shuffled. The aimless eddying became a river flowing through a door and down a sloping corridor, which echoed hollowly to the thump of boots and the clack of heels. I tagged along, toward the rear, knowing at all times where Emily and Barbara were, but keeping well back in the pack. Following, sheeplike, to the exit, across the wharf and up the steep gangplank.

A seaman, his blue serge pressed and gold buttons shining, inspected my ticket and me. Wordlessly, he cut me from the herd, indicating stairs that went straight down into darkness. I hesitated.

"Uh, can I not go up? I mean, I'd like to be upstairs. Somewhere I can see out. I thought my stateroom would be up...one with a porthole. I don't know...I've never been on a boat before."

He pointed at my ticket. "You're traveling steerage. You won't have a stateroom, just a bunk. It's down in the lower decks. Down these stairs. You'll find a bunk down there. Just follow the passage way. Yes. Here. You see...number six." He indicated the numeral scrawled on my ticket. "Down there." He pointed again. He half smiled at my look of consternation and disappointment. "It's not bad, you know."

"Oh, um, yeah. Okay, I guess." Being unsure of my ground, I thought it better not debate the matter further. I descended.

Below the first stairs was another. It also went downwards. I humped my suitcase ahead, holding it with one hand while grasping the handrail with the other, the worn leather of my boot-soles finding uncertain purchase on the narrow treads. The number of steps and the direction they were taking convinced me I would end up well below the waterline. Unhappily, I continued.

The second stairs ended in a narrow gloomy passageway with all the ambience of a mine shaft. It was lit by small bulbs in wire cages. Yellowed paint, dark varnished woodwork and brown linoleum underfoot, sucked hungrily at the weak light, leaving barely enough to navigate by. The passageway emptied into a room that, by its shape, had to be directly under the foredeck.

My first impression was that of a cavern with bunks terracing its walls and crowding upon each other. Beyond, through an open door, in a room slightly brighter, were tables with railings around their edges, and again, beyond them, more gloom. A hot stuffiness engulfed me, swaddling me in a thick fabric of stale odors—cleaning compounds, oil, paint, mold, onions, body odor, tobacco smoke, tarred cordage, old cooking fat.

Strange clankings came shuddering down through the decks above my head, and the ghostly sighings of fans and the whine of pumps whispered around me. I hesitated, unsure what to do next. I seemed to be the only one here, no one to ask.

I'd had mixed up, but generally pleasant, mental pictures of the interior of a ship. None of them, however, resembled any of this. I cast my eyes about. Out of all of these bunks, which was mine?

Then I noticed that affixed to the side boards were polished brass numerals, glowing satinlike in the dimness. I located number six. Until a few moments ago, when the seaman, above had combed that nonsense from my mind, I'd actually thought the six meant stateroom number six. I felt foolish. I should have known better.

I didn't know what oceans we were scheduled to cross—I had never given much thought to the coastline of British Columbia—but the side barriers on the bunks called up visions of vast waves and the ship standing on her beam ends. That they were there at all was both alarming and reassuring. I thought briefly of my forbears on my mother's side, all seafaring folk. Absently, I thought, here I am carrying on the tradition.

I threw my suitcase on the gray wool blanket and sat beside it, depressed. Confined, like a criminal, I thought, committed to a dungeon. Or was it called the brig aboard ship? Suddenly, I felt very lonely. My bright vision of shipboard travel had become badly tarnished.

I'd thought I was alone, but I wasn't. Across the way, in a lower bunk, a figure lay motionless, propped on one elbow. In the gloom, about all I could make out was that he was Chinese and that he was dressed in dark clothing. He had a little round hat on his head. He stared unblinkingly at me. I imagined nothing good in that stare. Abruptly, there rose within me a powerful urge to be out of there, to climb back up those stairs into fresh air and daylight.

However, to get to the upper decks I would have to argue my way past the seaman, an exercise not likely to succeed. I'd got the impression he could be very firm and that I was not welcome anywhere but where I was. My ranging the upper salons, I supposed, would somehow contaminate the first-class accommodation.

I was not bold enough to try subterfuge. I didn't know the passageways, so a circuitous route was out of the question. Above all, I was not about to risk getting thrown off the ship for trespassing where I wasn't wanted. So I sat on my bunk and covertly watched the Chinese man across the way staring unblinkingly at me.

We were not alone for long. More passengers arrived, those

whom I guessed were not well enough off to travel first class or, like me, were being shipped by some company. Some went directly to their bunks, others proceeded to the other room and gathered around the tables. Soon, decks of cards appeared, and shortly afterward, bottles were produced. The smell of liquor became pronounced. The conversation around the table was generally loud and boisterous.

They were a mixed lot, all men, a sampling of those I had become familiar with, those who had frequented the same areas of the city I had, primarily the waterfront. I knew their type. They lounged on its streets, occupied chairs in the lobbies of the shabbier hotels and ate their meals in the cheap restaurants. Some had done for years. They were leaving the city, perhaps like me, finally going to jobs, logging jobs, cannery work and God knows what, heading north to the camps and out-ports.

McGrath had said there were others destined for Ocean Falls, but who they might be I couldn't guess. Perhaps, unlike me, some of them might be better off and riding in the staterooms overhead.

I seemed to be the youngest in the room.

One huge individual with a protruding belly, and wearing the remnants of a business suit, arrived singing and waving a much depleted whiskey bottle about. He took up a weaving stance in the middle of the room, roared discordantly something about belonging to Glasgy, then made a beeline for a bunk and collapsed into it. He took a pull from his bottle then, hugging it to his chest, lapsed immediately into snoring. I noted that he was wearing high-top boots, the bottoms bristling with caulks and shining like a metal hedgehog. I dreaded to think what they might do to the bedding, which although not luxurious, was clean and without holes, so far anyway.

A deep throaty moan of a steam whistle filtered through many layers of steel plating reached me. It was one signal I recognized. I had heard it many times while I loitered on the docks. It was a warning to latecomers that they better get a move on. From where I was in *Catala*'s bowels, it was hard to know when our leaving would actually happen. In a few moments, however, I felt her come alive; bulkheads creaked and machinery thumped. Then came an alarming shudder. (I learned later it always accompanied a reversal of the screws.) It had me ready to abandon ship until I realized no one else was showing signs of panic.

I was determined to witness something of our going. So, resolved to plead my case to the seaman one more time if I met him, I picked up my suitcase, ascended the first set of stairs, tackled the first door I came to and found it exited to the foredeck. A couple of deckhands were tidying up, but neither paid any attention to me. The other seaman, I guessed, was probably now occupied with running the ship and wouldn't have time to concern himself with the likes of me. I wedged myself into a corner and watched.

The docks were behind and the First Narrows Bridge was swiftly approaching. I waited until we passed underneath its spidery steel, and Stanley Park became a green smudge with Point Grey an indistinct pointing finger beyond it, then retreated back inside, out of the wind of our own creating.

There was little to do but lie on my bunk and listen to the pounding of the engines and the raucous voices around me. I had nothing to read, and engaging any of my rowdy shipmates in conversation held little appeal. As far as I could tell, nobody, other than the Chinese man, had noticed me. And that was just fine. I was not big enough nor fierce-enough looking to deter anyone with a warlike bent, and the further the evening progressed and the more that was consumed from the bottles that were circulating freely, the more pugnacious some of them became. I lay in my bunk and said nothing while the arguments washed around me.

I had survived, largely unscathed, for more than a year in and around the seamier side of Vancouver by not being noticed. My natural instinct was that of the rabbit; when threatened, keep quiet and blend with the surroundings. "Avoid drawing attention to yourself," said my inner voice. And always there was Father's voice in my subconscious, admonishing me, as it had since I was big enough to understand the meaning, "Don't be conspicuous." I had kept myself free of unwanted attention by listening to these voices. I had ranged the tenderloin of a major seaport at a time when there were thousands of desperate characters subsisting on what could be gleaned from the unwary. They were there waiting to relieve the weak and the careless of anything of even the slightest value. I had never run afoul of any of them. I had witnessed just about everything from muggings to mayhem without any of it being directed at me.

I had no idea of the time, but eventually the crescendo passed. The arguments diminished as the contents of the bottles that had produced them ran out. Snores chorused from the bunks. I began thinking about undressing and crawling in between the sheets. I stuffed my suitcase in the corner of the bunk and pulled the blanket over it. It contained everything in the world I owned, and, such was my conditioning, I was sure that if I fell asleep, someone would pilfer it.

I had just started to take off my shirt, when the Chinese man bestirred himself and shuffled over. He had stared at me all evening, and I had grown uneasy, seeing only evil in his flat expressionless face and the brown unblinking buttons of his eyes. He came close and looked down at me.

"You got money," he hissed, scarcely above a whisper.

I shook my head nervously, certain he was about to rob me. I was trying to decide whether I could handle him myself—he was no bigger than me—or whether to holler for help, when he said, "You got money, you hideum. You puttem inside you undawear, right down next to you balls. Some bad mans here. I know him. You go to sleep, he stealum. You hide him in you undawear." With that he shuffled back to his bunk.

Surprised, I nevertheless did as he said. I tucked my five-dollar bill down into my shorts.

The sheets were white and crisp, the pillow full and clean. Sleep did not come immediately, and when it did, it came accompanied by a parade of disconnected dreams broken abruptly by panicky waking to grope for my suitcase and feel for the lump in my shorts. After awhile I must have fallen into a deep sleep because the next thing I knew breakfast was being announced. I vaguely remember that we had stopped somewhere in the night, there being a cessation of engine noise and an increased clanking overhead. I was relieved that, despite my unconsciousness, my valuables were intact. The Chinese man's bunk was no longer occupied.

Nothing could have been more tranquil than the waters of the inside passage that day.

As I was finishing breakfast, served at one of the tables in the room where the card playing had gone on the previous evening, a slim dark man of about thirty-five sitting across from me asked, "Are you Jones?"

Surprised, I said I was.

"How did you know?" I asked.

"McGrath. He told me you were going to the Falls. Said to keep an eye out for you. You're the only one that fits the description."

"Oh." I felt somewhat flattered that McGrath had considered me that important. "Is that where you're going?" I asked.

"Yeah. Me and that guy over there." He pointed at a simian type at the next table who was shoveling pancakes and sausages into his mouth and grunting with the effort of chewing them. He glanced around and shrugged. "There's a few more here somewhere, but he's the only one I know about, other than you and me. Uh...my name is McDonald. Ken McDonald." He extended his hand across the table and we shook.

"I'm Paul," I said.

He eyed me closely. "How old are you, anyway?"

His question caught me off guard. "Twenty, I mumbled," not looking at him. I had decided that being only eighteen was a disadvantage and I would lie a little. His look said he didn't believe me. He lit a cigarette and extended the package. I shook my head.

"You don't look twenty."

I thought it best that the matter of my age be dropped.

"Are you going to work in the finishing room?" I asked.

"I suppose so. That's where they need help right now. But I'm not going to stay there. There's better jobs, with more money. I'm going to get on the paper machines. You can make more than a dollar an hour on the machines."

I hadn't thought beyond getting there and starting work in the finishing room—and that, with trepidation—so I didn't offer anything like "that's what I want to do, too," because I hadn't a clue what a paper machine was. Any ambition toward a better job would have to come later. We chatted for a few moments then he said, "Lets go on deck and breathe some fresh air. This place stinks."

"Are we supposed to. I mean...I thought we had to stay down here. The guy when we boarded said...."

"Why the hell not? We're paying, well, at least somebody is

paying for us to ride on this bucket. We should be allowed outside. Come on."

I followed him up to the foredeck. After the gloom, the sunlight was a bright sword flashing in front of my eyes. There was no wind—the net effect of a following wind keeping pace with *Catala*. The sky was blue and without clouds. And having grown used to the mixture of smells below, the air seemed freshly scrubbed. With a newfound confidence, handed me by McDonald, I picked my way through the clutter of winches and cables to the forepeak and looked straight down. Fascinated, I watched the steel bow knife through the small chop and peel white-crested waves away evenly on either side. This was the glistening saltwater of the ocean, the first I had actually seen, far different from the gray leprous pollution of Burrard Inlet and False Creek.

Both sides of the channel were an unbelievable blue-green, the rounded hills, a soft petite-point against a backdrop of jagged mountains. Some of the higher peaks, even this late in the summer, still had snow encrusting their tops. A thread of sea-polished granite glistened brightly at the tideline, demarking the separation of forest and water, curving away into distant bays and inlets and reappearing again at the next headland. I leaned against the rail and soaked up the sun, lost in admiration of the magic fretwork of a coast I hadn't dreamed existed.

Overhead, seagulls floated effortlessly, like paper kites on invisible strings. And for a few minutes, a pair of dolphins arrowed in from somewhere and rode the pressure ridges at the bow. I hardly knew there were such creatures. And I couldn't believe that an animal as wild could derive such obvious pleasure from flirting with that knife edge and racing it. A few moments of entertaining us and they streaked away, leaving me awed. If this was going to sea, I could understand why my forbears had spent a lifetime at it.

I leaned against the steel of the foredeck bulwarks, not wanting to talk to McDonald or anyone else. I just wanting to look and absorb.

On the decks above, first-class passengers promenaded, sauntering in twos and threes. I caught a glimpse of Emily and her mother walking side by side. Barbara trailed behind, still showing her independence. My eyes couldn't help themselves; they followed her. I wondered idly where they were going.

As I stood there watching and dreaming, a feather of steam blossomed from the whistle mounted on the forward funnel, and then a stunning blast practically lifted me from the foredeck. It went echoing back and forth against the hills on both sides.

"Alert Bay," McDonald said. "We'll stop here. Do you want to go ashore?"

"Do you think they'll let us?"

"Sure. Why not? We won't go far. We won't be here very long anyway."

Alert Bay. My first glimpse of a fishing and cannery town. It glistened in the sunshine, white buildings with green roofs, people lounging on the wharf. Heaving lines arced out from *Catala*. Waiting hands hauled on the thick hawsers and snugged her into the wharf. Her derricks were already moving. A few passengers, suitcases in hand, descended the gangplank. McDonald and I followed, me with an uneasy sense of daring. Would I get left behind?

There was nothing to do but walk on the dock. Nowhere to go. No shops to look in unless we really got venturesome and explored beyond the wharf. The few people who belonged, mostly Natives, were busy with freight. They paid us little mind.

I was relieved to get back on board.

Bella Bella, our debarking place, another fishing and cannery town, on Campbell Island, was announced by another blast of *Catala*'s whistle. Excitement welled up in me. I hurried below and retrieved my suitcase.

I descended the gangplank behind McDonald and joined a cluster standing on the wharf. Some I recognized from steerage; the remainder must have been traveling first class, although none of them looked any more well to do than us. We were all dressed in a hodgepodge of threadbare clothing, the mark of those who had not worked for a long time, and each of us had a suitcase at his feet, mine appearing not much worse than some of the others. Standing to one side was the character from the breakfast table, looking more apelike than ever. I wondered if he too was to work in the finishing room.

"Over here! All you guys for Ocean Fall, over here!" The call came from a barrel-chested man who came striding up a slanting gangway toward us. His tin pants were stagged-off just above the tops of his caulk-encrusted boots making his legs look long and skinny. The heavy canvas of his trousers hung from his checkered-shirt-covered shoulders by broad, striped suspenders that could easily have supported one of the slings of freight being lowered from *Catala*. In addition, a wide leather belt, shiny with use, cinched them to his middle. He paused and pointed with his pipe at a tow boat that was moored at a float below and whose short mast extended above the edge of the decking. We moved as one, filed down the slatted gangway and clambered onto her deck.

Her bows and stern bore black letters announcing that she was the *John M.* out of Ocean Falls. The man paused to set fire to his pipe and then entered the wheelhouse. The diesels snorted and came to life.

I watched, nostalgically, as *Catala* dwindled in the distance, like a picture framed against the backdrop of blue-green hills—like the one on the fly-specked poster in the waiting room. She rounded a headland, leaving only a smudge against the sky.

I was thankful the weather was clear and warm; there was no possible way that the small cabin on *John M.* could have accommodated all of us had it been stormy.

Conversation over the roar of diesel engines was not worth the effort, so we just sat or lounged and watched the scenery go past. I stretched out, put my head on my suitcase and dozed. I would be glad to get there, but nagging in the back of my mind was the thought that, very soon, I was going to have to start making paper, and that whole process was a huge mystery.

The *John M.* was built for hauling, not for speed, and at her present rate, she was pushing a vast amount of water away from her bows. It was four o'clock when we rounded the point and there was Ocean Falls appliquéd across the side of the mountains. The great phallus of the stack dwarfing all else. Then, for the first time, I smelled the odor of rotten eggs—"that's the smell of money," I was told—that is the characteristic smell of all pulp and papermill towns. And for the first time, I heard the long, drawn sonorous moan of the whistle that would govern my comings and goings, night and day, for years to come.

The town as seen from a boat entering the harbor.

A view of the paper mill from high on the mountainside.

We trooped up the gangway to the wharf, all sixteen of us, and were met by one of the tallest men I had ever seen.

"I'm Cyrel Hague," he announced. "Welcome to Ocean Falls. If you'll follow me, we'll go over to the time office and sign you in. Then we'll fix you up with a place to live. You'll be in the bunkhouse. There's three of them. They're in behind the hotel there." He gestured toward a large white building with a veranda running across the front.

We crossed the bridge separating the mill from the town and crowded into the office where a short pleasant man with only one arm handed us forms to fill out and sign. I was last, having hung back to see how the others handled this task.

"You're in number one bunkhouse, room seven," the short man said, having finally got around to me. "I guess they told you in Vancouver that the rent is $8 a month. They're not bad rooms, plain but comfortable. You'll eat in number two diningroom; they call it the bullpen. That's $1.15 a day. Any question?"

"No. I guess not," I said. "Except, when do I go to work? They said I'd be in the finishing room. Where is that?"

"Oh yes. Yeah, you'll work in the finishing room." He looked at a list. "Yeah. You'll start at midnight tonight. When you have supper, ask them to pack you a lunch. Be here at eleven-thirty and somebody will show you how to punch the time clock and find your way around."

That shook me. Start work at midnight? I had seldom stayed up until midnight.

We trooped back across the bridge to the townsite.

My room was no larger than necessary to accommodate an iron cot and a small two-drawer dressing table under a window that was too high to see out. It smelled of Lysol and ancient tobacco smoke going back to the dawn of the smoking habit I was sure. On the wall across from the bed, was a shelf with a rod underneath. A tangle of wire coat hangers hung at one end. The walls were thin, so thin that normal breathing could be heard on the other side. Footsteps in the hallway, no matter how lightly trod, echoed the full length of the building. In the middle of the building opposite the door was a room with wash basins, a couple of showers and two toilet stalls.

Plain they had said. Yes, it was indeed that. Comfortable? I had my doubts.

I hung my jacket on a hanger, slid my suitcase under the bed and lay down. The mattress was lumpy and the blankets thin.

I lay waiting for suppertime and, afterward, midnight—when I would go to work.

The wooden streets and apartment buildings of Ocean Falls.

CHAPTER 6

The Longest Night

I have only a vague memory of that first night on graveyard shift. One thing, though, I am certain there has never been another one as long.

It began at eleven-thirty when I arrived at the time office, a brown bag containing lunch in hand, my self-confidence at low ebb and feeling grainy-eyed and lightheaded from already having stayed up too late. From there it went on interminably.

I had tried to prepare myself by sleeping during the evening, but it had been hopeless; I couldn't will myself into slumber. For one thing, I was worried I might not wake up. I had lain on my cot, my mind churning and my body tense. What demands might be made of me I couldn't even guess. The very fact that I would be up all night and expected to work at a job, about which I was sure I would know absolutely nothing, was enough to play havoc with my imagination. I had lain there listening to the clump of feet in the hallway, the flushing of toilets in the washroom next door, voices that seemed needlessly loud and argumentative and later, a discordant choir of snores vibrated in the flimsy walls ranging from high piccolo sopranos to heavy tuba basses.

I had eaten supper in the bullpen. I found it on the ground floor of the hotel. I hadn't thought to ask where it was when we signed in, but I remembered somebody had mentioned it being in the hotel. It was side by side with number one diningroom. I actually entered the latter first, but immediately realized I was in the wrong place. Tables covered with white cloths, napkins folded in triangles and standing smartly erect beside twinkling goblets, somehow didn't square with the title bullpen. I got it right on the second try.

Whoever had coined it, the title was apt. Though hardly resembling a cattle yard, there was little of refinement about it. Its furnishings, stout tables and benches made to withstand brutal treatment, were strictly utilitarian. Its wooden floor, chewed by the trampling of countless pairs of caulk boots, resembled a shag rug. It was not a place to linger in polite conversation. It was a place to get in, eat and get out, nothing more. However, the oilcloth on the tabletops was unstained. The cutlery, although bent, was free of grease, and the dishes, though crazed with long use and chipped around the edges, were clean. The kitchen, I later learned, was common to both dining rooms, the food no different in either.

Whatever the faults of the bullpen, a scarcity of food certainly was not one of them. In fact, there was more food presented at that one meal than I had seen in a long while. However, I just couldn't do it justice. My stomach was reacting negatively to the happenings of the last few days.

As I entered I felt conspicuous, stirring my natural aversion to being noticed. Although it was only a few minutes after opening time, it seemed I was already late; the room was almost full with a loud and boisterous crowd. It was probably my imagination, but I felt every eye follow me and all the voices hush. None of the waitresses scurrying back and forth to the kitchen paused to pay any attention to me. Apparently there were no allocated places.

I scanned the crowd for a familiar face. There were only two, those of Ken McDonald and the simian type who had traveled with me on the *Catala*. Ken was at a table on the far side of the room. It was fully occupied. And although there was room at the apeman's table, I had little inclination to sit there. I slid onto the end of a bench at a table with two men who gave me only a cursory glance.

There was no menu, but there were a variety of dishes. I was reluctant to dive right in as most were doing, although had I done so, I doubt I would have created much interest. I sampled a few things, but I have little recollection of what I actually ate. I did, nevertheless, have the presence of mind to order a lunch.

"Whaddaya want in it?" barked the waitress, dragging an order book out of her uniform pocket and a pencil from her hair. It seemed I was keeping her from more important things; she looked everywhere but at me. She was a bulky young woman whose white uniform struggled mightily to contain her ample figure. Her lipstick, a bright red, had been applied generously, perhaps with a trowel. It extended upwards, in a cupid's bow, high into the dark hair on her upper lip. Her eyes kept wandering as I mumbled something about meat sandwiches.

"You want pie?"

I nodded.

"What kind?"

"Ah, apple?" I suggested, hesitantly.

"Two meat and apple pie, that right?" she blared. Even over the surf of conversation, those in the far corners of the room could hardly have helped but learn what I was going to have for lunch sometime in the small hours.

There were five others waiting, all newcomers, standing in the pool of light outside the time office when I got there. Although I didn't know any of their names, I recognized them all as having arrived with me that afternoon on the *John M.*

A burly man with an unhealthy pallor, and the pronounced limp of someone with an artificial lower limb, exited the office. "I'm Tommy Grey," he said. He had a sheaf of time cards in his hand. He read off our names and dealt them out. He then went into a long, detailed instruction on how to punch the time clock. He made pushing a card into a slot until the mechanism clunked seem extraordinarily complex. That done, he led us through a door into a large gloomy room where the polished satin of well-used machine tools glinted softly. The only light came from lamps suspended over the passageways, the most of which was absorbed by the black of the oil-impregnated concrete floors. The rest, long banks of fluorescent tubes over the machines, were turned off. There was the smell of oil and grease, and of coal and heated metal. That last, I recognized, in fact I knew it well. I located its source, two blacksmith's forges, over against a far wall. With an expansive wave, Grey indicated the shadowy array of silent machines. In the gloom I could pick out a couple of lathes and a drill press, but the rest, I had no idea what they were. "This is the machine shop," he said. "They don't work nightshift here." What seemed self-evident did not deter him from launching into a long monologue on the occasions when there might be a need to work more than one shift. "And," he concluded somewhat proudly, "it's the biggest, most complete shop north of Vancouver." Nobody seemed ready to challenge that point. Indeed, to my eye it did look impressive.

To the left, above a pair of swinging doors, was a barely legible sign that said "Locker Room." He shouldered his way in. We followed him into a long low room that reeked of sweat, unwashed clothes, dirty steam pipes, dead soap, cleaning compounds and cigarette smoke.

"Other than the offices, this is the only place in the whole mill where you can smoke," he announced. "If you get caught smoking anywhere else, you could get fired. So don't get caught."

"Oh yeah. What do you do if you just gotta have a smoke?" a lank raw-boned individual inquired. He was middle-aged with long black hair leaking out and down his neck from a tattered cloth cap. He stood slouched, with his thumbs hooked in the pockets of his jeans. A large package of cigarette makings peeked out the top of his shirt pocket. His look of blank disbelief said, "You must be kidding."

"I ain't joking. If you gotta smoke, you sneak away and come down here. Nobody says anything if you sneak away once or twice a shift. Everybody does it. Anybody asks, just say you gotta take a leak."

"Pick yourselves a locker," he continued, his arms casually indicating the entire room. "Anywhere...anyone that's empty and has a key hanging in it. There's showers in the back there. Most guys like to shower when they come off shift. Leave your coats, but bring your lunches, that is unless you want to eat down here. Kind of stinks though."

He led us out and through the machine shop to a corner where a staircase with metal treads that rang hollowly with our footsteps, ascended steeply to the floor above. He had trouble climbing; his leg must have been hurting him. He clung to the handrail, grimacing with pain as he hauled himself up.

A slim, hawk-nosed man with thin, sandy hair met us. Our guide introduced him as Dave Donald. "You'll be working for Dave here," he said. "He's the night foreman. Any questions?"

We stood, shuffling, looking around. There were no questions. He nodded at Dave and turned to leave. "They're all yours, then."

It was just midnight. The room was huge and brightly lit, almost as bright as daylight, from dozens of high-wattage overhead lights. Paper, in rolls of every size, in stacks, on palettes and every shade of white through brown, filled the room. The far walls were obscured behind mountain ranges of paper. Narrow isles snaked between the stacks, through which jitneys, their engines roaring and their forks buried deeply into palettes stacked high with paper, wheeled at breakneck pace. The hum of machinery, low and pervasive, rumbled from somewhere in adjacent rooms, blanking out local sounds. The air carried a warm tropical dampness and the corrosive smell of sulfite.

Dave stabbed a finger at me. "You come with me." He turned to the others, "All you guys, you go over there and see Pete Brown. He's over there running that cutter." He pointed at a long red machine on which several huge rolls of paper revolved slowly. "He's a Scotchman. You'll know it as soon as he opens his mouth. He's wearing steam-engineers striped cap and overalls. He'll tell you what to do. You go find him."

He turned back to me. "We're doing bag roll," he said, matter-of-factly, as though I would know exactly what that was.

"Ah...what's bag roll?" I asked.

"It's paper they make paper bags out of...the kind you get at the store," He didn't quite roll his eyes, but by his expression, I half expected him to add, "What else, idiot?" But he didn't. He said, "It's shipped to Vancouver to the converting plant, a subsidiary company, Bertram Bag. That's where they make them. Okay?"

At least, I now knew where some paper went, but I still hadn't the faintest idea where it came from. Somewhere in this vast conglomeration of buildings somebody had to be making it, but where? Nothing in the immediate vicinity indicated where or how. My curiosity would have to be satisfied some other time.

The "doing" of bag roll turned out to be putting wrappers on rolls of brown Kraft paper destined for Bertram Bag. They were about the size of regular oil-drums and probably weighed several hundred pounds. I was the only green hand. Dave showed me where to go—about half way down and to one side of an inclined platform. A blond young guy waiting on the other side directly across from me eyed me speculatively.

"This is Earl Cochrane," Dave said. "Your name is?"

I told him. Earl smiled and extended his hand. Further along, a pair of youngsters watched, taking my measure. Was I going to fit in or was I a square peg?

"Earl here will show you what to do," Dave said. "Well go slow until you get the hang of it."

A few rolls started coming, rolling along the narrow platform. They first paused on a pair of revolving steel rollers where Dave whipped a heavy wrapper around them—the wrappers were longer than the roll by a few inches. He then nudged them off and sent them along the platform to Earl and me. Earl showed me how to insert a protective header inside the overhanging wrapper, and crimp the surplus end down over it. I waited for him to continue with further instructions, but he just stood there waiting for the next roll. There has to be more to it than this, I thought. This can't be all I'm supposed to do. But that was it.

Earl went back to his own side of the platform and the rolls started coming in earnest. I crimped as fast as I could, but somewhat sloppily.

We sent the crimped rolls on, along the ramp, to the other pair who were in charge of an air-driven press. They each had a bucket of glue, a wide brush and a stack of heavy heads the same size as the rolls. They liberally slopped glue onto the heads (and in so doing, onto themselves—the fronts of their pants were rigid and glistened with it) held them in place over the crimped ends with their fingertips until the one with the control lever closed the press to hold them there. There were frequent yelps and loud yells of "stupid bugger," as all too often the one without a control lever didn't get his fingers out in time. In a matter of seconds, the glue having set, the lever was banged the other way and the press gasped, as though it had been holding its breath, and opened, letting the roll continue on down the platform to be weighed, receive a label and stenciled address.

That first task of putting in headers and crimping ends seemed frantic until I got used to it. I felt like a dog chasing its tail, but without the option of stopping. We sat on old upended rolls of paper, a pile of headers beside us. It was replenished now and then from a loaded palette delivered by a young Japanese who drove his jitney like a racing car. It was reach out, grab a header, stuff it in and fold the overhanging wrapper flat over it. The rolls came to us at just the right height. There was nothing complicated about it. As Earl said, after the first half-hour, "A monkey could do this, you know." It was my first brush with assembly line type of labor. There was little to challenge the imagination.

Once we got going, there was no break. They just kept coming—brown rolls, from where I still hadn't figured out, but obviously from an endless supply. They were delivered to the upper end of the platform by the same Japanese cowboy and his jitney.

We were a team—Dave stressed that fact—the five of us. "You have to work as a team. It's the only efficient way for this type of operation to work," he said. We nodded. Whether it was or not we didn't know. And I doubt anyone cared. Anyway, nobody seemed to want to contradict him.

I got the hang of it. This is pretty easy, I thought, harking back to my days in the chain factory. And indeed it seemed so for the first couple of hours, then the mindlessness of it set in. After I had mastered the simple art of crimping, there was nothing to think about, except the ache in my shoulders from sitting hunched over. There never seemed to be a long enough break to get up, stretch and look around to see where the rolls were actually made and where they went after we got through with them, or what else was going on in the far reaches of this cavernous room. If we hurried to get ahead, Dave sent next roll that much sooner. The only bottleneck was at the press. If we could plug up the guys at the press, we could get a break. The glue, even the quick-setting type they were using, did, after all, need time to set. Earl took a delight in harassing the guys at the press.

We could talk, and we did. The hum of machinery was not loud enough to drown out conversation, and nothing we were doing was noisy.

I learned that the two young people running the press were local kids, George (Wong) Lee and Gwyn (Hank) Adams. I say kids, though they were only marginally younger than me. They had been raised at Ocean Falls. Both had graduated from high school the previous June and had been automatically absorbed into the workforce. The company looked after its own. Earl had come out of Trail, by way of Vancouver. He had been there for a couple of weeks.

We settled into the routine. I lost track of how many rolls I crimped.

As had to happen sooner or later, joking and banter grew out of the tedium of repetition. Mild horseplay followed, anything to relieve boredom. It started at the press with the spattering of glue on each other. It gravitated along to Earl who entered right into the spirit. As long as we kept up, Dave let it go. However, after one burst, where the ends of a couple of rolls got smeared with glue, Dave read the riot act. That settled things down for a while. It sobered me.

I'd never before encountered horseplay in the workplace. Work had always been a serious affair. It appeared I was the only one taking things seriously. It must have shown. George, a redhead with freckles, leaned over the top of a roll and nodded at Dave. Grinning, he said, "Don't worry about old Donald Duck there. He's not really a foreman; he's just running bag roll for a few nights. You should hear him squawk when he really gets mad." Whether Dave knew it or not, that name had stuck to him. Everybody throughout the finishing room knew who Donald Duck was. He had a squawky voice, but the rest of him bore little resemblance to the cartoon duck.

The man stenciling addresses and affixing labels was Stan Coldwell. Like the majority, he was from somewhere else. He had been there for a month or two. Older than the rest of us, dark and serious, he was close mouthed about his background.

As the first hour progressed into the next and the next, my thought process became blurred; the whole scene took on an unreality. Of all the things I had imagined about making paper at Ocean Falls, none of them had been remotely like this. Is this what I will do night after night, week after week, even year after year? I asked myself. The apparent answer was yes. By four o'clock I was going through the motions by rote.

We broke for lunch. We sat on the platform. I wasn't very hungry, but I ate the lunch that the bullpen staff had prepared—two ham sandwiches and a piece of soggy apple pie that had somehow got flattened in the brown bag. The apples were squished out from the sides of the crust.

"Did you look under the crust?" Stan asked, as I was about to take my first bite out of it.

"No. Why?"

"Cockroaches. The kitchen's full of 'em. The whole town, the hotel, the bunkhouses—they're everywhere. The place is alive with them, some as big as alligators. They get into everything. You gotta watch what you eat. Something like pie, there could be a couple under the crust. Apple, that ain't too bad, you can see them. But raisin...they're the same color, hard to find. You gotta be careful. Best not order any brown stuff. You'll probably eat a few. Won't hurt you though...protein."

My appetite for pie suddenly fled.

By eight o'clock, my mind had practically shut down. I punched the clock and walked out the gate with Stan into a wet, steamy morning.

"You comin' to eat?"

"I'm not very hungry, just sleepy," I said.

"You better eat. You're payin' for it you know. You don't eat, the company makes money off of you."

I went, and surprised myself by eating a platter of hot cakes and sausages. After breakfast, I crawled into my cot and sank into oblivion, my weariness eventually shutting out the thump and bang of the janitor's tools, the constant trample of boot heels, the loud voices and, over all, the drumming of rain on the roof.

I awoke sometime in the afternoon wondering where I was, the events of the previous night remote and unreal. As I lay there thinking about it, the realization set in that last night had not been an isolated incident; tonight would be more of the same—and the night after that, and on and on. God! Could I go on for years doing bag roll? Then I thought of the money—54¢ an hour, almost a fortune!

On the fourth night there was a change. A note on my time card said I was to check with the timekeeper. See the timekeeper? But why? Had I screwed up somehow? I entered the office, trepidation monkeying with my heartbeat.

Tommy, the man with the bad leg, was still on night shift.

"We want somebody to relieve the townsite watchman for a few nights," he said. "Bob Holmes is the regular watchman. He wants some time off for something. Do you know Bob?"

I drew a breath of relief. It was nothing I had done. I shook my head. "No, I don't know him. I don't really know anybody...not here. But I thought I was supposed to work in the finishing room?"

"Yeah. You are. It's only for two or three nights; then you'll go back up there. They said for one of you new guys to do this, but I couldn't find anybody else who wanted to. You could refuse of course..." He left it hanging.

I mulled it over for a few seconds. Did I want to show an unwillingness? By refusing, would a black mark be scored against me? Anyhow, being a watchman for a few nights was probably no worse than doing bag roll—and it would be different.

"Okay, sure," I finally said. "Where do I go?"

The watchtower was on the wharf, at the head of the gangway going down to the float where a few transient fish boats and fleet of pleasure boats was moored, in front of the townsite office and the Bank of Commerce. It was a small two-story building vaguely resembling a squat lighthouse. The upper floor, reached by an outside staircase, was glass on all sides. However, there the resemblance ended. Unlike a lighthouse, there was no friendly finger of light piercing the night to warn mariners of rock and shoal, the tepid yellow glow from inside, oozing from one small bulb hanging on a twisted cord, had barely enough energy to escape through the glass that was opaque with grime.

I opened the door and was nearly bowled over by the stench of stale tobacco smoke. A bulky man sat slouched in a wooden armchair. He was adding to the stench, a cigarette hung from his lips. Smoke curled up past his eyes, further masking his features that were already indistinct in the dim light. A red tin bucket labeled "Fire" in white painted letters, sat beside the chair. It was three-quarters full of cigarette butts.

"Hi!" I said. "I'm Paul. They said I was supposed to relieve you for a few nights."

"Yeah, that's right...for a few nights. I'm Bob." He threw his cigarette butt into the bucket where it lay smoldering. He turned his face to the light. It held little animation, just weariness, a woeful expression that I surmised had something to do with his wanting time off. Even his eyes looked tired. Above them, his partially bald dome glinted in the light from the naked bulb directly over it. Through the open front of his raincoat, I could see he was wearing a brown suit with a white shirt and tie. His shoes were shined...dressy clothes. I wondered why he would be dressed this way to walk around at night in the rain. A hat, a gray fedora with a broad brim, lay on a small table—the only other piece of furniture in the room—on top of a few dog-eared magazines.

The table was scored liberally with burn marks from cigarettes left smoldering along its edges. It also held a leather-bound case with a strap that hung in a loop below the edge, and beside it, a black beat-up lunchbox.

"I'll show you the route, tonight. It's not difficult. There's not much to do, just punch the clock." He looked at my threadbare windbreaker and my dripping hair.

"Haven't you got a raincoat or a hat? You're going to get pretty wet."

"Yeah, I guess so, but I'm used to it," I said.

"Well that's crazy walking around in the rain like that. You should at least have a hat. Didn't anybody tell you it rains here most of the time?"

"Yeah, but I haven't had a chance to buy anything yet. I just started work a few days ago. I don't have much money...not until pay day."

He shook his head. "Well for Christ's sake. Okay, let's go, then." He hoisted himself, tiredly, put on his hat and smoothed the brim with his fingers. I followed him down the steps to the rough timbers of the wharf.

The route bore left along the docks and the marine ways, up through "Jap town," dog-legged behind a couple of large apartment blocks and ascended to a street half way up the mountainside. It carried on, zigzagging across the upper reaches of town, circled back past the swimming pool, down the main street in front of the fire hall and the general store and back to the wharf.

Generally it was dark. At that time of night, there were few lighted windows. There were streetlights, dim yellow pools reflecting weakly on the rain-soaked planking of the stairs and narrow walkways, but the whole feeling was of gloom. There were dingy passages overhung with dripping foliage from which came strange rustlings. My inclination was to hurry and keep looking behind.

"Are there any animals around here...like wild ones?" I asked, trying to sound no more than mildly curious.

"Oh yeah, there's a few. There's cougars and wolves and a few bears," Bob didn't sound particularly concerned; he just ambled along, saying little, his shoulders sagging, his gaze seldom lifting from his feet.

Every so often, he'd pause, reach into a secret crevice and withdraw a large key attached to a chain. It fit into a slot in the leather-bound clock he carried slung over his shoulder. There was a small click as he twisted it in the mechanism.

"You have to remember where these keys are," he said. "It's about the only thing you have to remember. You don't want to miss one. The fire chief, Jack Raymond, he looks at the tape inside the clock. It's the only way he can tell if you really are making the rounds, and how long it takes you. A circuit is supposed to take about three-quarters of an hour. That gives you fifteen minutes to rest between rounds."

"What are we supposed to be looking for?" I asked.

"Fire," he said. "We're supposed to report any fires down at the fire hall."

"Oh," was all I could think to say. A fire was one of the last things I would have thought to look for in this dripping, moss-grown, sidehill maze of dwellings.

When I arrived at the tower the next night, there was a hat lying on the table. I supposed Bob had left it. He had taken pity on me. It was still raining so I wore it. It was not a dapper fedora; it was shapeless, well worn, but did have a broad brim. I fit more like an umbrella and came down around my ears.

It was lonely climbing through the warren of silent streets by myself. The gloom seemed deeper and the rustlings louder. Just after three o'clock, I was trudging up and down stairs, my thought process at low ebb. The bushes overhanging a short flight of stairs began swaying violently. There was a grunting and what sounded like hard claws raking on wood. My heart came up into my throat, beating like a trip hammer, nearly choking me. I stopped, ready to turn and run, but was paralyzed. A dark bulk emerged into the light and went ambling off down the boardwalk—a huge old porcupine.

By the time I came round again, he had somehow climbed to the roof of a house and was scrabbling precariously along its ridge-pole. He must have taken up permanent residence in the area. I saw him nearly every time I passed. And even though I was ready for him, he usually startled me.

On the fourth night, I want back to the finishing room. A week later, I changed to day shift, which went from eight in the morning to four in the afternoon. There was a bigger workforce on days, many new faces, and a lot of them were girls. I was no longer on the bag roll crew. I was moved around to a variety of jobs, all in some way connected with the bundling of paper for shipment. Few of the jobs required more than repetitive motions, and, once learned, the eyes and mind were free to wander. My eyes, followed by my mind, wandered to the girls, most of whom appeared to be in their late teens or early twenties. Some were high school gradu-ates. Like George and Hank they had been absorbed into the work-force.

CHAPTER 7

Fitting In

Ocean Falls, when I first knew it in those last few years leading up to World War Two, was a compact haven sheltering some 3,000 souls—a somewhat gloomy, rain-soaked Shangri-La, insulated from the real world by its remoteness. Few communities in those dwindling depression years could boast of a comparable lifestyle. Tucked away at the end of a lonely inlet, it still held practically everything essential to comfortable living. Unlike most towns of that era, there was full employment. If for any reason anyone found himself or herself unemployed, they didn't hang around; they took the next boat out—Mother Company saw to that. And indeed there would have been little point in staying since Pacific Mills Ltd. was the only employer. And the only support for anyone caught without a job might be the kindness of personal friends, which would have its limitations.

Although the population numbers remained static, there was a constant ebb and flow within the workforce. Each boat brought new faces and carried away an equal number who, for one reason or another, had failed to make it. Of the ones who stayed and progressed up the employment ladder, many prospered, becoming comparatively well to do within a few years. Some had lived there a very long time; in fact, a few had never worked anywhere else. And, not surprisingly, those who had been born and grown up there were reluctant to cut loose and try their luck in the uncertain world of the 1930s on the outside. The venturesome that did, often returned within a year. Many had never known anything but the close-knit life of a company town.

For the "web feet," those who could live with the isolation and the rain, there was the kind of security unknown elsewhere, where families, sheltered from the gnawing poverty of the rural areas and the seamy destitute congestion of the large cities, could grow in comparative safety and comfort. Toddlers could play in the streets unsupervised, without fear of molestation or of being ground under the wheels of vehicles. There was next to no crime, there being nowhere for a criminal to hide or run to—the only means of escape being the next steamship. A detachment of two RCMP officers under the command of Cpl. Lance Potterton—who could pick up nine billiard balls with one hand—kept the lid on normal rowdiness.

Families who could afford it, mostly the upper strata who had risen up through the well-paying trades, had engaged in the actual making of paper by running of the huge machines or the professionals such as the engineers and accountants, sent their sons and daughters off to universities outside. A goodly number of these kids then returned to take up well-paying positions. The young people who were not so privileged, generally unworldly, knew little more of the outside than what they had been exposed to during brief holidays. Hardly disadvantaged, however, they moved naturally from school into employment where, even without a secondary education, there were opportunities galore for the choosing, be they in the trades or in the huge unskilled workforce. And not just within the mill, but in the marine component, such as the rafting of logs and the operation of the towboats that moved them. And although there were no elected officials or bureaucracy, there was still a many-faceted townsite to maintain.

Wages, even in the lower echelons, were good. There were recreational facilities, entertainment and if they married and settled down—a number of school romances had quite naturally progressed into marriage—there was comfortable housing, at reasonable rent.

Settling in. Becoming a member of a new community, shedding the awkwardness of a latecomer, a new boy, and finding a sense of permanence, were challenges I'd never before had to contend with. I'd never had to make a place for myself, by myself. Only once in

105

my life, had I ever had to adjust to a strange community, and that, when we'd moved from the small Alberta village, where I'd been born and grown to adolescence, to Vancouver. And then, I'd not had to do it alone. I'd had others to fall back on. I'd been part of a family. And although the upheaval had strained the ties, we had hung together. They'd been there, Father and Mother, Olwyn and Owen—anchors to windward. Now I had no one I was close to. At the end of the day there was no sharing. A lot of mountainous real estate, tortuous channels and gray restless water lay between me and everyone and everything I had known. I felt a long way removed from them.

From the moment I arrived, I had kept my eyes open and enquired for the one person in Ocean Falls I knew—John McConaghie, the man who had been instrumental in getting me hired. But it was almost two weeks before our paths crossed. We had been on opposing shifts. Even in a town as small and compact as Ocean Falls, it was possible to go for weeks without seeing someone who was on a different shift.

"So they finally got around to sending you up here, 'eh?"

A familiar voice, one with the soft Irish that couldn't be mistaken, I turned. He was leaning on the railing of the porch that ran along the front of the store. I felt a thrill of pleasure. Finally, a friend, someone I knew and who knew me.

He took me home with him. We chatted as we walked to where he lived in a private home. His landlady, a motherly woman, made tea. We visited for the afternoon.

He was a warm and friendly man, a man to like, but there was an awkwardness between us, despite which we managed to talk the afternoon away. He was well entrenched. He knew things about Ocean Falls that made it easier, things that I would have had to ferret out for myself. We talked about our families and what had been, but there was no sense of closeness. And I could see that there wouldn't be. We lived in different worlds. He was more than twice my age, and that alone would move us in different orbits. He had done me a favor by getting me hired, and for that I would always be grateful. He brushed off my thanks. As he said, it was a favor that had really cost him nothing. I felt I owed him but, for the present at least, there was little I could do to repay him.

The paper mill.

Ocean Falls hydroelectric dam and powerhouse.
View from the bridge connecting the townsite and the mill.

It took a while to get over being a stranger, to see myself as something more than what I was sure others saw me as—a rank, down at the heel newcomer. I wanted to belong, like the other young men I saw who obviously belonged. They exuded a confidence that I hadn't seen in the men of similar age I'd encountered lounging around the Vancouver streets and waterfront. It was a confidence born of being employed and having money to spend. I watched them strolling around town and going to dinner in the diningroom, dressed in jackets and ties that practically sparkled with newness and in shoes with intact soles, polished until they shone. I wanted to dress as they did, to be one of them. They were the living proof that there was a way of life other than on the edge of poverty. I wanted that way of life so bad I could taste it. I wanted to think about other things than where my next meal was coming from.

There was no magic wand. I resigned myself to that. To achieve what I wanted would take time, longer than a few weeks and, of course, money. I would have to be patient, but I would watch and I would learn.

And it did take time, time and getting used to hauling myself out of bed to go to work every day. Despite what McGrath had said about four days a week, I actually didn't get a day off until Christmas. I had to accept that the horn-pipe to which I was destined to dance was the groaning blast of the mill whistle, morning, noon and night, winter, summer, seven days a week. Every plan I made, all my eating sleeping and leisure habits would, as long as I lived there, be governed by that whistle and the rotation of shifts.

That kind of routine more than anything, was the key. By changing shifts round the clock, seeing the same people day after day, eating with the same crowd and sleeping in the same bed, what had seemed new, became the norm. The loneliness slowly ebbed away. Without thinking about it, the town and the paper mill, most of which was still a mystery hidden from the eyes of the world in a bowl of rain-washed mountains, gradually became my home. Less and less did I feel an alien that had merely paused on the way to somewhere else. I guess I had taken out citizenship papers without realizing it.

Even in the first few days, I could see that there were opportunities in this shut-away community that offered more future than I had ever dreamed existed. There was suddenly a destination to travel toward. But just what shape the future might take would depend entirely on my ambition and how I took advantage of what came my way. Tentatively, I began looking at other than the finishing room, to the shops, the trades and, in particular, the electric shop. Plans began taking root in my mind, but as yet without clear definition. It was the first time in my life I had been able to look ahead with any degree of optimism.

After three weeks, I still had the five-dollar bill that mother had given me. To this point I had not needed money. I was being housed and fed without need to fork out any cash. And so conditioned had I become to being without money; there was never the slightest urgency to spend just for the sake of buying something. In fact, I had become almost paranoid about parting with even a nickel. There were many things I needed, but because I had developed such a pinchpenny attitude, I pushed them into the back of my mind. It would be a long time before I could actually go into a store and buy something without feeling guilty and that I had to somehow justify or explain why I had done so.

A single need finally breached my fortress of denial. And despite my trying to ignore it, it became a matter of urgency. I just had to have a reliable timepiece. The alternative of continuing without one, as I had been, depending on the foghorn blast of the mill whistle and the clock on the wall in the bunkhouse, had become too chancy. The mill whistle gave me no lead time. When it blew, I should already have been there. And the clock was inconveniently out in the hall, by the washroom door, necessitating getting out of bed to see what time it was. And as I became accustomed to my bunk bed, thin and narrow though it was, and to the noise that at first had been so intrusive but had gradually become the sounds of normalcy, I was sleeping longer and sounder. Several times I had narrowly missed being late for work because I was loath to get out of bed to look at the clock in the hall. I had gone without breakfast and without a bag lunch, just because I had tried guessing the time and had been wrong.

There was nothing else for it, a dependable means of telling time was not only worthwhile spending money on, it was essential.

I debated at length on an alarm clock or a watch. I needed both, but the watch won out.

It cost me a dollar and a quarter in the jewelry department upstairs in the company store. I bought a Westclox Pocket Ben, with a shiny case, a black face that glowed in the dark and a loud comforting tick that, even in the depth of night, left no doubt that it was running. It didn't keep particularly good time, but by keeping it wound and frequently adjusting it to the time clocks at the gate, it at least gave me ballpark accuracy.

I collected my first paycheck with barely suppressed excitement. Alas, the wealth I had anticipated was a short-lived dream. By the time the accountants had got through carving board, room and boat fare on *Catala* from it, there wasn't a lot left. I looked sadly at my eviscerated check. Things I had anticipated buying would have to wait, perhaps the next one... I did, however, purchase a money order for $15 and sent it to Mother. Strangely, I sent it to Mother. Without consciously thinking about it, I must have taken some perverse delight in not sending it to Father. I felt good about sending the money. It was proof positive that I was working and prospering. I resolved that come what may I would send that much each month. Being next to broke a while longer was no big deal.

Seeing how other single people lived bred dissatisfaction with what I had. And out of the conversations that washed around me while eating and working, I discovered there *were* more attractive alternatives to the bunkhouse and the bullpen. In fact, there were a number. However, all were more expensive and would have to come over the long term. I did sort out in my mind what order I would pursue them when I had the means.

My first goal was to leave the bullpen and eat in the upscale number one diningroom, primarily because I had envisioned myself as one of the well-dressed individuals who ate there. But until I could afford new clothing, I knew I wouldn't fit the image I had created and would feel out of place. Following that, I would move from the noise and the bare-bones comfort of the bunkhouse.

The word was, that in winter all the bunkhouses were "colder than a whore's heart." And indeed it was not at all difficult to imagine the cold seeping through the paper-thin walls. I would get out before winter. Occasionally, there were vacancies in the hotel—

slightly better than the bunkhouse, comfortwise, but every bit as noisy—and in the hotel annex, a newer, quieter building that had been built to take the hotel overflow. This latter was more desirable than either the hotel or the bunkhouse, but it had few rooms and there was a waiting list for them. Seemed most of those arriving to flesh out the workforce that was enjoying a modest expansion due to an awakening Canadian economy and a burgeoning paper market, a response to rising European unrest, were single people. There just weren't enough company rooms to go round.

There was however a homegrown industry that had sprung up to take care of the deficiency. Married couples living in company houses had seized the opportunity to enhance their incomes. Anyone with a spare room, rented it out, even if it meant doubling up the children two or three to a room to create one. The going rate for a room was about $15 a month. The bathroom was shared with the family, there being few, if any, houses with more than one. I let it be known I was looking for a room in a private house.

In the meantime, the rough and ready bullpen filled the need. It was a place for working men, a place where, if they arrived straight off the booms wearing boots with caulks a half inch-long, dripping water from their raingear and with their tin pants sticky with tree pitch, no eyebrow was raised. Or if they came from the Bull Gang—the stevedores and yard workers—bringing with them a yellow coating of sulfur from the docks, or from the acid plant, or from the smelter with their hair and beards whitened with lime, they were admitted without comment. It was taken matter-of-factly, if they came directly off shift in the digester room, their clothes rife with the rotten egg stink of sulfite. And if they came fat eyed from having just arisen or sleepy and just going to bed, nobody intruded into the semilucidity of their thoughts.

The bullpen was ruled over by Goldie, blonde and quick of tongue. She took no lip from anyone, not that she had to as she had been there a long time and was pretty well respected. And apart from the occasional loudmouth drunk, whom she had lots of volunteers to help squelch, she had little that was unpleasant to contend with. Most exchanges were good-natured banter.

She was assisted by a variety of, usually, young women fresh off the boat, few who stayed long. Either they took the next boat out or found a niche somewhere else—not easy to do, it being only coincidence if a vacancy occurred elsewhere in town when somebody wanted to make a switch. Word had it that a few courtships had blossomed into marriage all within the few days or before the arrival of the next boat—one solution to being unemployed, even if only in short term.

Eating in the bullpen wasn't dining, it was more a stoking of fires. It kept fuelled those who worked outside in the rain or in the remote dungeonlike corners of the mill. And sometimes, feeding time at the zoo was more civilized. The tables, about twenty of them, held eight men seated four to a side. They were covered with white oilcloth. A shelf suspended over their centers ran full length onto which the food was delivered in big serving dishes with portions for eight hungry men. Most times the dishes arrived with a crash and a shouted warning, "Look out! It's hot." They hardly had time to come to rest before eager hands reached for them—hot or not. Appetites were, in the main, prodigious.

I had just thrown my leg over the bench to sit beside Stan at breakfast. He nudged me and inclined his head at a short stocky individual with a shaved head and a huge handlebar moustache, who was sitting waiting across from us and at the far end of the table.

"Just watch that guy. Bet you've never seen anybody eat like him," he said quietly.

"What about him?" I asked.

"Just watch. Watch how he eats."

Goldie delivered a bowl of porridge for eight. Handlebars was fastest on the draw; he took it, poured the contents of the cream jug on it, spooned a mound of sugar over it and with his face only inches away, began furiously scooping it into his mouth.

"Well...Jesus. Hey Goldie! More porridge," came the chorus from the rest. Handlebars never looked up. It was like that with everything—bacon, eggs, pancakes—and not just breakfast either. If he got there first, he took it, all of it, no matter what. And he ate it, no leavings on his plate.

"Who is this guy?" I asked Stan.

"I don't know. There's supposed to be a story about him, but I've only heard some of it."

We didn't always sit at the same tables, but after that, no matter where I sat, I kept an eye on Handlebars. I couldn't help it. Anybody who could eat like that fascinated me. And I found out there was, indeed, a story about him, although I never did get more than bits and pieces of it—very little of it from him. There was no logical reason for me to delve into his past, but the very fact that he was different and the vague reference to adventure in his early life piqued my curiosity. Once or twice I attempted to talk to him and draw him out. He didn't draw out easily, perhaps because I was an inept interrogator and too obviously curious about things that didn't concern me. His English wasn't good and he was disinclined talk about himself. A veil of suspicion usually slid down over his eyes, like the hasty lowering of a theater curtain to conceal some unscripted mishap from the audience, and his face took on an inscrutable flatness, at any direct line of questioning other than concerning the time of day or the weather.

There was a story all right, perhaps even a book, but like many others, it would never be written. According to what he'd let drop to those he worked with, he'd been raised on the shores of Lake Baykal in southern Siberian Russia. At an age little more than adolescence, rather than become embroiled in the Russian revolution, he had left home, on foot. And without any particular destination in mind, other than to get outside the boundaries of Mother Russia, he had starved his way through Mongolia and China to a port on the Yellow Sea. Somehow he had found himself a berth aboard a ship that eventually off-loaded him in Vancouver, then sailed away leaving him there. The last chapter, how he had got himself hired at Ocean Falls, was never really revealed. However, he was there, working on the Bull Gang and determined to make up for his years of starvation. Strangely, he wasn't fat. He had a little round paunch, but that was the only testimony to his eating capacity. What his real name was, nobody seemed to know or care. He must have had one, and perhaps the office knew it, but to those of us who ate with him, he was called Handlebars and addressed as such, that's all. Only in later years did I become aware that in Ocean Falls there were many like Handlebars—men whose lives had been rich in adventure, but also been warped by deprivation.

Only we who were recently come and hadn't had time to catch

up were without money; everyone else evidenced trappings of prosperity, visible primarily in how they dressed. The single people hoarded it or spent it on clothes with there being little else to squander it on, except, of course, liquor. The liquor store, although carrying only the basics, did a land-office business. Most recreation was next door to being free.

It didn't take much of an excuse to flaunt new togs. Even to go to the one movie house was an occasion for suit and tie. And on special occasions, like Christmas and Thanksgiving, a few tuxedos might appear at dinner in the hotel dining room, even though the wearer might be dining alone.

My need for clothing became dire; I was practically in rags. The men's wear department in the store, presided over by Keith McAllister* and Stuart Askew, carried everything for the ordinary needs. Anything out of the ordinary was purchased while on holiday or by mail. There *was*, however, one other source for clothes—Wylie Nicol.

Wylie sold men's clothing such as suits, overcoats and, for the fastidious few, tailor-made shirts. He came once a month and stayed between boats. He had a standing order for a room in the hotel. He would arrive, lay out his samples in his room, and then, dressed in the latest fabric, stand on the street in front of the hotel. Word got around, "Wylie's in town." He was a big man, fleshy but not excessively so, pleasant well groomed and exuding an aura of confidence, professionalism, friendliness and shaving lotion.

There was a ritual to ordering a suit from Wylie. During the handshake and the murmured greeting in which it was established that a garment was being contemplated, his eyes were undisguisedly active, roaming the figure in front of him, assessing the quality and cut of the clothing presently being worn and, from that, making a snap decision on whether the person's wallet was deep enough and his taste sufficiently sophisticated to warrant proceeding further. If he considered his time would be worthwhile spent, his eyes would then take on a distant dreamy look as he mentally flipped through his catalog of samples, visualizing how the figure before him might look draped in one of his many weaves and patterns.

---

*Keith McCalister left Ocean Falls early in the early 1940s to settle in Kamloops where he partnered with Poli Howard to open a menswear store. The store, owned by McCalister and Howard, is still in existence on Victoria Street, although now owned by others.

Following was a trip upstairs to view the samples and, if a deal was struck, a precise measuring. The size of deposit was then agreed upon and provided. It was all very low key, no pressure whatsoever. Three weeks and the suit would be there, the remainder of the purchase price payable at the post office. To my knowledge, Wylie never misfitted a garment.

I was not yet ready for Wylie Nicol. My next paycheck went for serviceable shirts, pants, underwear and socks. I bought a "tin" coat, made from heavy cotton duck. It was the coat of the outside work crews—one of the best purchases I ever made. As it became wet, the weave swelled and shed rain like a shake roof, just getting heavier and stiffer as the day wore on and rain fell on it. It wasn't warm, needing sweaters under it, but it was practically a lifetime garment. It just didn't wear out. I bought a hat to match. I bought steel-toed shoes, which were a mandatory item and subsidized by the company.

Later, having overheard whispered references to Rapunzel, I sought out Bob Beaty, the white-haired, diminutive barber who had cut hair for years in a little shop in the hotel basement. I got the first professional haircut I'd had since I was a little kid in Alberta. I paid Bob twenty-five cents. I came out feeling light headed and pleased with my reflection in the mirror.

"See you got you ears lowered," cracked Dick Green, next time I saw him. "Didn't let old Bobby do it, did you?"

"Yeah. Why?"

"Jeez, you're lucky you got out with your head. Why'nt you go to Kenny Shigawa, down in Japtown? That's where I get mine done. Old Bobby's more concerned with what's on the floor than what he leaves on your head."

I never did go back to Bob Beaty.

Dick Green, like me, had been hired to work in the finishing room. He had come about the same time as me. I came in August and he in September, but somehow we missed each other until sometime in October.

He was tall, with dark hair and eyes and a ready smile. He had boundless energy that was infectious. We first encountered each other one nightshift on the bag-roll crew. Thereafter, our lives meshed. Although markedly different in temperament, or perhaps

115

because of it, we got along. For a lot of years we were practically inseparable, while at the same time pursuing different interests and careers.

For the first years, up until the war, Dick lived with his sister Kay Morrow, and his brother-in-law Cecil Morrow who headed up the order and sales department. Kay was a good deal older than Dick and she mothered him. And because I frequented their house, she mothered me. Both she and Dick nudged me into doing things for myself I wouldn't have thought of or just hung back from doing.

"Why'n hell don't you get 'em fixed?" Dick asked one day when I was complaining about a toothache. "Go see old Fox there. He'll do a job on them. Going around hurting like that is crazy."

I went to see Dr. Fox in his little office on Main Street. It was a pretty tiny place—two small rooms, one a waiting room and the other with his chair and tools.

His professional mask barely concealed his look of horror at the condition of my teeth that had never before been looked on by a dentist. He probed and scraped dug and pried.

"Well it looks like we'll have to do quite a bit of work here," he said. " A few weeks, we'll have to set up a schedule. How's your shifts?"

We worked out a schedule, not only for the dental work but also for paying for it. The upshot was twenty-six fillings, three extractions and a bill for $45. I paid for it over three months. I suffered, but it was with new confidence that I faced the world. I was able to smile without having to keep my lips closed.

I continued working in the finishing room at a variety of tasks. I packaged paper of all sizes and shapes—reams, quires, bundles and bales...brown, white, striped, butcher's paper, newsprint, fruit wrap, even Christmas wrap. And I wrapped thousands of counter rolls. I helped load huge rolls onto the cutters that chopped them into sheets to be packaged and sent off to China, Australia and places I'd never heard of. All of these tasks were mundane and required little thought, so little thought that I almost got myself in hot water with Jimmy Bird, the superintendent, a couple of times.

I got so I could wrap, tie, glue, label and truck with my mind and my eyes elsewhere. I was working strictly for the money and not with any interest in what I was doing. I was, frankly, more interested in the girls I was working with. Standing beside them for hours on end was playing games with my mind. Most were young and attractive and ready to joke and banter. Because of them, I had become obsessed with my appearances and how to enhance it. I was thinking more along social lines than was healthy.

It couldn't last. Bird yanked me back to reality by suggesting that I'd better buckle down. I guess my inattention had been pretty obvious. That's all it took. I reset my sights on my main objective to become something of substance.

CHAPTER 8

Friends

Two significant events occurred between my August arrival at Ocean Falls and Christmas of that same year. The latter was the more significant of the two. Although I didn't realize it at the time, it would have a profound effect on my life.

The first event came as a surprise, but with less long-term impact than I at first thought it would have. It occurred in October.

"Dear Paul, We've bought a house."

The letter from Mother opened just like that, without preamble. A simple statement, but it caught me off guard. Mother's letters were usually couched in her very best English and carefully constructed—as an example to me. She had never given up being a teacher. Occasionally, she would correct all my mistakes, spelling and otherwise, and send my letters back with an apology for doing so, but stressing that it was for my own good.

"You've what!" I guess my face must have betrayed my amazement, and perhaps my exclamation was a little loud. "Bad news?" a woman I didn't know asked. We were sharing the cramped space of the post office outer room.

"I don't know. I'm not sure yet whether its bad news or not. It's surprising news, though," I said. "It's from my parents. They've bought a house. I just...it's just hard to believe."

The woman shuffled through the handful of letters and thick magazines. She gave each piece a brief glance and without looking up, she smiled and said, "Is there something wrong with that? People do it all the time you know."

"No. I guess not. It's just..." Still disbelieving, I wandered out.

I sat on my bed and read the rest of the two pages. "Owen has found a job. He's working for B.C. Plywoods, in a large plant down on the Fraser River. And what with both of you working and both able to afford $15 a month, we thought we would be better off to buy than to carry on paying rent. It's a new, small, two-bedroom cottage on the corner of Fifty-Eighth Avenue and Ontario Street."

There was more, but I couldn't help but return to and dwell on that first passage. The rest was of little consequence.

My emotions were mixed, but blended in was a liberal lacing of resentment. I was locked in. They had locked me in, as they had locked Owen in. We were committed, both of us, each to fifteen dollars a month. They had just gone ahead and done it without consultation or the slightest warning, not taking into account what might happen if one or neither of us could send that much. It was Father. I knew how his mind worked. He felt we owed him. And the very fact that neither of our jobs was cast in stone—in those days all jobs hung by very thin threads—had little bearing. He wanted money from each of us, every month, for what seemed at the moment forever. Well, all I could do was try. Forever was a long time. Things could change and probably would.

The other event happened in early December. George Lee's mother invited me to their home for Christmas dinner with the family.

Ever since that first night on graveyard shift on the bag-roll crew, George and I had got along and had become friends. I'd been to the Lee house a few times. Dwight Lee, George's father, was townsite foreman, in charge of maintenance. A big man, red haired and with the pale skin that is characteristic of redheads, he was though without the volatility that is supposedly another trait of redheads. In fact he leaned the other way. Mild of manner, he spoke softly, usually around the stem of a large briar that gave him a scholarly look. A third generation Canadian, he had gone overseas with the Canadian forces during World War One and served in the trenches of France. While on leave in Brighton, England, he had found Mrs. Lee.

Mrs. Lee, Daisy—or Dais, as Dwight called her—was half the size of Dwight. A short, round, motherly woman with a ruddy complexion, due in part to a heart condition that on occasion had her in hospital. She piloted the family ship with a firm but kindly hand on the tiller.

They were a warm tight-knit family. Not only were they affectionate, they demonstrated their affection outwardly. They hugged and kissed at the slightest provocation. It took a little getting used to. In our house, particularly in latter years, even a brief hug was seldom come by.

There were two girls younger than George. Arline and Gwen, with Arline the eldest. From our very first meeting, I had eyes only for her.

She was a neat, vivacious blonde, in the final years of high school, who could cook, sew and play the piano. There was nothing in my immediate world I wanted more than to be in her company. And because of my blind fascination, I probably attributed more to her friendliness than was actually there.

"You'll come and have Christmas dinner with us, won't you," Mrs. Lee had said.

"Yes, thank you very much. I would be delighted to come," I said, while looking at Arline.

I hadn't given much thought to Christmas, except the fact that I would be alone had crossed my mind briefly, and that I should do some shopping for my family. To be taken in by the Lee family was more than I could have hoped for on this first Christmas away from home. It did, though, pose an immediate problem. I could not, would not, appear in the clothes I went to work in. I needed a suit, or at least a jacket and dress pants.

Wylie Nicol was not in town, and even had he been, there was no time. I went to Keith McAlister, upstairs in the men's wear department of the company store.

"Oh yes. I don't see why not. It'll be tight, but we can get you a suit in time for Christmas," he assured me.

He measured me and between us we selected, from his limited array of samples, a navy blue serge with a pin stripe. It wouldn't be as prestigious as a Wylie Nicol suit, but the price tag was more in keeping with my budget. I sweat it out for the next two weeks.

"How are you fixed for shirts and ties?" Keith asked, when I came to pick up my suit a few days before Christmas. He was probably relieved to get it out of the store; I had pestered him with "Has it come yet?" after the arrival of almost every boat. I didn't own a dress shirt or a tie.

"Ah...could I maybe charge them? I don't have enough cash right now, and I need a pair of dress shoes. I can pay most of it next payday."

"Hmm...I suppose." He looked a little wary. "Yeah I guess so. You're not leaving town or anything like that are you?"

"No. No. I'm going to be here." I was a little aghast that such a thought had entered his mind. "I'm going to Lees' for Christmas. And I'm going to stay here. I'm going to transfer to the electric shop and learn a trade." It was a bold statement, made on the spur of the moment to satisfy McAlister that I did indeed intend to stay around and pay him. At the time, though, I had little assurance that what I had said would come to pass. There was some truth there, but it was actually the first time I had voiced it. I had, in a vague sort of way, formulated my long-range plan around becoming an electrician. Now I had said it. It was out in the open. The plan suddenly had substance.

We selected a white shirt and a burgundy tie.

"You'd better buy a pair of socks," McAlister said, eyeing the pink peeking through the gray wool of the pair I was wearing. He was sitting on the stool fitting me with a pair of black dress shoes. By that time I was on a high. What the hell...why not?

"Yeah. I guess so."

I bought the biggest box of chocolates I could find, three pounds I think it was, and it cost me $3. I had the women in the drug store gift wrap it.

I was hesitant to leave my room. I had never worn a suit and felt elated, but at the same time awkward in it. The mirror that was part of my room's furnishing was about a foot high and half that wide. It was nailed solidly to the wall at eye level and I could see little more than my face. The morrors in the washroom were slightly larger, but still too high.

I spent a long time fitting my tie under the stiff new shirt collar and knotting it. Still dissatisfied—a limp rag was how I thought it looked—I gave up wrestling with it, resolving to have someone educate me in the skills of tie tying.

Christmas Day dawned mild and sunny. It stayed that way—a good thing too as I had no raincoat and would have had to pull my 'tin' work coat on over my suit. The idea was abhorrent.

Chocolates under my arm, I presented myself at the Lees' door. That Christmas was a beginning. The warmth I experienced there, the love that was evident between family members, and the unreserved sharing of the occasion with me, a perfect stranger, was an overwhelming emotional feast. Here was a chart to steer by. I somehow knew that the values I had seen demonstrated in the Lee household that Christmas would become the pattern upon which I would fashion my own home, if I ever had one.

In fact, my relationship with the Lee family, developed over the next two years, set me on a course from which I would never deviate. I spent a lot of evenings slouched in the comfort of their living room, listening to music from their modest collection of records: Gilbert and Sullivan, Franz Lehár and much from the English music hall. And there were sessions at the piano, Arline playing and the rest singing. Upstairs, in the narrow, slant-roofed playroom was a Ping-Pong table where fierce contests took place while the rain drummed on the roof.

There was also the *Gwen Dee,* the Lee family's boat of questionable parentage. Twenty-six feet long and shabby of appearance, she was powered by a one-lung Easthope engine that, when going full out, pushed her along at about eight knots. Not fast, but adequate for what was expected of her. As a boat for young people to mess around in, she was ideal. She was a stable platform from which to jig or pull crab nets and she could hold trolling speed for hours on end. I was introduced to her the following spring.

The Lees' also had a cabin at Wallace Bay, a half moon of quiet water a few miles around the point and out of sight and sound of the town and the mill whistle. It was built on the rocky shore, high above the tide line, and had two bedrooms and a screened sleeping porch. Their weekends were spent there as soon as the weather became tolerable in the spring. Since only in the warmest days of summer was the water warm enough for swimming, fishing occupied most of these leisurely weekends. There were ground fish, shellfish, crabs and, of course, salmon, all in abundance.

I first experienced the pleasure of saltwater fishing from the

Ocean Falls. Skipper, Dwight Lee and company aboard the
Gwen Dee.

Ocean Falls. Cecil and Kay Morrow, Dick Green and author
in Morrow's boat on Link Lake.

deck of the *Gwen Dee*. And I got to experience sleeping with the sound of gentle swells lapping rocky beaches in my ears, from the sleeping porch of the cabin at Wallace Bay.

Beyond the concrete dam, about half way along the sixteen-mile, deep, fresh-water reservoir that was Link Lake, my other friends the Morrows owned a cabin. High on a rocky point, it had a view of practically the whole length of the lake. Looking straight across, a silver thread of a small cataract spilled down the mountainside from a nameless high-elevation secondary lake that was joined by tunnel to Link Lake. The tunnel was known as the hole in the wall, and where its outflow tumbled into Link Lake was a prime fishing location.

The Morrow's boat, a fifteen-footer that hadn't warranted christening, was a lesser boat than even the *Gwen Dee*. A fair-weather craft, wide open to the elements and with marginal freeboard, she chugged along at the urging of a four-horse, one-lung Easthope engine. She was, nevertheless, a fun boat to mess around in. She was stabled in a boathouse in the boat basin just behind the dam. Cecil Morrow, whose lukewarm interest in boating was limited to a semiannual fishing excursion, had pretty well turned her over to Dick Green to do with as he saw fit.

Dick, being the person he was, renovated everything on her that could be renovated. Our days off didn't always occur together, but when they did, they were usually spent working on the boat, huddled under tarpaulins fishing at the mouths of any of a dozen streams entering the lake, or fixing up the cabin's amenities, which were skeletal at best.

For me, those pre-war years, making friends and getting to know boats, were good years.

In February, 1940, Ralph Hamilton arrived at Ocean Falls. He and my sister, Olwyn, had become engaged the previous Christmas. I had met him, as they had been going together when I left Vancouver, but I didn't really know him. Had I, things may have turned out differently.

He was a tall slow-moving slow-witted man, with latent cowboy tendencies. His high-heeled boots and ten-gallon hat raised eyebrows in that up-coast rainforest setting. He'd never quite shed the Alberta ranchland of his childhood. And although he had never been a cowboy, he had lived in Vancouver since his early teens, he fancied himself as one. By his mid-twenties, he had never worked at anything for more than a few days. He had lived with his mother, a sister and a younger brother in a big old house on Barclay Street. His father, who seldom made an appearance, paid the rent and kept food on the table by working as a bull-cook in logging camps on Vancouver Island.

Olwyn had met him early in 1939 through a mutual friend. And although he had little to recommend him, other than he was big and paid her a lot of attention, their relationship evolved to the point

Ocean Falls. Boat houses on Link Lake.

where she agreed to marry him. It was understandable—a decision made out of a desperate yearning for change, to leave home where the full weight of housekeeping and caring for Mother had fallen squarely on her shoulders.

I was living in a private home, upstairs, in an attic with two bedrooms. Since Ralph was to be my brother-in-law, I suppose I saw it as natural to share the space. Besides, the rent was less for the entire attic than for two individual rooms elsewhere. I arranged with the landlady, Mrs. Hastings, for him to move in.

It didn't take long to find the arrangement was flawed. I just couldn't abide the man. He was dull and with slovenly habits. And although he had his own room, he seemed to want to spend an inordinate amount of time in mine, just sitting, looking at me and saying nothing. I began harboring severe misgivings. His impending marriage to Olwyn was a recipe for disaster. I became convinced of that, but there was nothing I could do about it. Writing a letter to voice my doubts as to their suitability would do little but alienate her, and I didn't want that.

I put up with him for a month and then moved out. I went to live with an elderly couple, Mr. and Mrs. Crawford, in an apartment building. They were a gentle pair, he a school janitor and clock fancier. Their rooms were crowded with clocks of all descriptions. I thought all hell had broken loose the first time I heard their chimes kick in all at once.

Ralph was put to work in the sulfite mill in the digester room. Not the most ideal environment in which to work, but at least it was inside, out of the rain, and others had tolerated it. In fact, some had worked there for years.

Rumors began circulating that he wasn't too swift, that he just wasn't cutting it. However, he survived, in the short term that is. And in late April he took a couple of weeks off, went to Vancouver and married Olwyn in St. Giles United Church. They came back together, she a dewy eyed bride, ready to settle in and make a home, he as dull and uninspired as ever going through the motions of working.

They lived in a room in the hotel for three months. The handwriting was on the wall, he wasn't going to make it. Despite Olwyn's tearful pleas, the company declined to assign them a house. He was let go and they left in August. Olwyn was already pregnant.

Owen came in the fall of 1941.

His job at the plywood plant had not lasted and he was at loose ends. At Mother's urging, he had sought out the Pacific Mills hiring office. She was afraid that he would come to no good hanging around Vancouver without a job, and besides his monthly payment had suddenly dried up.

He had two things going for him: a natural charm that probably impressed McGrath, and the fact that the market for paper was expanding and Pacific Mills needed people. He was hired and shipped out within a couple of days.

He was put to work in the finishing room. Being a people person, he fit right in. He joined our loose clique consisting of Dick, George, Hank and a few others.

Back row, left to right: George Lee,
Arline Lee, Dick Green.
Paul Jones in front.

CHAPTER 9

War Begins

And then I will stand among you,
a seafarer among seafarers.
— KAHLIL GIBRAN

In its early years, 1940 and 1941, the conflict that was still largely confined to northern Europe, but would spread and go down in history as World War Two, held little interest for me. It was a long way off, so remote as to be unworthy of my attention. There was little reason to fret about it; it would be looked after by Europeans and would be over and done with in short order. It would not affect me, or so I thought—if I thought.

Older and wiser heads warned otherwise. "This is no short-lived skirmish," they said. "It's going to spread and Canada can't help but be drawn into it. Just you wait and see."

Even so, I remained blissfully unconcerned. It was impossible to ignore it entirely, it being the main topic of conversation in the work place, the coffee shop or wherever people gathered. But despite all the talk and gloomy predictions, I remained indifferent. I just couldn't seem to get worked up over what was happening in Poland and the Baltic countries. Their shapes and where they were located on the map was about all I knew about them.

In one of her letters, Mother cautioned: "This war in Europe... It seems to be growing without check. It's only a matter of time.... Think twice before you get involved in it. Remember what happened to your father...what he went through."

Hers was a reminder I did not need. I replied. "I have no intention of rushing off to take part in what appears to be another tiresome European squabble." How naïve I was.

Opinions differed, of course, as to the actual seriousness of Germany's expansionist activity. Some thought Britain and France would nip it in the bud and send Hitler packing. Others, those who had lived through the previous war, shook their heads in grave doubt, certain that history was about to repeat itself. For me, however, it remained something to avoid thinking about at all, even though the news media did its best to focus my attention on it. It was there whenever I was inclined to read a newspaper, and when late at night the radio reception firmed up, there was little else but the reporting and analysis of war for entertainment. Even the music harked back to 1918: "Pack up your troubles," and "Long, long trail awinding," a desperate attempt to rekindle the esprit of the last fracas. I would lie in bed twisting the dial, seeking less somber fare. Perhaps half the world was attentive to what was being said, but I was merely exasperated that war was all they could find to talk about. I listened as eventually the low countries were overrun and the Allied forces were evacuated from the beaches of Normandy. Just another radio play it seemed and not a very good one. But unlike a radio play, there was no end to it. Its dreariness went on and on. Occasionally though, and unaccountably, as I listened the gravity of what was happening would strike and a noble urge would come unbidden from somewhere within me. I suppose it was some primal instinct floating up through the gene pool that spawned me, an ancient response to imminent danger to my tribe, the same response that roused my ancestors to deal with the threat of the Vikings and the Roman legions—a call to arms so to speak. "I should be girding myself, preparing to face the enemy." The feeling, however, was always short-lived, evaporating with the click of the switch as I shut the radio off. Deep down, I must have known that eventually events would overtake me, but I somehow lacked the will to act. It was not a deliberate avoidance, I just couldn't come to grips with it. "Should I do something? And if so, what?" So I did nothing, preferring not to dwell on it.

I had been raised in a home where almost daily war, or some aspect of it, was referred to. Father, a veteran of the "Great War," and with shrapnel scars to prove it, was determined that no one, and in particular his children, would go uninformed or would be allowed to forget what he and his generation had been through. I had grown up firm in the belief that war was unnecessary, a barbaric way for humans to settle their differences and without any sense that serving in one was heroic. On the other hand, I also had it drummed into me that not serving was showing the white feather, the ultimate cowardice.

To add to my confusion, this was a different war. It didn't fit the picture portrayed by Father. Which was real war—this highly mobile slash and burn type, this *blitzkrieg*, the boundaries of which changed daily or the static mud-slogging trench warfare, the sordid details of which I had learned as bed-time stories since childhood? Any logical conclusion escaped me.

About the only direct affect it had on me at this stage of its evolution was that I was reaping a benefit from it. I was working longer hours. Industry was feeling the change. An air of resurgent energy, almost an excitement, was taking hold, an awakening after the somnolence of the depression years.

Throughout the paper mill, overtime work became the norm. A day off was something to remark on. Orders for pulp and paper were suddenly flooding in. Every paper machine was going full out. And not only was the sawmill's huge band saw running around the clock, slashing pulp wood, straining to keep a stream of blocks bobbing along the flumes to the chipper and ground-wood mills, it had been pressed in to cutting "aeroplane" spruce—clear, straight-grained wood from ancient old-growth forests, rafted in from remote forests on the Queen Charlotte Islands. Deck loads were being slung weekly onto coastal freighters to be ferried to small mills where the squared off timbers would be reduced to structural members for fighter aircraft. When viewed within that context, that it might take part in the great air battles over Britain, this pale yellow wood took on special qualities indeed.

However, other than earning a good deal more money, nothing to do with war was making any real impact on me or the pack I ran with. It had not yet intruded far enough into our lives to trouble us. Life went on pretty much as it always had. Shift after shift, the drone of the mill whistle prompted our comings and goings. The rotten-egg stink of sulfur still permeated everything—so inured had we become, that only occasionally was it noticeable. And the low pervasive hum of machinery kept overriding the constant patter of rain and the chuckle of water running down through the wood-planked streets.

In Canada, even into 1941, full-scale conscription had not been implemented. The threat was there, but politically it was too hot a potato. The thin edge of the wedge had nevertheless been inserted and was opening the way. There was the National Resource Mobilisation Act of June, 1940, that gave the government authority to conscript, but only for service within Canada, a sort of half-hearted attempt at preparedness. A few, probably no more than a dozen, were called up to take basic training, but they came back after thirty days and resumed their lives having had only a brief taste of what army life was all about.

There were, of course, a few leaving to join the Air Force and the Army, fully intending to go to war. But even they were of little interest to us, since most were not close friends. They were generally a little older, men in their late twenties and thirties, and people we didn't know very well. And they went one at a time, leaving behind a sense that there had been no real urgency to enlist, that they were just going off on some romantic crusade because it was more interesting than working in a hole-in-the-wall mill.

Even the attack on the Hawaiian Islands and Pearl Harbor did not immediately strike us as something greatly significant, it being a place somewhere in the remote reaches of the southern Pacific that, until it was bombed, we'd scarcely heard of. Its importance as a strategic Japanese target was lost on us.

Everything to do with war was unreal and very far away, and I, for one, would have been content to have it remain as far away as possible. So I suppose I shut it out, fearing it might interfere with my lifestyle. I wanted things to remain as they were: I had money in my pocket, I had friends and was enjoying life as I had never done in the past. There was certainly no sense of physical danger to me or the town I had adopted as mine.

The first concrete evidence that all was not well came with the sudden evacuation of the Japanese. It was a rude awakening, hammering home that even this hidden community was not immune; it too was subject to what was going on in the rest of the world.

At first the whole exercise struck me a ludicrous. It seemed irrational to believe that Kenny Shigawa, the guy who cut my hair, could be anything but what he appeared. And there was Mrs. Omoto, a motherly woman who did my laundry. That she could be a threat to anyone was beyond all reason. It was ridiculous believe that this tiny woman who regularly apologized for charging me so much—every week it was the same, "one dolla fi-cent, one dolla will do,"—could be evil.

But the whispering had started. Questions were asked. Ordinary mishaps suddenly became suspected sabotage: "Did a Jap put sand in that bearing, the one that failed on number three paper machine last week?" And other suspicions: "Are those fishing boats out there spying for Hirohito's navy?" I began seeing evil in the familiar faces of the jitney drivers. The small stooped man covered in glue who had spent years down in a dark corner of the basement making cores for the huge newsprint rolls became someone to notice. Were people such as he the enemy? I couldn't logically believe they were, but the germ of suspicion had been implanted and was carrying out its purpose, infecting us all, until even we the skeptics became almost believers.

Once started, the exodus went swiftly. Suddenly the wharves were lined with fishing boats, combed from the remote channels and inlets and herded into the inner harbor. They were layered one against the other, tied six or eight deep, a swaying forest of spars, a wealth of nets and floats stacked on their afterdecks, everything for sale. Word went around that there were bargains to be had. The contents of the homes in Japtown were on the block at sacrificial prices. Pieces of furniture and household effects were seen being carted through town, bought for a song. Mrs. Omoto, bowing apologetically, told me she could no longer do my laundry. There were tears of embarrassment in her eyes and I felt like putting my arms around her diminutive motherly figure, but I didn't. Might such a gesture be construed as consorting with the enemy?

So they went, gathered together in families, dressed in their best, the dark material of their suits and hats becoming darker yet as they stood waiting in the rain, their hands occupied with suitcases and bundles, too full to hold umbrellas. They filed up the gangways under the watchful eyes of extra police constables brought in for the occasion. They went onto the ships that would take them away, at this point, few knowing where they were going. They went without protest in what seemed stunned silence, leaving behind virtually everything but what they could carry, not looking squarely at the bystanders who for various reasons had turned out to witness their exodus. To some observers it was almost a carnival event: "About time they got the bloody Japs out of here. Good riddance." To others it was an occasion for tears.

CHAPTER 10

A Raw Recruit

It seems that whenever my life changes direction, the pivotal day is blessed with good weather. The first day of April, 1942, was no exception; it dawned warm and sunny. Harry Chase and I wandered out of the drugstore cafe where we had been dawdling over mid-morning coffee.

Across the street, on the hotel porch, a Royal Canadian Navy lieutenant stood at relaxed attention, not lounging against the railings with the regulars, but balancing on the balls of his feet. (I learned later it was against Naval regulations for an officer to lean on anything.) He was taking in the sun that glinted warmly on his cap badge, the gold braid on his sleeves and the double row of brass buttons on his jacket. A tall man with chiseled features and beautifully straight white teeth, he looked like he had stepped out of a recruiting poster. He, a doctor and a clerk had arrived on the *Catala* the previous day. This small recruiting team would stay between scheduled steamships and then move on to the next coastal village, gathering those with a seafaring bent into His Majesty's Navy.

Harry was about to go one way and me the other when we paused. We looked at the lieutenant and then at each other.

"Hey, Paul. How about we join the Navy? Harry asked.

A picture of myself wearing a Navy uniform had crossed my mind when I saw the blue-clad trio debark the previous evening, but it had quickly faded. "You mean, like right now?" I asked.

"Yeah. Right now."

Caught off balance, I guess I nodded assent. It was one of those spur-of-the-moment decisions that didn't get the thought it deserved. That my life might be altered irrevocably hardly entered into the thought process. I have never really decided whether it is a strength or a weakness that prompts me to grasp eagerly onto suggestions by others and run with them regardless of consequences. I guess in the back of my mind I was looking for such a prompting, knowing full well I couldn't dilly-dally much longer. I would eventually have to join something but, typically, I was putting it off. And had Harry not mentioned it, I would probably have procrastinated further. Here, however, was a ready-made logical choice that I didn't have to wrestle seriously with. Hadn't my mother sprung from a long line of seagoing people? Wouldn't it be natural for me to follow in their footsteps? The alternative, of course, was to hang back and be conscripted into the Army. But any thought of the Army included an image of Father, so I rejected out of hand anything to do with that branch of the service. And even though the romantic notion of flying was appealing, I had to cross the Air Force from the list of options, since I hadn't the required education. So that left only the Navy.

"Why not." I said.

The lieutenant eyed us speculatively. "Ah, at last, a couple of live ones," probably running through his mind. Business had not been good thus far.

In somewhat less than two hours, we were inducted into the Royal Canadian Navy. With hand on bible, we had sworn allegiance to the crown, at the moment being worn by King George VI—a most unkingly man to my way of thinking. The doctor had gone over us, the clerk had fingerprinted us and noted any scars or disfigurements that might identify us if the worst came to the worst, and we had signed multiple legal-looking documents without reading any of them.

The lieutenant shook our hands.

"Congratulations. You're in the Navy now," he said, smiling.

"Thanks. When do we go...like with you? Tomorrow?" we asked innocently, I at least envisioning myself—by what magical process I couldn't imagine—as being immediately dressed in a natty suit with gold braid and oak leaves, exactly like that being worn by the lieutenant, and waving goodbye to the local folk from

135

the bridge of tomorrow's Union steamship *Cardena*.

"No, not tomorrow," the lieutenant said. "It'll not be for a few weeks. You'll receive your travel documents sometime within the month. That will give you time to attend to your affairs here. You'll take basic training in Vancouver at HMCS Discovery, a shore establishment. It's located in Stanley Park."

Back on the street, Harry and I looked at each other. What had we done? Were we really in the Navy? The magnitude of what I had committed myself to began to sink in. This was no momentary diversion. This wasn't something I could just shrug off and carry on with what I had been doing. There was no way I could go back and say, "I've thought better of it, just tear up the forms." I had signed on. I was in the Navy, and that was that.

In the weeks that followed, I had a hard time keeping my mind on the job.

During the summer of 1941, I had successfully negotiated a transfer from the finishing room. Matter of fact, Dick, George, Hank and Owen and I had all escaped the finishing room at about the same time, me into the electric shop and the rest into the machine shop. Dick, George and Hank had begun apprenticeships; Owen and I, our educational background being insufficient to be apprentices, had to start as helpers.

Mike Stevens, the journeyman electrician I was helping, was the first person I told. A slow-moving, laconic individual, his only comment was, "Well, we'll miss you...I guess." Since he didn't consider helpers as people, I knew that the fact he was about to lose me as such wasn't going to markedly ruin his day.

The next person I told was Jack Stevens, the shop foreman. He shook his head resignedly. There was nothing he could do about it, and he had probably rationalized that what was now a trickle of able bodies leaving to join the forces, soon would become a full-scale freshet.

"Have you told anyone in the office?" he asked.

'No, not yet," I said.

"Don't you think you should? Maybe they'd like to know."

"Oh, yeah, maybe I should." I said. It hadn't dawned on me that I might actually be leaving a hole in the workforce. My sense of worth was not yet that well developed.

I didn't have much in the way of affairs to put in order, just the purchase of a trunk and the packing of my belongings—mostly clothing and a few books. I had accumulated a sizeable wardrobe in the preceding two years; I would ship them to my parents' address in Vancouver. My first inclination was to leave everything as it was. I would go and fight this war and then come back and resume my life. I still had trouble putting things into their proper context: I couldn't visualize being gone for very long.

The travel documents arrived as promised.

The night before my departure, Owen and I sat up late talking. He was feeling down. He pretty well knew he was going to be odd man out. His eyesight was so bad nobody would want him. Dick, George and Hank were all going through the preliminary moves of enlisting, Hank into the Navy, Dick and George into the Air Force. Owen had become resigned to remaining a civilian. (Try as he would over the next year, he was rejected by every branch of the service.)

Harry and I had been the only ones the lieutenant had been able to recruit. We said our goodbyes, for how long we didn't know, but I knew I would return sometime. At that moment of parting, as *Cardena* pulled away from the wharf, I realized that Ocean Falls had become my home—the place I would tell people I was from.

I felt no insecurity about leaving. I knew my job was guaranteed, held for me pending the end of hostilities, whenever that might be. There was never any doubt in anyone's mind that our side would be victorious and that life would be regenerated in its present pattern. I would pick up where I'd left off provided I hadn't got killed or seriously maimed and that scarcely crossed my mind—that was something that happened to others.

Two days later, in the peaceful setting of Coal Harbour in Vancouver's Stanley Park, in a gray-painted building that appeared more like a yacht club headquarters (which it had been) than a Naval establishment, I was issued a uniform and the war became more tangible, except that it was being carried on in parklike surroundings and the only wounds were to our egos as those in charge began molding us into fledgling sailors.

The uniform I was issued was not, alas, like that of the recruiting officer. Mine was a "round rig" designed by someone with a diabolical sense of humor—someone back in the days of Drake and Nelson I judged. Getting into it could be managed single-handedly but with difficulty. But if the uniform fit reasonably well, getting out of it was impossible without help to peel the jersey off over the head. And despite all of us having been shorn to one inch of our scalps, the collar was still unchanged, the same as it had been for centuries, designed to protect the back of the jersey from the pigtail clubbed with tar worn by the fashionable sailor of the 1700s or thereabouts. The hat that fit naturally on the back of the head, could not be worn there. Regulations insisted that it be squared off one inch above the eyes, in order, I was sure, to extract the maximum discomfort from it.

HMCS Discovery, the basic training headquarters in Stanley Park, was not a barracks per se, it was strictly a daytime training establishment. Everyone, trainers and trainees alike, lived ashore—meaning anywhere in Vancouver. I lived at home with Mother and Father.

Their house was small, but it did have a spare bedroom. I moved in as a matter of course. It didn't occur to me that inserting myself into their life pattern might be inconvenient, that I might be a too-large chick to return to a too-small nest. However, I was only there at night and on weekends. Daytimes, beginning at 6:00 A.M. and ending at 6:00 P.M., I was either on a streetcar coming and going, being drilled on the parade ground that had once been a parking lot for yacht club members, being route-marched around Stanley Park or across the Lions Gate all the way up to the Capilano Suspension Bridge. My intrusion, if it did put undue pressure on them, was somewhat mitigated by the board and lodging allowance paid by the Navy, and that I turned over to them in its entirety. I was there for three months.

Marching around Stanley Park and being shouted at was different from anything I'd encountered so far, but it still wasn't war, nor was HMCS Naden, at Esquimalt, that followed. Naden was big, a full-scale shore training center with barracks. There, I was introduced to sleeping in a hammock and naval armament, but the only sounds of hostility came from the mouths of the drillmasters, the petty officers and chief gunners-mates. The war was still on the other side of the world.

I had no problem with discipline. Father had drummed into us since babyhood that, "In the Army, you do as you are told, when you are told." The Navy was no different. It never occurred to me to think otherwise or behave in any way to incur the wrath of those in charge. I was never singled out for any disciplinary measure.

There was a brief stint at Comox, primarily a small-arms training base, where I earned the dubious title of Comox Gun-Layer and was entitled to wear crossed rifles on my sleeve. Following, was a dreary winter in Prince Rupert at HMCS Chatham. There, I became a sail maker. The title, a misnomer like so many other holdovers from the days of sailing ships that still cluttered naval way of doing business and its jargon, there being nothing resembling sails to make. There were, however, other canvas things to sew—boat covers, gun covers, awnings and bags. I learned to fashion all of these odd shapes in a draughty old building through which the Prince Rupert winter wandered at will, under the watchful eye and the whiplash tongue of Petty Officer Nutter. He was a career Navy man who looked upon us, the hostilities-only types, as having diluted the real Navy. We were something to put up with for the duration, yet another, maybe even the primary, reason for him to hate the enemy.

Following HMCS Chatham came my first tour of duty on a floating vessel. A ship of war, though, it wasn't.

Prince Rupert is one of the world's finest deep-water harbors. It is also one of a handful of seaports on the globe that boasts tidal fluctuations that exceed seven meters. In its frantic effort to fill and empty the harbor through the narrow gateways, the ocean's ebb and flow can reach millrace velocities.

As soon as Japan posed a threat to West Coast shipping, the port facilities were seen to be an attractive target. The Navy therefore had caused a submarine net to be strung across the harbor's southern entrance. Fastened to the shores at both ends, the net hung from surface to sea bottom like a great theater curtain, the center section of which could be drawn aside to allow legitimate shipping to enter and leave. Two gate vessels, little more than barges, positioned either side of the gate itself, housed the diesel-engine-driven winches that actuated the gate. They were also home to the dozen or so seamen who operated them. I was posted to *Gate Vessel 5*, the

Mother and author in front of their house
at 58th Ave. and Ontario St., Vancouver,
in 1942.

senior of the two vessels, in March, 1943. *GV5* was senior because
the officer who was in charge of both vessels hung his hat there.
The officer held the rank of "Skipper," the bottom rung of the ladder of commissioned ranks. Skippers were actually fishermen who
had been lured into the Navy and given commissions, the original
idea being that they would remain as fishermen, but would provide
eyes and ears for the Navy. They were handed, instead, all the unsa-
vory duties shunned by proper officers, lowly commands that had
little to do with the harvesting of fish.

During the following six months aboard *GV5*, I became a vir-
tual recluse. Chatham barracks in winter had been bad enough, but

Author and Father in front of their house at 58th Ave. and Ontario St., Vancouver, in 1942.

at least it was a simple walk up town after hours, even if there was nothing to do there. Leaving *GV5* entailed a voyage of about a half an hour on the open deck of the tugboat that serviced the gate vessels at regular intervals. It also meant that once up town, there was no returning until the next boat.

Prince Rupert had little to offer in the way of recreation, and what there was had to be shared with the thousands of servicemen from every branch of the Canadian and American forces. It had burgeoned from a small city devoted to fishing and operating its port facilities to one with thrice the population carrying on war activities. There were two movie houses that were always full, two hotel beer parlors that were jam-packed and rowdy, and a few restaurants and coffee shops with long lineups. I found it hardly worthwhile to go through the tiresome ritual of pressing a uniform, shining shoes and standing inspection to ride the tug and arrive uptown wet and disheveled to wander for hours in the rain waiting to get inside something, and always keeping in mind the boat schedule and how much time there was to kill before the return trip. So my trips ashore became fewer and fewer. I put up with the boredom, the endless make-work of scrubbing down bulkheads and when the weather permitted, slathering gray paint on everything in sight. I stood my watches, and during my off-duty hours, I lay on my bunk and read or gazed from the window at the rain dimpling the water and at the misty shoreline a few hundred yards off. The only thing breaking its monotonous gray-green, was the twice-daily trip of the single-coach bud-car making its way and hooting derisively at us from the rail line that ran to and from Port Edwards.

Only two brief events livened my tour of duty on *GV5*. Once, a huge whale became captured in the harbor, likely having entered when the gate was opened to admit a ship. It entertained us for almost a week, humping its way along the submarine net searching for a way out, rising unexpectedly a few yards away and blowing its breath across anyone standing on deck. It disappeared one day, probably the same way it came, underneath a ship.

A week later I was almost swept out to sea.

Sometime previously, in the early dawn, a weathered, old, twelve-foot long rowboat had come drifting by on the ebbing tide. The duty watchman, a slick-haired seaman we called Tarzan, had seen it coming and reached out with a boat hook and snared it. He tied it alongside. The Skipper, an easy-going sort, turned a blind eye to this derelict appendage dangling at the end of his command. He also ignored the use of the leaky old tub by off-duty personnel to vacate his ship for an hour or so, to fish or just row around. It was our proud possession—one we could lord over those on *GV6*, our companion gate vessel, who had no such craft at their disposal. Nobody, not even Tarzan who had captured it, claimed personal ownership and anybody could to use it, except, of course, those envious souls on *GV6* .

One rare sunny afternoon, I sat lazing in it looking down into the crystal clear water, watching ground fish drift across the sandy bottom of a little cove a quarter mile outside the net. I wasn't paying proper attention to my anchorage and the gradual straining of the anchor line as a large chunk of Pacific Ocean began its headlong rush out of the harbor. By the time I awoke to reality, hauled anchor and unshipped the oars, the tide, bound for the Orient, was running a good ten knots. Panicked, I began rowing, but much too late. Within minutes I was in deep water beyond the depth of the anchor line. Helplessly, I watched the shoreline pick up speed and *GV5* recede rapidly into the distance.

I looked at my watch. I was due on duty in less than an hour. I was not going to make it—that is without divine intervention. I was heading in the wrong direction. Before the tide's six-hour cycle would deliver me back from whence I had come, I was in for a long and uncomfortable voyage in a boat that let water in through its bottom rather freely. If I hadn't made it back by dark, there was also a good chance of getting lost in the clutch of small islands that dotted the local seascape. Beyond that I hated to think. I would have been "absent from place of duty" long enough to have incurred the wrath of even the easiest-going skipper.

"How come you're out here all by yourself in that kind of a boat?" the swarthy Native fisherman asked as he leaned out of the cockpit of his double-end troller and made my painter fast to a cleat on deck. "I thought the Navy was supposed to be fighting a war someplace. You can't fight much of a war in that boat, can you? She's not much of a boat, is she? I never knew the Navy had a boat like that. You got any guns or any of them depth charges in that boat, 'eh?" His flat dark face was serious, but there was a glint of humor in his eyes.

I said nothing except to tell him where I wanted to go. He could lay any ridicule he liked on me as long as he got me back to *GV5*. It had started to rain and a breeze of wind was getting up to make things interesting. My teeth were chattering. I sat hunched, breathing the fishy slipstream and listening to the satisfying thunk, thunk of the one-lunger that was towing me home, thankful he'd come along. I owed one to St. Christopher or whoever was looking after sailors cast-adrift on that particular day.

The Skipper had gone ashore for the day and a genial beak-nosed seaman named Cook had covered for me.

The boat? It disappeared one night leaving a frayed tag end of rope tied to a stern cleat.

Ocean Falls. Owen and Hank Adams.

Chapter 11

Losing Mother

Mother died while I was in Prince Rupert aboard *Gate Vessel 5*.

The call came midmorning from Lieutenant Commander Lee, the officer in charge of the port defenses. He wanted to speak to me.

"Hey Jones!" Johnson's voice came funneling down the stairs from what passed for a bridge on *GV5*. "Lieutenant Commander Lee wants you on the phone." Johnson, a towhead with a big mouth, was always pulling something.

"Oh sure, so does King George."

"I'm not kidding. Old Lee wants to talk to you. You better get up here."

My God! What had I done, nothing less than a major breach of discipline would warrant a phone call from a lieutenant commander to me. This was no social call, of that I was sure. With trepidation, and still uncertain that Johnson wasn't setting me up, I picked up the phone.

"Able seaman Jones speaking," I said.

"Jones?"

"Yes, Sir."

"Lee speaking," his raspy voice cut through the hiss of the habitually wet telephone line. "I have some bad news. Your mother died."

There it was. No preliminaries, just that stark statement. In all fairness, there is probably no way to soften such news. It eventually has to come out. He did follow it with an offer to approve two weeks compassionate leave.

I was struck dumb. "Yes, Sir. Thank you, Sir," was all I was able to say.

I wanted to ask how he knew, how come someone had told him and not me, and a dozen other questions, but my presence of mind had deserted me. For the remainder of the day, in something of a daze, I went through the motions of requesting leave, filling out the proper forms and getting them signed by the skipper. I took them ashore to Lee's office, where, good as his word, he signed them without the usual rigmarole. I would leave on the next boat south.

While ashore I tried to phone, but over the cluttered telephone lines from Prince Rupert it was impossible. I gave up after several frustrating attempts. I would have to wait until I got to Vancouver to find out what had happened.

In the afternoon, on my return to *GV5*, the mailbag produced a letter from Mother, written four days previously. It was her usual letter, full of chitchat about inconsequential things, news of Owen, Olwyn and Olwyn's daughter, Lynda, who was growing apace and spending her days at Grandma's house. Not a word about an illness more serious than usual—nothing that would give me some insight to why she had died.

The small house on the corner of Fifty-Eighth Avenue and Ontario Street seemed empty and more spacious with only Father in it. And *he* seemed to have shrunk. He was smaller, grayer and more rumpled than I remembered him from only a few months back. He hadn't shaved for several days and his clothing needed washing. It was evident that the props had been knocked out from under him. The loss of Mother had shaken him to his roots.

He gave me a perfunctory embrace and then turned away. He pulled out a hanky and wiped his eyes. As soon as we began to talk I sensed that a subtle change had taken place in our relationship; he was no longer the Alpha male. I got the impression he was passing the mantle to me. He was looking for someone to explain to him why his life had suddenly turned upside-down and what he should do about it.

I wasn't sure I was ready to accept the power shift. It had come too suddenly; I needed time to think about it.

Olwyn, who lived across the street, had been keeping him fed and shored up as best she could. But she had problems of her own. She was working downtown at Spencer's department store, and with Mother gone she was having trouble finding and paying for alternate daycare for Lynda. This situation and Father leaning heavily on her had her feeling the pressure. Her life had become complicated, and she was getting little support from Ralph, who was working out of town. She wanted to shed some of the responsibility for Father onto me.

My first question, of course, was what had happened; why had Mother died? The answer was simple: pneumonia, the most virulent kind. Mother had had no defenses. She had been taken to St. Paul's Hospital, but had succumbed despite the best efforts of the staff in intensive care. There was no one to lash out at, no focus for blame. All we could do was accept.

Owen arrived from Ocean Falls, and our cousin John and his wife, Thelma, from Victoria. John was in the Army stationed at Work Point. It was the first time we had all been together since we had lived as a family, crowded into the tiny log cabin on the Alberta homestead where we'd had our beginnings. We had been children then.

Mother's piano, a scarred old upright with cracked and yellowed keys, that she had bought without a down payment and was paying five dollars a month on, sat silently in the livingroom. There was only one wall in that small room it could go against, and even then it protruded across the bedroom door at the one end and prevented the front door from opening fully at the other. Her music, a book of *Favorite Selections*, open at "Whispering Hope," the last thing she had played, was still open above the keyboard. On top of the piano was a pile of dog-eared sheet music, old pieces, things she'd had around for years—Mozart, Beethoven, Chopin, a hymn book side by side with selections from light opera and musical theater. I knew most of them well, heard her play them countless times.

We were drawn to that piano. John, who somewhere in his travels, had learned to pick out tunes, played, while the rest of us gathered around and sang. Father was horrified. Where was our respect? What would the neighbors think? But our singing wasn't just lighthearted amusement. There was no lack of respect, it went much

147

deeper than that. It was more a tribute to Mother. She was there; we all felt it. There was nothing she liked better than a singsong, playing for those clustered around the piano. Her spirit was with us.

The funeral service was held in the chapel of a funeral home, not in a church as I had expected. The arrangements had been made before I arrived. Mother, an avowed atheist, illogically, still attended church whenever she felt up to walking out to Main Street and hauling herself aboard a streetcar. She usually went to St. Giles United, down on Tenth Avenue and Ontario Street, the church we had found when we first arrived in Vancouver. I was a little surprised, but I didn't question.

It wasn't a well-attended funeral. There were only a few neighbors and the vice-principal from Sexsmith School, across the corner. In her last year, Mother had returned to her first love: teaching. She had become a volunteer at the school for a few hours a week.

The casket, covered in gray fabric and without adornment, rested on trestles. It was open. I couldn't believe it was Mother lying there.

It was the first time I'd had to confront death. I had never before lost a family member. My grandparents, on both sides, had departed long before I was born, as had several aunts and uncles. I'd never even lost a close friend. Somehow I'd always assumed that Mother and Father would go on forever, notwithstanding the ill health that had dogged them as long as I could remember.

Illness had been a way of life in our house. As children, we were always being cautioned to tone down our natural boisterousness because either Mother or Father wasn't feeling well. Illness was so normal I had hardly associated it with death. And we had always assumed that, in the unlikely event that one of them had to go, Father would be first, he being the one with war-related maladies, the bad heart and the many and varied things he'd complained of over the years. Mother, although actually the frailer of the two, had always been stronger in spirit. It just seemed natural that she would endure.

I stood looking down on her. This wasn't my mother. Even with her hair combed the way she had always worn it and wearing her best dress, a navy print with tiny white flowers, this wasn't my mother. This was someone else. This was a very old, tired woman.

To this point the reality of her passing hadn't sunk in. Now, here was the finality of death. I felt an awful tightening in my throat and the urge to cry came upwelling from deep within me. I wanted to cry, for me and for this woman who was owed so much and had had so little. She was young, only fifty-four, but had seemed old for so long.

I choked back my urge to cry. Men in uniform didn't cry.

We buried her in Mountain View cemetery. Probably no more than a dozen people witnessed the lowering of the coffin.

After the funeral, I stayed on. Lee had been generous; he had included traveling time with my leave, and I still had most of my two weeks left. Before I had to catch a boat back to Prince Rupert, I wanted to restore something of a firm footing under Father. We were all a little concerned how he would manage. Would he cook for himself? Did he think he could look after himself and the house…perhaps with some help from Olwyn? He evinced little interest in any of this.

John's leave was up. He and Thelma left for Victoria. Owen had to go too. I went with him to the boat.

"I wish I could stay around," he said, "get the old man settled. I don't know whether he's going to be able to manage on his own. Doesn't seem to care about much. I guess Mother took some of him along with her."

I didn't want to push Father, but I needed some assurance that he was going to be all right. Knowing I would eventually run out of time and have to return to Prince Rupert, I asked him right out. "So, do you think you'll be able to manage here by yourself?"

He wouldn't meet my eyes. He looked a little embarrassed, almost guilty. He said, "I'm getting out of here. I'm not going to do housekeeping."

"What do you mean? Where are you going to go? What about the house?"

"I'm going to sell it. It should be worth something. I don't need any house. I don't need very much. I'll find something, a room somewhere. I know how to live like that. I did it for years, long before any of this…before you were born. I'll manage."

Shocked, I tried to reason with him. The house was small,

149

wouldn't take much looking after, a nice neighborhood where he had friends, close to Olwyn.

He would have none of it.

"I've called the real estate company. There'll be a guy here this morning to put it on the market."

"What about the furniture? What are you going to do with it?"

He smiled ruefully and shook his head. "Yeah, sure. Look at it boy. Take a good look at it. What is there?"

I looked. He was right. What was there? In the kitchen, only a wood and coal range and a table with four chairs. I knew the bedrooms had iron beds with thin mattresses and nothing else. The living room had the piano, a sofa and a chair. And in a corner by the front window was a stand with a potted fern on it. It was a roughly made stand. I recognized Father's carpentry.

"But you can't just leave it. You have to do *something* with it."

"Olwyn can have what she wants. The second-hand store can have the rest."

There was no talking him out of it.

By the time I left for Prince Rupert, the house was sold and everything in it had been disposed of. Father had moved into a basement room across the street, taking with him his clothes and not much else. The last vestige of home had disappeared.

I stood alone on the deck of the night boat heading north into the gloom and rain of the upper coast. I let myself cry.

CHAPTER 12

HMCS *Capilano*

My first impression of the North Atlantic, colored I'm sure by the events of the preceding three years, was that it was cold and unfriendly. A dark and truculent ocean, it would not suffer gladly those who would venture upon it. I would not get over feeling threatened by it. First impressions etch deeply.

I saw it from a bad angle that first time, coming as we were from the south, riding the Gulf Stream and having been entertained for the past weeks by flying fish and schools of playful porpoise. Suddenly we were being asked to leave behind the blue warmth that we had lately become accustomed to and, all within a day, dive into the dank fog shrouding the coast of Nova Scotia.

A sea was running and the air was raw as we entered the shelter of Halifax Harbour and snugged HMCS *Capilano* into the wharf. It was October 22, 1944.

A brand new frigate, one that only a few months ago had slid down the ways at Yarrows shipyard in Esquimalt, we had completed our first voyage, circumnavigating half a continent in doing so. She, and we who had brought her, were destined for duty shepherding the convoys that were still the lifeline between the old world and the new.

We didn't know it then, but the war was winding down. There was an air of optimism. Daily, the newscasts were more favorable. Even so, the Canadian Navy was not yet ready to lower its guard. Underneath that surging gunmetal sea, littered with the bones of

151

war, lurked the remnants of the still-dangerous submarine wolf-packs.

I had come a long way from the north coast of British Columbia, and by a circuitous route, but at last I had reached a theater where war was real. I had done what I set out to do, for better or for worse.

My time in Prince Rupert had run out. Perhaps the card with my name on it had come up when the deck was shuffled in the great naval game of "move the troops around." Whatever the prompting, I was drafted out to HMCS *Givenchy*, a shore base in Esquimalt. I wasn't sad to leave the gloomy backwater of Prince Rupert; however, the return to the rigid disciplined routine of an advance training and staffing base was like a cold shower. It jerked me back to reality. I had grown slack, as had we all, in the informal atmosphere of that rain-streaked northern outpost.

There were enlisted men who had spent the entire war, thus far, in *Givenchy*, holding down humdrum jobs and quite content to ride out the rest of it in the same way—a safe berth, for however long it took. But not for me. It took only a couple of days after my return to discover that life in and around a naval base held little appeal, confirming what I'd felt all along. I may not have had any firm convictions when I enlisted, but after a year in which I had done little of consequence I was asking myself why I was here, and if there was something meaningful in all this why it had it eluded me. My time as a naval rating had not counted for much, but I was growing more determined that it should. I had joined up expecting to go to war, and by God, to war I would go if at all possible. And when my grandchildren asked, "What did you do in the war, Grandpa?" I wanted to be able to tell them that I had been somewhere in the forefront and had lent a hand to win it. I couldn't ask why things were the way they were. Able seamen didn't question the system, but it seemed the scheme was one of rote—don't ask, just go through the motions for the sake of the motions. I wanted either out or a sea-going ship, the latter I judged to be the most readily attainable. To say "I've had enough" and walk away just wouldn't wash.

Thankfully, *Givenchy* didn't hold me for long. Within a week I was drafted aboard HMCS *Bellchasse*, a Bangor-class minesweeper, plying the straights of Juan de Fuca. Not exactly a war zone, as there was no visible enemy, but at least it was a ship at sea.

For six months I "slung my mick" in *Bellchasse* while she patrolled between Port Renfrew and Sooke, back and forth, night and day, four days out and four days in port lying against the wharf in Esquimalt. None of us knew exactly why we were out there doing what we were doing, but we all assumed that we were performing some useful service. Perhaps there were hostile forces lurking on our western doorstep and sowing their seeds of destruction; however, we never saw any. All we saw was the detritus of

Esquimalt. Aboard *Bellchasse*, author third from left.

civilization, junk set adrift by the shore dwellers on both sides of the straights who used the sea to dispose of things unwanted. One sunny morning, out of boredom and a dearth of things to report, I called from my lookout station on the wing of the bridge, "Bearing green four-oh, a dead pig, Sir." For a moment I thought Captain Redford would have me join it.

June, 1944, I was drafted back to *Givenchy*. More than ever, having had a taste of shipboard life, it was a letdown. I felt useless, cast up on the beach without cause. In that huge brick and asphalt conglomerate, I saw myself as nameless flotsam stranded at the tide line. I wanted only to get back to sea in any kind of a ship—a blue-water ship if at all possible.

I became a gadfly hanging around the offices, weekly requesting drafts to sea-going ships. Careful not to push too far or too fast and rouse a backlash from those in charge, I nevertheless kept myself in front of anyone who had anything to do with staffing the new ships that were regularly being launched from the western shipyards. My persistence paid off. Those at the drafting office finally relented, doubtless to rid themselves of me. I was told to report to the duty officer aboard HMCS *Capilano*, a new frigate just off the ways. Bigger than a minesweeper, but smaller than a destroyer, she looked sleek and businesslike. This was more like it. Elated, I dragged my sea bag and my hammock down to the wharf and joined a dozen or so others reporting aboard.

The commissioning ceremony took place on the morning of August 25, 1944. A colorful pageant: bunting fluttering from the halyards, sun glinting on gold encrusted uniforms and from the tubas and trumpets of the HMCS *Naden* Naval band, a light breeze stirring the summer dresses of the officers wives, and we of ship's company drawn up smartly in ranks on the afterdeck among the depth-charge racks. The band's rousing rendition of "Hearts of Oak" was followed in somber counterpoint by the chaplain's voice over the loudspeakers soliciting divine protection. "God bless this ship and all who sail in her."

The feverish activity of outfitting followed. All within a month, *Capilano* was provisioned, armed and her compass swung. On September 27, we let go her lines, eased her out of the harbor and pointed her bows at the Pacific Ocean. We were a new ship and a new crew that hadn't had time to become a single unit. There were rough edges to round off before she and we would weld together into an effective fighting machine. That would come, and it did, day by day, with the experienced molding the inexperienced—naval discipline, tradition and practice, practice, practice being effective tools. At any hour of the day or night the shrilling of the action-stations bell roused us. This was repeated time and again, until we were closed up in thirty seconds. We became so jumpy that any sharp sound, the mere tinkling of a glass in the mess, sent us flying for the companionways, squirming into lifejackets.

My regular watch station was lookout on the starboard wing of the bridge. My action station was on the afterdeck on the forward port depth-charge thrower.

Esquimalt. Launching *Capilano*.

Off watch and in between practice sessions, I was assigned the unenviable (at least I considered it so) task of the chief petty officer's messman, known to some as a "jammy number." There were three of us—Johnstone, from Rossland; Terleki, from Montreal; me from the northern rainforest. Waiters, dishwashers, deck scrubbers and fetch-and-carry boys, we were all of these, rotating with the watches. Chief Petty Officer Lightfoot, the coxswain, ruled the mess. Built like an out of condition fireplug, his little piggy eyes saw everything. And if what he saw displeased him, which was much, his mouth issued snarling expletives, some of which I'd

Esquimalt. Christening *Capilano*.

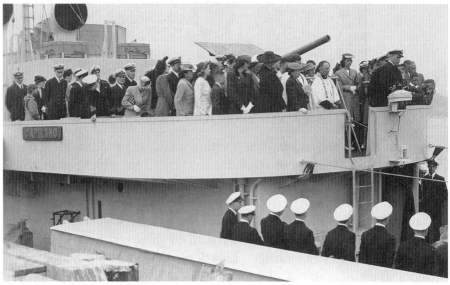

Esquimalt. Commissioning ceremonies aboard *Capilano*.

never heard before. A career navy man, he brooked no shirking or half-hearted attention to duty. There were four other chief petty officers, all of whom we were at beck and call. It was not a job I could warm to, but I put up with it, biding my time. I knew there had to be a way out, but it would take a while to figure something.

It came sooner than I anticipated.

One of our tasks was to draw the chief petty officer's rum ration. It was doled out each day at eleven o'clock. Five two-and-a-half-ounce tots of rum were measured out by the steward on duty at the time, put in a enamel teapot (an exact duplicate of the one used for tea) and taken to the mess where it was consumed at the petty officer's pleasure. (All ranks lower than chief petty officer who drew rum—there were two options: grog or temperance—were required to drink it in front of the commissioned officer observing the doling out) Thinking about something else, as I usually was, while cleaning up after the midday meal, and not paying particular attention to the contents of the pot in my hand, I emptied it over the side. A major gaff; alas, it was not leftover tea. Chief Petty Officer Lightfoot was not amused.

It was carelessness, not a breach of discipline. There was no basis for punishment, but I immediately became *persona non grata*, I was cashiered as messman and sent packing back to the seaman's mess, Lightfoot no doubt thinking he was exacting retribution by depriving me of a coveted position. To appear contrite while trying to keep an inner elation from seeping out around the edges was not easy. I about-turned and marched smartly off, trying desperately to hide a grin.

Thinking that the sewing skills I had acquired under the watchful eye of Petty Officer Nutter at Prince Rupert would sidetrack me out of the mainstream of general duties, the chipping painting and scrubbing that is the lot of the able seaman, I let it be known I was a sail maker. To that position, I was duly appointed. Turned out, though, there was little in the way of sails or anything else to make, we being in a new ship in which everything made of canvass had been provided and was still intact.

It followed that I was not allowed to sit around waiting for something in my line of work. In the meantime, I was handed my share of scrubbing and painting.

Never before had I lost sight of land. Never had I not had something solid to reference to. Now, here in this open western ocean, there was nothing but water in any direction. Like a hick, neck-craning tall buildings, I gazed at the swells, marveling at their magnitude. My whole world was in motion. Silas Marner's *Ancient Mariner* came to mind. Water, water everywhere, and not a drop to drink. I kept looking, mesmerized. And too, this was clean water, no garbage or strayed saw logs. Nothing to see except for the slim-winged, wandering albatross—the habituates of the lonely oceans, soaring effortlessly impossibly close to the water, riding the air currents thrust upward by the swells, letting them lift them over the crests, then sliding into the troughs inches above the slick. I never tired of watching them.

Our position was not routinely passed down from the bridge to the mess decks, but it got there anyway. The unofficial word was that we were 200 miles off shore. And, of course, anybody with half an eye for the sun and the slightest sense of direction, knew we were on a southerly course. "We're taking her round," was the buzz. That was nothing new; we'd known, or at least suspected it, since the day somebody had discovered tropical white uniforms being brought aboard.

The humid heat became increasingly oppressive as we stepped down the latitudes. Day after sunny day, as *Capilano*'s bow knifed into the Pacific and her wake, straight as an arrow, unwound like foam-flecked road behind us, the sticky heat became more pronounced. The mess decks felt it first. Their stuffiness became unendurable. Running under wartime restrictions, even though we weren't considered to be in a war zone, darken ship was rigidly enforced. Deadlights closed as soon as darkness fell, not a glimmer showing anywhere. With portholes closed and fans without sufficient muscle to scavenge the fetid air, the atmosphere below decks climbed and became ripe with the sweat of 130-odd bodies denied sufficient fresh water for bathing, cigarette smoke and stale food odors. Nobody wanted to stay below.

The word came down. "Permission is granted to sling hammocks on the upper deck." There was a rush for spaces with anchorages the right distance apart from which to suspend hammocks.

Whether the captain, Lieutenant-Commander McCarthur, and the "jimmy", Lieutenant Best, had hatched a plot for their own amusement or decided it was simpler to prove an arrangement was impractical by demonstration rather than prohibit it outright was never established. Whatever the case, it didn't take long for the point to be made. Nightly, usually at the end of the first watch or the beginning of the midwatch, the fireworks began. Great blades of lightning came slashing up from the western horizon to knife open the bloated rain clouds that assembled over us as soon as the sun went down. I'd never seen anything like it. Torrents, they lasted no more than a few minutes, just long enough to fill every nook and cranny capable of retaining water. A hammock made of canvas, containing a mattress, two blankets and a snoring *matelot*, holds a remarkable amount of water. A mad, cursing scramble below decks to sleep on top of lockers with gear laid out to dry did nothing to deter those off-watch the following night from blissfully slinging their hammocks and getting their heads down above decks. Same story.

October 10. Our first landfall. Punta Mala, Panama.

0700 hours: Anchored off Balboa, the western gateway to the Panama Canal. No shore leave. U.S. Customs officers came aboard, and a pilot to ship-handle us through the canal.

0800 hours: Entered the first lock. An amazingly simple operation. Dark skinned men in broad hats, effortlessly firing heaving lines to our decks and attaching our hawsers to diesel donkeys that draw us into the lift locks, stepping us up to Gatun Lake. Bright sunshine suddenly disappears and we get drenched in another downpour. Then sun again.

"This is me standing on this deck, and that vegetation over there is tropical jungle, and this ship is going through the Panama Canal," I keep telling myself. Unreal. I am awed and excited by the sights and sounds and strange odors. I have read about the Panama Canal, how in its construction, hundreds of workers died in the tropical heat. That scenario I can understand. We, who are all products of temperate climate bloodlines, are lethargic, suffering in the unfamiliar oppressive heat. One minute we are drenched in the downpours, the next we are frying in the blistering sun. Any effort at all and the sweat runs.

October 11. Berthed in Colon. Drew first-watch gangway duty. Huge insects: moths bigger than bats throwing themselves headlong into the floodlights. Half the crew ashore. We're into tropical whites, but that they are cooler is a myth. Tomorrow I will go ashore.

October 12. The cantina, the one we chose at random, like all the rest that line the back street, has no front. We, Curwin, McQuade and I, are to one side of the bar, sitting in its gloom on spindly metal chairs at a small metal table that rocks on the uneven floor. We sip Panamanian beer and watch the flow of nighttime humanity in the weak incandescence lighting the street outside. It is a filthy, narrow street. The crowd washes past, most dark-skinned, but representing every race. They are scantily dressed, their clothing nondescript. The language is Spanish, as is the music that blares into the night. The look is suspicious of us, definitely not friendly. We are in this cantina because for the moment we are lost and have sought sheltered moorage while we consider. We have strayed, against better advice, from the more brightly lit streets. We took a wrong turn somewhere. *Capilano* and the waterfront lie somewhere over there, the direction, were not sure of. We will have some beer and think about it.

A man enters, shuffling in from the street. He is shouting what sound like Spanish epithets. At first I think he is a dwarf, but then I look again and decide he is not. It is just that he has no legs. His legs are missing from just above his knees. He is hobbling on two stumps. His crotch is scarcely more than a foot above the floor. He has pieces of wood tacked into the bottoms of his chopped-off trousers. These are his shoes. He is barrel-chested and has thick arms, a man who would be big if he had legs. His features are Caucasian but cooked to a saddle-leather brown by the tropics. His shiny, bald head glistens in the lamplight. He stumps along aided by two thick wooden canes. He is being abusive, perhaps he is a little drunk.

He shouts something at the bartender, a slim curly-headed black man. The bartender shakes his head, shouts back and points to the street. The shouting exchange gets louder. Only we pay any attention. The other patrons ignore everything but what is directly in front of them. Shorty becomes more agitated, shouts louder and waves his canes. The bartender leans over the bar and says something—obviously the wrong thing. Shorty reaches up and lays a cane dead center of the bartender's woolly thatch. There is a loud crack and the bartender sinks below the bar. Shorty then starts breaking things, swinging his canes right and left, smashing anything within reach. With one swipe he clears a pile of glasses from the bar, shattering them. Glass flies right across the room. A shard catches McQuade under the eye and slits his cheek wide open. Blood flows, first running down his cheek and then onto his freshly washed white jumper and pants.

McQuade swears and grabs his cheek then looks unbelievably at the blood on his hand that has run so quickly between his fingers and down his arm.

"You sawed off son of a bitch," he shouts.

McQuade is a husky lad, with broad shoulders and long arms that end in lumpy fists, and it takes much less than what has just happened to make him mad. He is getting mad now. He swears and gets up from his chair, knocking it and the table over in his rush to get at Shorty. Our beer goes flying. He will wreak vengeance on Shorty, regardless of Shorty's handicapped stature. I can see it coming. The problem is, Shorty obviously has allies. The other patrons look at us and start getting up from their tables. Nobody seems to have sympathy for McQuade. It appears they are aligning themselves with Shorty. We, in our white uniforms, are aliens here. I glance around—not another uniform in sight, not Army, not even a United States serviceman who seem to be everywhere else in great numbers. We are alone. There is going to be unpleasantness, major unpleasantness. Some of the crowd is moving in from the street. Shorty is still venting himself smashing things.

Curwin, looking around, says, "McQuade! For Christ's sakes let it go. Let's get out of here!"

"Yeah, let's go," I echo. I don't like what I'm seeing.

I grab McQuade on one side and Curwin grabs him on the other.

"I'm gonna kill that little bastard," McQuade says.

"Kill him some other time," says Curwin. "Let's go."

We muscle him out into the street before the crowd gets organized. He is mumbling about stomping Shorty into the deck, and at the same time holding his cheek and wiping at the blood that is smearing his uniform. We run, not paying attention to direction, shouldering our way through the throng, bowling a few over and hearing Spanish curses follow us. There are women sitting on chairs beside dark doorways, mostly fleshy dark women in loud print dresses. "Hey Sailors!" they call. "You want some fun?" Their laughter follows in our wake. We ignore them. We want only to get out of this labyrinth of unfriendly streets.

After a few blocks, we heave to, to get our bearings. Everybody seems to have lost interest in us. Getting McQuade to a doctor becomes uppermost in our minds. There is a lot of blood.

I look down an intersecting street. It seems brighter in that direction. We follow the light and come out on a busy street that we recognize. We are not far from the waterfront. Relieved we hurry back to *Capilano*.

The sick berth Attendant says McQuade needs stitches. The medical officer, Dr. Jones, is ashore, but when he comes back aboard he will get him to look at McQuade's wound.

I sit in the mess deck looking at my only souvenir of Panama, the only one I will have, since we leave tomorrow. It is a bracelet bought at a stall in a huge marketplace that has a roof but no walls. There were dozens of vendors selling the same things—rings, bracelets, earrings, necklaces and pendants, all made of what they call Mexican silver. It looks like silver but, from the price, I doubt it is. I selected the bracelet, after looking at a great many, because it seemed to have been made with a little more care than most. It is a series of links and inset in each is a square of glass behind which is a tiny landscape fashioned from iridescent fragments of butterfly wings. I have someone in mind to give it to, someone living in a cool remote inlet miles from here. I wrap it in tissue paper and bury it in the bottom of my locker.

October 13. Sailed from Colon.

We saw little during the next ten days, just the low outlines of Jamaica and Cuba and any number of unidentified clusters of islands that straddle the shipping lanes in the Caribbean. We passed them by, well offshore, bent only on our trek northward and our long climb, up the rungs of latitude to where we were needed.

CHAPTER 13

Londonderry

The city ahead, seen through the rain of the December afternoon, seemed a dour spot to end a long voyage. A dismal place, if it held any warmth, which at that moment I seriously doubted, it was well concealed behind a cold and dreary facade. The gray church spires and the jumble of slate rooftops grimed with the smoke of years, materializing out of the mist as we snaked our way up the Foyle River, held little promise. Not very cheery looking, I thought. But, perhaps I was making an unfair comparison. Still fresh in my mind was Hamilton, Bermuda, with its bougainvillea draped walls, red-tile roofed cottages, white coral beaches and surrounding warm blue oceans.

This was no Bermuda. I was shivering. The dank chill, born on a sharp wind that was following us through Lough Foyle, was seeping through my duffle coat that was becoming progressively saturated by drizzle. Well whatever it turned out to be, even if this cluster of gloomy buildings hugging the banks of the Foyle did not exactly exude gaiety, it was better than another day at sea. It must have a pub or two, and there must be girls. I hadn't talked to a girl since we'd left Esquimalt. If nothing else, it would be a change and a relief from tension, crowded mess decks, food that had grown tasteless and the routine of watch keeping, if only briefly.

Londonderry, North Ireland, was only new to me and a handful of others. The bulk of *Capilano*'s company had been here before in other ships. And if I had wanted to believe all the enthusiastic chatter that had gone on in the last few days, I'd have thought that at least half the fleshpots and pleasure palaces of Europe were congregated right here in this small Irish city. Some could scarcely wait to don their number ones and go ashore. I, however, was unable to muster much in the way of excitement. I stood looking at it without anticipation, with my back to the wind, heaving line coiled and ready in my hands that were turning blue with cold.

Again, *Capilano* was entering a port for the first time, having come by a circuitous route to get here. There was a lot of water between us and Halifax, our last Canadian port.

I hadn't seen much of Halifax, having only two short shore leaves that I spent wandering the streets adjacent to the waterfront. Then, following a boiler clean, refueling and provisioning, we were again at sea, ordered to proceed to St. Margaret's Bay, around the corner from Peggy's Cove, to begin work-ups in earnest. Despite the practice we'd had bringing *Capilano* to Halifax from Esquimalt, we were short on actual skills needed to wage submarine warfare. The only firing we'd done from her guns and depth-charge throwers was to ensure they actually worked.

We got down to business in St. Margaret's Bay, a cold and windy place where shooting at a target in the flat light caught between an overcast sky and a pewter sea was an exercise in frustration. The target, about the size and color of a submarine's conning tower and drawn at the end of a long cable by a towboat, proved annoyingly elusive, seeming able to dodge at will.

"Shoot the bloody thing out of the water and let's go back to Halifax," was wishful thinking. It was stay with it until the gun crews manning the twin four-inchers forward and the twelve-pounder aft gained an acceptable level of proficiency. The anti-aircraft gunners fared better. Their twenty-millimeter Oerlikons found the drogue, towed by a slow-moving biplane, much easier to hit. Besides, hosing tracers up into the sky was more fun than humping four-inch shells.

St. Margaret's Bay was only the beginning of work-ups. It was primarily a target range, and there was much more to submarine warfare than shooting. In most cases, the real targets lurked far below the surface. There were Asdic and Radar echoes to interpret. There were depth-charge patterns to lay and Hedgehog to fire. And, above all, there was the learning how to cope with ship damage, such as how to affix a collision mat and how to shore up a bulkhead and, that worst scenario of all, how to abandon ship. For these other exercises we again entered the warmth of the Gulf Stream, ordered to Bermuda where training increased in variety and intensity.

We were a month in Bermuda, based in St. George's Harbor, working with officers specializing in turning ships into fighting machines. Everything that could have been tested was tested, time and again, until the margin of error became acceptable. We made mistakes and did it over. Things happened that almost, but not quite, cost us dearly.

There is little sea running, just a chop with a brisk wind blowing the tops of the small waves and casting them like handfuls of jewels at us, the depth-charge crews working on the afterdeck. The spray is warm, as is the sun. We are practicing depth-charge runs using live ammunition.

For the last few days, we have been working with a submarine that was lately liberated from the Italian Navy's fleet. While working with it, we fired only small charges that did little more than make a noise, but their proximity was recorded by the submarine as hits or misses. Now the submarine has gone off somewhere and we are simulating. We are pretending that he is still with us and is weaving a devious course. We are testing our efficiency in getting charges away and reloading.

We have fired two patterns and are loading the third into the throwers. We have used the charges from the top of the storage racks and are having to hoist the next ones from the bottom to replace them on the rollers, ready to be pushed into the throwers. This morning, I am working on the portside forward thrower. My job is pushing the charges into the thrower from the top of the rack. They should move easily on the rollers. That is the theory anyway, but they don't. I question the mental powers of the individual who assigned me this task; I weigh in at just over 140 pounds, while the charge weighs 450 pounds, all of it being Amatol, a very high explosive. Seldom can I muster sufficient muscle to load the charge with one clean push. I struggle. Sometimes I have to hang by my hands from the top of the rack and actually boot the thing in with my feet. Mostly, I need help to get it the last few inches into the thrower. This particular time, while I am struggling, I miss some of what is going on at the bottom of the rack below me.

The man affixing the tackle to hoist the next charge to the top of the rack is having trouble hooking on. He has taken the retaining bar out and has rolled the charge out onto the deck, where he can get at it.

Suddenly *Capilano* rolls to starboard. She is turning. Under the direction of the training officer, she is following what he has dreamed up as the evasive course of a submarine. The man still hasn't got the tackle hooked to the charge. It rolls, knocking him over. He screams and falls to the deck. He is holding his leg and screaming that it is broken. The remaining charge in the bottom of the rack, with nothing to hold it, rolls out and together the two roll across the deck. They hesitate as *Capilano* rights herself, and start to roll back. A shout goes up, "Watch those bloody charges. Get a hold of them."

Two crewmembers grab one and start to wrestle it back to the rack. Meanwhile, the other one remains loose, rolling around. I make a grab for it, but it is too heavy and I can't hold it and have to jump out of the way. All of this is happening in seconds and the danger is just becoming apparent. We don't know what might happen. If a blow can detonate the explosive inside these gray drums, we don't know, but the thought occurs that it can. *Capilano*'s deck cants again and the charge takes off for the rail. It catches O'Neil, a baby-faced seaman, and takes him with it out between the railings. In an instant he is gone.

"Man overboard! Man overboard!" Seems everybody is hollering at once. For a moment we think maybe somebody else has gone, but a quick headcount establishes O'Neil as the only one.

The officer in charge of the depth-charge crew attempts to inform the bridge via the headset, but he is overridden by the order to fire coming the other way. It takes precedence, so he hollers "Fire!" and the pattern goes over the side—fourteen charges, four from the throwers and ten from the rails, all set to explode at depth. How deep, only the Asdic Officer and the Leading Torpedo hand, who is setting the detonators, know. There is the expectant lull between firing and the explosions. The man with the broken leg is groaning and trying to pull himself upright. Nobody can help him because we can't leave our stations. This is supposed to be war and we are reloading.

We look for O'Neil. Somebody shouts, "There he is!" He is bobbing in the wake.

Even after hearing what has happened, Captain McCarthur is not about to slow *Capilano* down and get her stern blown off by her own depth charges—not for O'Neil, not for anybody. He keeps her going at attack speed. It's only a matter of seconds, but O'Neil is getting smaller and disappearing between the swells. "He's a goner," someone says, gloomily. "He's gonna get blown to hell, right out of the water."

The deck comes up and hits the bottom of my feet. One after another the stunning explosions shatter the surface, heaving it like a vast belch, flattening the chop, but without sending up geysers. The charges have been set deep. We count. They all go off. We expect to see O'Neil fly out of the water like a cork from a Champagne bottle, but there is no sign of him.

"Secure depth charging," comes down from the bridge. *Capilano*'s speed drops and she turns to retrace her course. Everybody is looking at the wake and the acres of disturbed water.

"Anybody see him?" somebody asks quietly.

"Naw, not a sign. Aw shit, fish bait. Nobody could live through that."

Capilano is down to slow-ahead. She has come about onto her reciprocal course.

"There he is! I see him, dead ahead," The cry comes from somebody on the bridge.

O'Neil looks alright. He waves. A ladder is thrown over the side and he grabs it. A couple of hands reach down and hoist him inboard.

The man with the broken leg is carried to the sick bay. He is the first casualty aboard *Capilano*.

There is an investigation, a lot of investigation. There is also a lot more practice hoisting depth charges under the direct supervision of the work-up officer. He has a sharp tongue and not much patience or humor.

O'Neil has not suffered, only because the charges were set deep. The force of the explosions was dissipated before it got to him. He says he didn't feel anything. He joins in the practice.

Later on in the week, we all go over the side.

The buzz has it that we are going to practice abandoning ship, but nobody knows when. The leading hands, who don't know any more than the rest of us, tell us that when the order comes, "Over the side you go. No hanging around putting on bathing suits. You just jump."

The order comes when we're least expecting it. Nothing has been said for a few days so we figure maybe they've forgotten about it or decided not to.

I am on the port wing of the bridge when the loudspeaker opens up. "Abandon ship. All hands abandon ship." I look down. It is a long way to the water. I look fore and aft. The decks are much lower there. Despite what the leading hands have said, I see guys pulling off clothes and folding them in neat piles. I think I will go down to the foredeck and do the same. My line of thinking is interrupted. A voice behind me says, "Hey you! You deaf or something? Abandon ship."

"Yes, Sir," I say.

I take off my hat and hang it on the signal lamp, climb over the railing, cross my arms and grab the arm holes of my life jacket so I won't fall right through it when I hit the water and jump clear. I was right; it is a long way to the water. I hit feet first and go down , down, down. Then I start upwards. I'm running out of air when I pop to the surface. *Capilano* and I have drifted apart; she is hove-to a cable's length away. I start to swim. I realize just how cumbersome clothing can be. I can hardly move my arms. Around me is most of the crew, a good half of them naked. I seem to be the only one fully dressed. I look upward. Captain McCarthur and the work-ups officer appear to be the only people aboard. They are looking down and smiling.

Sonofabitch! It's a long swim to that boarding ladder. Good thing this is not the North Atlantic.

Only in the final week was there any shore leave. A few of us boarded a train and spent the day in Hamilton.

I saw my first convoy on December 6. We'd had trouble finding it. We'd been in thick fog for three days with our radar out, north of Bermuda. One of the escorts, a corvette from the group we were joining, found us and shepherded us into position.

It was a magic sight. Gray ships spread out as far as the eye could see, all low in the water, their holds bloated with the materials to wage war and maintain life on a ravaged continent. It was a fast convoy. By noon of December 11, we were 140 miles from Ireland. A Sunderland flying boat came out to meet us and stayed with us, flying unbelievably slow and at not much more than mast-head height, until daylight started to go. By the next day, we had rounded Ireland, to the south, and had swung north into the Irish Sea.

We went to action stations at 1600 hours. Asdic had picked up an echo. We ran in on it followed by HMCS *Longueuil*. We fired three patterns each, then hove-to, listening for sounds of propellers or the breaking of bulkheads. An oil slick appeared. No telling whether we had hit and disabled or sunk a U-boat or whether it had dumped oil to fool us and was readying to sink us. We stayed closed up at action stations until after dark, then left *Longueuil* to keep watch and rejoined the convoy that was starting to break up, each ship proceeding independently to its designated port.

My first leave in Londonderry has in no way made me reconsider my first assessment of it. It is cold and gray, a tired town that has been used to the hilt by the crews from the escort vessels that it has harbored since the war began. Yes, there are pubs handy to the waterfront and there are girls who frequent the streets in the same downtrodden area. We calculate that the traffic through both has been considerable. The standard greeting is Newfie slang: "Hiya gitt'n an Bye."

There are eating places, all with pretty much the same menu—sausages, eggs and potatoes, and fish and chips—an unlimited supply, even in wartime. Even so, it is a welcome change, and at first it tastes good.

We have been paid in pounds, shillings and pence, my first acquaintance with English currency. The two women in the restaurant are patient. They sort out our handfuls of coins on the counter. "These are shillings. And twenty shillings make one pound, you understand? And five shillings make crown. No I don't know why it's like that, but you'll get on to it." Their patience pays off; we leave a large tip. It's not like it's real money we are spending.

We roam from pub to pub, the last weeks at sea forgotten. We sample whatever is in bottles, of which there are many—Bushmills and Jaimisons, the smoky whiskeys of Ireland; Guiness stout and Youngers ales, nut brown or pale. "Together then, is it? Aye, Sir, with your whiskey. Oh, not in the same glass then; you'd like it separate. Is that it?"

There's no shortage whatsoever, no ration cards or wartime restrictions. We crowd together in the small, worn, dark-paneled rooms. The jokes are ribald; the stories long on rhetoric, short on truth, the bantering goes back and forth. The singing gets louder as the evening progresses, the jokes more vulgar. A few arguments break out, quickly squashed by the Publican. All this in an atmosphere of smoke so thick it can be cut in chunks. The locals, all older, sit quietly, accepting the generosity of those around them, nodding. "Yes, yes, you're absolutely right, no doubt whatever. Oh yes. I've heard Canada is a wonderful place. Oh thank you very much." Their soft brogue, agreeing with everything, scarcely heard in the din. They've seen and heard it all. And tomorrow there will be new faces, new stories and new rounds of drinks.

"Time gentlemen, if you please," eventually comes. Find the way back, sling the hammock and try to get into it, the uniform so freshly pressed a few hours ago, in a heap on a locker or on the deck.

Wakey, wakey comes early. The inevitable turning-to follows; the business of maintaining a 300-foot ship of war, provisioning and readying her for sea never ends. The tongue is thick, the reflexes slow. Never again, I think.

Christmas, 1944, was spent at sea. Twice action stations interrupted the rigmarole of the captain trading places with the youngest rating, an old tradition handed down from the Royal Navy. Christmas dinner suffered from reheating.

Three days out of St. John's, we picked up another echo and stayed with it, closed up at action stations for hours, the adrenaline slowly dissipating and being replaced by boredom. Depth charging was not conclusive.

The following day, about midmorning, the wind started picking up. By noon it was gale force and the sea had built. *Capilano* was taking green water over her decks, and the spray, torn off the wave tops, was cascading clear over the bridge. During the next twenty hours we could do little but ride it out. We hung, nosing into the mountainous swells, just maintaining steerage way. There was no sign of the convoy; it had scattered, each ship looking out for itself. In those conditions there was little danger from U-boats; they would be deep, below the turbulence. They, as we, would be waiting out the storm, waiting to continue the war.

Looking astern from the bridge, in the thin light of day break next morning, watching *Capilano*'s slim length corkscrewing, I marveled at her ability to flex. How could her stern and head continuously twist in opposite directions without breaking, snapping one way then the other hour after hour? I said a brief thanks to the Yarrows ship builders for their diligence, for the sound construction of the thin-skinned vessel under me. One bad weld and...

Below decks was a shambles; anything that could move was doing so. The off-watch hands were flaked out on top of lockers or on the deck, just trying to stay in one place. Work was impossible. Many were suffering from sea sickness. Thankfully, I was born with a stomach that didn't object to the gyrations going on around me. Hot food was out of the question. There was cold meat and sea biscuits with jam if anybody wanted them, but there were few takers.

We arrived St. John's on January 3, 1945, more or less intact. Shore leave in St. John's was a mirror image of that in Londonderry, except for the icy wind and the snow, heaped in vast drifts that inhibited wandering. Once into a tavern there was little inclination to leave its warmth unless a fight broke out. The atmosphere was more hostile than that of Derry, making shore leave much less attractive. No matter where, in the taverns or cafes or movie houses, explosive violence could occur at a moment's notice between civilians and Navy, Navy and Airforce or Army or a combination of any or all. Even in the mess decks, resentments that had smoldered while at sea could erupt into open warfare primed by a few drinks ashore. A few of us less warlike souls minded our peace. We let tumult wash around us, finding solace in writing letters, reading and doing dhobeying (washing clothes).

January 8. Waded through pack ice as far as the eye could see in all directions. The grinding as *Capilano*'s bows sliced their way through it was fearsome below decks. The thin plating, the only thing separating us from the vast white expanse frequented only by harp seals, seemed more fragile than ever.

We again deplete our supply of depth charges in the shallow waters of the Irish Sea. Whether the echoes come from U-boats lying in wait or from long-dead wrecks that litter the bottom, we have no way of knowing, but we don't take a chance. Nothing conclusive comes of the action.

The train leaves Londonderry in the evening and slides in early darkness through Coleraine and any number of small, dimly lit villages on its way down the coast to the ferry terminal at Larne. The terminal building is dark and its wooden benches uncomfortable, and always there is the damp cold. Three of us, McQuade, Curwin and I, are dressed in our number ones and carrying only attaché cases. We are off to London on four days leave.

The ferry runs between Larne and Stranraer on the Scottish coast. It runs blacked out. Like a thief in the night, it sneaks across the North Channel. Most of the passengers are service people and we all feel uncomfortably vulnerable on this small, unarmed craft. Rumor has it that one of its sister ships was shelled and sunk. The sooner this one deposits us in Stranraer, the happier we will be.

We board the train at Stranraer and find a vacant compartment. We think for a moment that it will be ours and we will be able to flake out on the seats and sleep, but then others start shouldering themselves and their baggage in with us until there are eight all told, jammed together. This is not at all bad; four are ATS girls and the other is a sailor from the British Navy.

It is cold in the coach. There seems to be no source of heat and there is snow outside that is not melting. The cold alone is sufficient reason to sit close, and we arrange it so the girls are interspaced with us—to ensure they are kept warm, of course. A blanket appears from somewhere. We spread it across the intervening space between the seats where our legs have managed to become entangled. It is big enough to cover us all and we all huddle under it. Under the blanket is a very friendly place. It does not take long for everyone to become acquainted. Later things go on there with little being said. There are movements that are better not interpreted.

The train glides stealthily, without a light from a window or even a headlight to help it find its way. Only its whistle splits the night. Its incessant cries, trouble me. They are not those of a proper train, I think. They are not the long lonely calls that I associate with real trains, like those that echo for miles across the vast open spaces of the Canadian prairies. They are the shrilling of a toy whistle that shrieks of crowded cities, of villages that follow one right after the other, of roads, bridges, canals, and of the hundreds of barriers that slam down as we approach intersecting roads. Its incessant bleating grates on me.

In darkness we slide around Solway Firth. We pause in Carlisle and Sheffield and Birmingham and other blacked-out cities that I don't identify, and hurry down through the English countryside in the early morning light. It is not a long way by Canadian standards, but it seems so. We arrive in London, at Paddington Station, stiff with cold, hungry, lightheaded from lack of sleep and hoarse from having sung every off-color ballad that was ever composed. The British sailor knows them all. We say goodbye to the ATS girls and the British sailor. They know where they are going. We don't.

There is an information place in the station. We ask their advice on places to stay. They suggest the Canadian Legion in Bayswater. Outside the station, we ask a pinch-faced man with a drippy nose, in a uniform that is not one of any service we recognize, where we can find a taxi. It turns out he is a dispatcher of some kind. He pulls a whistle from his pocket, gives it a blast and waves at a line of taxis half way up the block. He holds out his hand for a tip. We pile into the taxi that to us looks antiquated but, we find out, is the typical London cab. It skirts around collapsed buildings, blocked off streets and water-filled craters. It doesn't take much brainpower to figure bombs created these obstacles.

The room at the Canadian Legion is huge. It is heated by a gas fireplace with a slot on the side that eats shillings by the handful.

One shilling supposedly provides an hour's heat, but it varies markedly and the heat provided is only felt directly in front of the grate. The window looks out on piles of rubble and the skeleton of what once was a brick building. The room has three beds.

Our leave goes quickly. Even though we go to bed late, we also sleep late. The eating places and pubs we wander into are usually crowded, mostly, with service men and women from all the Allied forces.

We board the underground railway, the stations of which are host to many whose homes are no more. They lie along the walls, wrapped in blankets, quilts, greatcoats and whatever will cheat the cold and soften the concrete under them. With the guidance of any number of helpful souls, we find our way to the landmarks: Buckingham Palace, St. Paul's Cathedral, The Tower of London, all sandbagged and can only be looked at from the outside. And we walk miles, not knowing where we are and not caring. When we run out of the will to continue there is always a taxi or someone to direct us to the correct underground train to get us home through the smoke, fog and blackout.

There is a thread that ties me to London, a thread that goes a long way back, to a time before I was born. This city is one that my parents knew, where they were married, in the dying days of the first war. It is a tenuous attachment, I know, but an attachment nonetheless. In just being here, I know something more of their early life. Now when we speak of London, Father and I will, at least in this respect, be on common ground.

Phyllis Dixie is playing the Windmill Theater in Piccadilly Circus. The whispered word has it that she capers around the stage stark naked. The female figure revealed in its entirety, attracts us.

We locate the Windmill. It has a plushy, bordellolike naughtiness about it that whets the anticipation. Only later, do we learn that there is nothing illicit here.

In England, persons can and do appear completely naked on stage, provided they remain stationary while disrobed. Phyllis gets around this legal roadblock to free expression by skillfully draping herself with two white doves, a fan and a flimsy veil whenever she moves, which she avoids as much as possible. Caper, she doesn't. Most of her time on stage is spent standing buff-naked, singing or just talking, which is pleasant, but not particularly entertaining. The people around us obviously find her English music-hall style of humor hilarious, but it is largely lost on us. We think her act doesn't exactly live up to its advance billing. Nevertheless we feel our money is well spent, since the others in her troupe, although partially clothed, are accomplished singers and dancers and put on a good show. Nudity, we decide is not everything.

We arrange to be back to a pub that is within a stone's throw of our lodgings, well before closing time. We go upstairs, load the gas grate with shillings then sit in the pub until the temperature is livable, and the beds have lost some of their damp chill. By bedtime we don't feel the cold as much anyway.

It doesn't worry us, but it does cross our minds that London has been the target of the *Luftwaffe* on numerous occasions over the previous three years. Indeed, evidence of the bombings and the historic battles for the skies overhead, is there in the shattered buildings, piles of rubble and cratered roadways. However, we have been assured that the RAF has things pretty well under control and that we need not overly concern ourselves. Be that is it may, we know from the newscasts that the second wave, the V1 and V2 bombs are still a menace. Occasionally the air-raid sirens go and twice there are shattering blasts that jar the vicinity we are in. Once while we are eating in a restaurant.

"Its just one of those 'doodle bugs' you know." Perhaps the waitress feels compelled to explain to reassure herself. "It's not like the bombers you know. Oh, my, they were bad. Were you here then? At least these come only one at a time, and if they don't hit you with that one, there isn't another one right behind it...not like the sticks from the bombers, you know." No one in the restaurant pays much attention; after a momentary lull in conversation in which they looked at each other, they resume eating and talking.

The second one wakes us. It has landed somewhere close, in Bayswater we judge, and is rather a blessing in disguise.

We have loaded the grate with shillings before going to bed. Sometime in the night, the gas must have been interrupted and the flame extinguished. Later, the gas has come back and it fills the room. I can hardly breathe. I holler and stagger to the door, barely able to get there. It takes a while to get Curwin awake; his bed is closest to the source.

We arrive back in Londonderry broke, slightly hungover and tired, just in time to prepare for sea.

There is a sameness about the ocean, but there is also a constant changing. There is the play of light on the hills and valleys as the great swells bear down on us. There are cloud shadows that change the color of the water from aquamarine to leaden gray, minute by minute. The very pattern of the convoy alters in the time I swing my binoculars slowly from dead ahead to dead astern and back. The gray hulls rise and fall. They disappear in the swells and reappear, their relationship to one another having changed, the angles having shifted. The total motion is hypnotic. The only thing stationary is my relationship with *Capilano*. Every few minutes I have to swing my eyes inboard, to look at some solid fixture—the stack, the *Oerlikon* anti-aircraft gun hooded in gray-painted canvas or the rectangular shapes of the bridge fixtures. At night, under cloud cover, there is nothing but blackness and the faint luminescence of the water. When there is a moon and the seas are flat, the scene is pure magic. But then is when vigilance might mean living or dying.

From the wheel, the panorama is narrowed to a few degrees either side of dead ahead. The only view is through the square window of the periscope, sufficiently wide to watch the swells and ease Caplilano through them. The gyro compass-repeater, slightly to the right, indicates the last course sent down the voice-pipe from the bridge. The course changes in a designated pattern hour by hour as the convoy plods across the thousands of sea miles.

"Port ten."

"Ten aport on, Sir."

"Midships."

"Midships, Sir.

"Steer one four oh."

"One four oh it is, Sir."

And so it goes. Steering is something of an art, and those who steer pride themselves on being able to do so without having to make major corrections, no matter what kind of a sea is running. The yawing of a ship is felt below deck, and invariably someone asks, "Who the hell is on the wheel?"

We lost two ships the next time we entered the Irish Sea. Both were big freighters. The huge explosions vibrating drumlike through *Capilano*'s hull came during the morning watch, one right after the other. I was working on the quarterdeck and happened to glance in the right direction at the right moment. Plumes of spray were still towering above the gray hulls, white against the green-patchwork backdrop of Irish fields. Seconds later the action stations bell began its insistent clamoring.

We close up to actions stations bracing ourselves against the cant of *Capilano's* decks as she heels over in a tight turn to starboard; the beat of her engines has picked up and her speed is building. "Prepare for depth charging," comes down from the bridge.

We run in on the echo and let the charges go, followed by *Longueuil* and *Sudbury*.

The Irish Sea is a relatively shallow body of water. The charges, set accordingly, throw up vast columns of water. We slow then, wait for some sign. Nothing—no oil or debris. We stop engines and lie drifting, rocking gently on the flat sea. Nobody says anything or makes any loud noises. The asdic operator is listening.

By now both freighters are listing badly. One is also down at the stern. We watch. They are lowering boats.

"Prepare to pick up survivors."

Our scramble nets and ladders unfurl along the port side. We stand by to grab lines tossed from lifeboats and to help the merchant sailors to come aboard.

Sudbury and *Longueuil* must have again picked up a moving echo; the force of their charges booms through our hull.

Some of the freighters' crew are badly hurt, they can't scramble aboard. We go down into the boats and help hoist them inboard onto *Capilano's* decks. Most are in shock, even if not physically hurt. A few are fished from the water, having jumped overboard; they are suffering from hypothermia. We help them below decks where it is warm.

The captain of the one freighter thinks perhaps his ship is not in immediate danger of sinking and he wants to go back. He says that three of his crew are trapped in a stern compartment. He takes one of his officers and a couple of men and they row back, but before he gets there the ship slides stern first under water. She hangs there with just her bow sticking up, then the next time I look she is gone. The three men have gone with her.

We are ordered to deliver the survivors to Milford Haven, a

town on the Welsh coast. The convoy is pretty well scattered, proceeding independently to their various ports. *Longueuil* and *Sudbury* stay behind. They are sitting on the target, waiting it out. They have plastered the area with depth charges and hedgehogs. All they can do is wait and see if anything moves.

We are crowded below decks. I don't know how many survivors there are, but there must be thirty or more. Those with minor wounds are sitting or lying in the mess decks. They are quiet, just staring ahead saying little. Those more seriously wounded are in sick bay on stretchers. I glance in the galley in passing. I see a smiling black face that doesn't belong there. It belongs to a cook from one of the freighters. He is chatting animatedly as he peels potatoes. Turns out this is the third ship he's had blown out from under him. He says he's beyond worry; he has a charmed life.

A big towboat has put out from the Irish coast. It is approaching the disabled freighter that is now listing far over and is low in the water.

Milford Haven is a pretty town, or it would be but for the ragged forest of masts that have turned the harbor into an obstacle course. These are ships that were caught by the *Luftwaffe* sometime past. Unable to escape the tight confines of the harbor they were sunk, turning it into a graveyard. We thread our way among them.

We offload the survivors. The black cook scampers down the gangway. He is smiling, and well he might—he has again cheated King Neptune.

We set a course for Londonderry. There is only a slight glow left in the sky.

CHAPTER 14

The Vanquished

I needed to go home, at least my mind told me that was where I wanted to go. I still had an outdated picture of home as being my family all together under one roof, even though I knew full well that was no longer the case. Home now meant the remnants of a family in Vancouver and my newfound family, the people I had grown close to in Ocean Falls. I wanted to see them, all of them. I wanted to tell them where I had been and what I had done. And, too, I needed the reassurance that somebody cared, that I was not forgotten.

Since Mother died, letters out of Vancouver had been few. Father wrote now and then, duty letters that said little. Olwyn wrote occasionally and Owen, still in Ocean Falls, not at all.

The one person who wrote regularly was Arline Lee from Ocean Falls. Her letters came frequently and were full of news. I came to depend on them, and I guess I read more into them than what was really there. Anyhow, going home meant seeing her. Little else really mattered.

I had leave coming, so I applied, as soon as we arrived in St. John's. Lieutenant Best, the "jimmy" approved it without my having to stand at attention in front of him.

"Where do you want to go?" asked the uniformed clerk in the regulating office at HMCS *Avalon*, the shore establishment.

"I want to go home," I said, flirting with getting shouted at.

"Where's that?"

"Ocean Falls, British Columbia,"

"Ocean Falls? Never heard of it. Show me on a map."

I did.

"Holy Jesus! Why away up there?"

"That's where I live, my home, so, that's where I want to go."

"Your traveling time will be more than your leave."

"Yeah. I guess so." I couldn't help the smile.

Ocean Falls is about as far away from St. John's as you can get and still be in Canada. (In fact, the joke was that it was farther. At that time Newfoundland was not yet part of Canada.) The regulating petty officer was not at all amused. Quite the opposite, he was a little short, as these officers were known to be. He nevertheless saw to the sheaf of travel vouchers I would need for the many and varied carriers that would get me there and back. I would travel by RCAF plane from St. John's to Moncton, New Brunswick, and thence by train to Vancouver, then by coastal steamship to Ocean Falls. I would spend time, both coming and going, in Vancouver.

When a naval rating goes anywhere, his sea bag and hammock go with him; naval regulations are quite specific on that score. But the thought of humping a brown canvas bag full of gear and an outsized, banana-shaped, marline-hitched hammock containing a mattress and two wool blankets across Canada and back was daunting. God knows how many times I would have to reclaim it and transfer to some other means of transport. Nobody had said anything about me leaving *Capilano* permanently; so, regulations be damned, why take it? I stuffed my attaché case with everything it would hold, asked McQuade to keep an eye on the rest and walked down the gangplank. If I did receive notice somewhere along my route that I was not to return to *Capilano* or if *Capilano* came to grief in its next crossing of the Atlantic and took my gear down with it, I would be in the glue. But I put that thought out of my mind.

The RCAF plane turned out to be a wheezy old DC-3. It struggled free of the snow-encrusted tarmac of the St. John's airport and set, what I hoped, was a course for Moncton. The seating, dished indents in cold hard steel polished by hundreds of rear ends and without even a suggestion of padding or insulation, was fastened solidly, lengthwise, one row down each side. The backrest was the curving inner side of the fuselage. From my seat on the port side, I could see into the cockpit where two pilots were drinking coffee and joking, only occasionally glancing out the window. I had never flown before, and this lack of attention to business was in direct contradiction to what I understood about flying. It didn't seem to bother anyone else of the half dozen mix of servicemen who were hitching a ride the same as me, so I pretended indifference while white-knuckling it all the way.

The train left Moncton at nightfall. The layover next morning in Montreal was not long enough to leave the station and explore, although it would have been nice to see something of the city. There was just time to find a barber, a place to bathe and shave and then, refreshed, have a hearty breakfast prior to boarding the Canadian Pacific *Continental*.

I've always thought of a train as a place to relax. I had nothing to do but read and look out the window. The coaches were full, but I was content to remain aloof and think my own thoughts while letting the tension of the last few months drain away. Much of the time I just sat watching the country slide by through miles of evergreens and the gray rock of the Canadian Shield. Somewhere, I had picked up the knowledge that these were oldest rocks on earth. I could believe it; they were rounded and polished as though having been scoured by any number of ice ages.

My berth with crisp white sheets and a pillow was sheer luxury. Apart from a few nights in London, I had slept in nothing but a hammock since leaving Esquimalt. I slept solidly, the long drawn-out organ chord of the steam whistle only half waking me.

At last, the prairie, that I'd heard so much of, but had never seen, stretched for miles on all sides. It was snow covered, but even so, I found beauty in its very bleakness. I couldn't help the twinge of pride I felt in this huge country of mine. And oddly enough, I, who was born and raised in the west, was seeing it for the first time from the east.

Father was still living across the street from the small cottage he and mother had bought and lived in until she died. His landlady, Muriel Mellors, was a pretty woman in her thirties with one small child and a husband in the service somewhere. Father's room was in the level-entry basement, but because the bathroom was upstairs, and he took his meals in the kitchen, and he baby-sat occasionally, he more or less had the run of the house. Muriel also washed his clothes. It was a comfortable arrangement and well within his means. I had a choice: either share his double bed or find a hotel downtown. I opted for the latter. Olwyn's tiny house, only two houses away, had no space for an extra person, although she did offer to make me a bed on the floor. It was an offer I declined with thanks.

Father was much tidier. He looked better cared for. His clothes were pressed and he was shaved and his hair had been recently cut. Perhaps I just hadn't realized how much the years of caring for Mother had been dragging at him. Or maybe I hadn't wanted to see it. And her sudden death had probably been more difficult for him than I imagined. Maybe I hadn't given him credit for handling it as well as he did. I think I now had a better appreciation for what he must have gone through. Now, without that sapping his resources, he seemed to have found the will to carry on. Olwyn was close by and having her there helped, even though he didn't get along with Ralph, her husband. But he did see his granddaughter, Lynda, every day. This, and having a close association with Muriel and her son, was helping to take the edge off his loneliness. I looked at him in a new light. For years I had thought of him as an old man, but he wasn't. He was only fifty-nine, an age when a great many men are in their most productive years. That he would be more than he was, however, I doubted. He was off the main line, shunted onto a siding, content to remain uninvolved, to just live. One thing though, he wasn't as irascible, which made for easier relationship. He smiled more and he even told the odd joke.

Friendlier though we were to each other, it didn't take us long to run out of things to say. He was moderately interested in where I had been and seemed to take a certain pride in having me accompany him to the Legion at Forty-Ninth Street and Fraser where he could show me off to his cronies—his son in uniform. A congenial bunch, they included me in their billiard games and their conversation to a point. But it was obvious that Father and they still considered their war the premier event and that was the war they talked about. They were polite to me, but it was evident they don't consider mine a real war.

In addition to the Legion, two beer parlors, the Strand and the Metropole, had become his watering holes. Therefore, because I was staying downtown, he'd suggest we meet at one of them. And although I was not above having a beer or two, sitting for hours in the yeasty, smoke-filled atmosphere soon began to pall. Much of the time, we merely sat, saying little. He seemed content. There was nowhere else he wanted to go and there was nothing he wanted to do. Sometimes we were joined by Olwyn and Muriel Mellors, which made for livelier conversation for a few hours. But those occasions were few. Olwyn was working in Spencer's department store and Muriel was daycaring Olwyn's daughter and her own son, so their opportunities for pub-crawling were limited.

After a few days, it grew on me that this was a pretty sedentary way to use up a leave. I was growing restive; I wanted to go North where I'd wanted to go all along. Father couldn't understand my desire to leave. "You've just got here," was his plaintive comment. Why I would want to trade Vancouver and his brand of conviviality for an up-coast village, he couldn't fathom. I was reluctant to admit that the desire for a special girl had really been the impetus for this entire cross-Canada junket. Assuring him I would be back in a week, I caught a night boat for Ocean Falls.

In my last letter to Arline, I had told her I was coming. I hadn't said exactly when, because I didn't know. Nevertheless, she was there to meet me as I disembarked. My spirits soared. Here was this girl I had dreamed of on long nightwatches half a world away. She was there to meet *me*, no one else. Not only that, but she announced, "You're coming to stay with us."

For almost a week, I basked in the warmth of the Lee family home. George was away in the RCAF, so I had the full attention of the rest of the family. They pampered me.

During the day I wandered the town, seeking friends to visit with. But things had changed. The male workforce, at least the younger segment, had been decimated by the call of the Canadian Forces. There was no one left of my crowd. They had been replaced by men who had come out of retirement and young women—all imported from elsewhere. What had heretofore been strictly the province of men had lately become the territory of women, and much to the dismay of some of the old hands, they were carrying the load more than adequately. Owen, of course was still there, one of only a handful of lusty young men left. He was making money hand over fist and spending it as fast as he made it. He was having a ball. His eyesight was his only real impediment. It was keeping him out of the forces, but not out of much else. I saw little of him and, then, only in the company of others.

It was an idyllic week, but as the day of my departure drew near, I had to face the inescapable truth that what I felt for Arline was not mirrored in her feelings for me. She was not ready to make any kind of a commitment and her sights were set on something other than what Ocean Falls had to offer. In fact she was planning to leave. It was a blow, and despite initial denial I soon realized I would have to accept reality and cast out any thought of a permanent relationship. I also knew full well that purging myself of her would be no easy matter. It was not something I wanted to think about, not right then anyway. Things might change. Perhaps after the war, when I returned...

I left, thankful for that week, but hurting a bit. Father and Olwyn saw me off on the train that would take me back to St. John's. I had spent the remainder of my leave in Vancouver partying. There were a lot of servicemen loose in Vancouver and ready to party, some I had met along the way in Esquimalt, Prince Rupert and wherever. I found solace in their company. Father, of course, was miffed that I chose them over him, but I had the feeling he would have thought poorly of me had I not caroused a bit. He must have remembered what it was like to be young and in the forces.

The distance from Vancouver to St. John's seemed at least twice as long as the reverse direction. The prairies, although beginning to green up, had lost something of their charm. Gazing again at the dense evergreens and rock of the Canadian Shield was merely tedious. I needed to busy myself. Sitting was getting to me. I had too much time to think.

There would be no plane to take me across the Gulf of St. Lawrence. Instead, I would take the ferry that plied the Cabot Strait from North Sydney, Nova Scotia, to Port aux Basques, Newfoundland. I had again to change trains in Montreal to one that wound through the Maritimes. It eventually deposited me and a number of others in North Sydney.

The weather was dreadful. A series of late-winter storms had come marching out of Labrador. The rain, chased by storm-force winds, was gusting in sideways and the cold was enough to congeal the blood. The ferry wasn't running and wouldn't until the storms subsided.

I was without money; not a *sou* did I have. That last freewheeling week in Vancouver had roundly depleted my resources. I was in a quandary. I couldn't just sit in the waiting room on the dock. Who knew how long this gaggle of storms might last.

"There's a Salvation Army place up the way, there," said a taxi driver with a broad down-east accent. "You could maybe find a place to keep warm until the storm blows itself out."

"How far?" I asked. "I don't have any money."

"Ah, what the hell, Bye. It's a miserable night. I'll run you over there. It's not far."

The man in the Sally-Ann, hearing of my impecunious state, shook his head resignedly. He couldn't turn me away.

"I suppose we could give you a bed for the night. You don't have any money at all, 'eh?"

"Not a cent."

"Okay. They say things should improve tomorrow. The ferry will probably run."

In a draughty barn of a room, I was assigned the lower half of one of a row of double-decker cots arrayed down one wall. I was also given supper. I was their only customer.

I was there for four days, living on the good graces of the Salvation Army. I listened to the radio and read dog-eared magazines. I did not venture forth. Seemed only out of necessity did anyone do so.

Seldom, if ever have my spirits sagged as low. I was alone, broke and my self-esteem had taken a pummeling. Not only that, nagging in the back of my mind was the thought that *Capilano* might not be there to welcome me. Any number of things, the more I thought about it the worse they got, could have happened to her. I now regretted my devil-may-care departure. I was going to be overdue. This storm-enforced layover had not been calculated into my leave schedule. I could be keel hauled, at least.

The storm eventually abated, at least sufficiently for the ferry to venture a crossing. I thanked my Sally-Ann hosts, glad to be on the move again. There was still considerable sea running and the big-bellied craft made heavy weather of it.

Travel on the Caribou Express—affectionately known as the Newfie Bullet—bore little resemblance to that on the CPR *Continental*. I did not have a berth for one thing, and my day-coach seat defied any attempt to get comfortable. The seats, covered in a woven cane-type fabric, the same as had disappeared from all but the oldest Vancouver streetcars, had little padding; the backs went straight up at right angles, similar to a church pew. Thankfully the coach was sparsely populated making it possible to sprawl with feet on the opposite seat.

For some twenty-four hours the steam locomotive labored, winding through swamp and forest, stopping frequently for no apparent reason. At one stage there was a jarring crash that brought us to a halt. After half an hour or so, word was passed along that the locomotive had tangled with a moose, which was now being chopped apart by the engineer and fireman. We would progress when this task was complete.

Capilano and I arrived back in St. John's on the same day—me, I'm sure, more travel worn than she. I was not the only one delayed by the storm, and there being others of higher rank caught in the same situation, the leave overdraft was brushed under the carpet. I was happy to see that gray hull with the salt-encrusted bows.

"So how was the leave?" asked McQuade.

"Fine," I said, "had a ball."

Four days later, reprovisioned and re-armed, *Capilano* was again at sea. We picked up a slow convoy and slogged eastward, zigzagging in a great bight northward.

The day after our return to St. John's, VE Day was announced. All the details of the armistice came blaring over the radio. Every foghorn, every church bell and anything that would make a noise sounded throughout the harbor and the city. Bunting flew from every masthead and halyard. The war in Europe was over!

That evening the rioting started. All of the pent-up frustrations and resentments between the civilians and the forces were suddenly unleashed. McQuade and I had gone uptown, but what was happening—the window smashing and mob violence—we wanted no part of. We returned aboard. "Jeez, a guy could get killed up there." McQuade voiced my sentiments exactly.

So the war was over. What now? Let's go home. This was what was running through everyone's minds. Things weren't quite that simple, though. There were a number of U-boats unaccounted for. Where were they? Had they been sunk? Were they heading for South American ports, as rumor had it? Or were they out there refusing to concede defeat and lying in wait for those who had dropped their guard?

The war machine, although losing some of its momentum, was not ready to quit entirely. We would go one more time. There was grumbling, but deeply imbedded habit and discipline governed. *Capilano* bestirred herself. There was a trip to the ammunition dock, to the fueling dock and the loading of provisions, and then, the usual, "Hands to stations for leaving harbor," was being piped throughout.

The winds of change were blowing, however. Subtle undercurrents were washing through the mess decks and through the whole ship for that matter. The fabric of command was becoming threadbare. The natural individualism of Canadians that had been buried so long in the pool of common purpose, was asserting itself. The time of acute danger was past. There was an urge to throw off the yoke, open the ports and let the light shine out. There was no out and out rebellion, but the "Aye, aye, Sir," might carry a hint of flippancy that would not have been tolerated a few short months back. Tasks were performed, but without the alacrity that had been the norm. Thoughts were elsewhere—back to the farms, villages and logging camps. And yes, they were back to the breadlines of the cities and riding the tops of boxcars. What were we going back to? To the depression years? That was on everyone's minds. Some were already seeing themselves picking up the threads of the jobs they had vacated, and others who had never held a job didn't know what faced them. To some, being lost at sea was better than being let go by the Navy.

Londonderry has not changed. It merely looks a little more worn and tired. There are fewer ships at the wharves and fewer servicemen roaming the waterfront streets. The women of easy virtue are more blatant in their approach. They walk in twos and threes, chorusing, "Hiya gitt'n an, Bye?" They are frantically trying to hang on. Their livelihood is threatened. The escort ships from the convoys will no longer come. The pubs are not as well patronized—more locals, fewer servicemen. And the servicemen are not as free and easy. They are introspective; this will be the last that many, nay, the majority, will ever see of Londonderry.

Capilano lies quietly at the wharf. In a day or two she will follow the path of the discoverers, westward. This too will be the last time she will enter this port. The evening meal is over, but the normal boisterous chatter and horseplay as the off-duty men prepare to go ashore is missing. Nobody is in a hurry to get to the pubs.

As is usual though, we are invaded by the waterfront urchins. In the past, they have come in ones and twos, perhaps a big brother hauling a smaller one with him. Six to twelve-years old, it's hard to tell, they have the faces of old men. Tonight they come in flocks. They too will feel the pinch. They come to sing for their suppers and steal anything that is loose. They are gaunt and hungry; they dive into the leftovers and gobble it down like seagulls. They can sing, though, all of the Irish songs; their voices like those of angels coming from the mouths of young devils. Getting them ashore empty-handed and seeing they don't come back is the next chore.

We walk along the Foyle. Moored there are U-boats tied four and five deep along the docks. They have been directed there to await whatever is decreed by the terms of the armistice. So *this* is the enemy. The same thought runs through all our minds: *these* then are the people and *these* are the ships we have been intent on blasting into oblivion with our depth charges. We will never know, of course, how successful we were. And now it doesn't matter. The German sailors are moving around on the humped-back decks and in the conning towers. Strangely, they don't look evil. They look a lot like us. They lean on railings, basking in the sun, smoking and talking. Their future has not been decided. We, the victors, know that the cities and towns we are returning to are intact; they don't know what condition theirs are in. We don't speak to them. What do you say to the vanquished?

Capilano slips down the Foyle into the Irish Sea. The fields

Londonderry, Ireland. German submariners waiting to go home.

crosshatching the Irish landscape are emerald green. We are carrying a few deck passengers. They are hitching a ride home. A ragtag convoy accompanies us, more because we all happen to be going in the same direction than any need for our guns and depth charges.

We won't be going St. John's. Instead it will be Shelburne, Nova Scotia, where rumor has it *Capilano* will be refitted for the tropics. "Aye. We're all going to the Pacific, give the Yanks a hand, you know."

German submarines moored in the Foyle River, North Ireland.

"I'm not going to no bloody Pacific. My old lady's been by herself long enough. I'm going home."

"Oh, we're going to the Pacific all right, but just back to Esquimalt. We only borrowed this packet—supposed to return her when we're finished." And on and on.

Disarming looms as a substantial task. One last practice will ease things. We do a few depth-charge runs. We fire every gun we own. Hedgehog, those bomb-like depth charges that are fired from a stationary ship and fly like a flock of sparrows to land in a fan dead ahead, arc from the foredeck. One is defective and flies end over end. It comes down, narrowly missing the forepeak. We all let go pent-up breath. Even star shells, snowflakes and all the small-caliber tracers, the whole lot, go in a fireworks display. We are considerably lighter when we enter the harbor at Shelburne.

Almost immediately discharge notices come aboard. Half the crew is gone inside of a week, drafted back from whence they came, their divisional headquarters, where they will be given $100 clothing allowance and a slip of paper. Nobody says goodbye. From then on they go in ones and twos until the mess decks ring with emptiness. There is finally one officer left, a leading hand or two and a half dozen able seamen, me among them, and that's all. There is no real work, just tending lines and keeping things tidy. We take the whaleboat, twenty-seven feet long, with a gaff-rigged, loose-footed mainsail, a jib and a mizzen. We raid the galley for leftover canned goods and sea biscuits and spend the days sailing. The weather is fine.

My sea bag has been ready for days and each morning as I lash my hammock I wonder if I've spent my last night in it. As regulations dictate, I will have to take my gear with me. What I will do with threadbare uniforms and what's left of my issue kit, I haven't thought about. I doubt I will have any use for a hammock.

My turn comes. I load my stuff on the truck that will take me to the station, take one last look at *Capilano* and start the long trip home. When my grandchildren ask me what I did in the war I can tell them I sailed with the great North Atlantic convoys.

Esquimalt. HMCS *Capilano*.

HMCS *Capilano*: River class frigate. Built in Yarrows Shipyard, Esquimalt, B.C.

Launched April 8, 1944.

Commissioned August 25, 1944.

Paid off November 24, 1945.

Displacement: 1445 tons.

Length: 301 ft. 6 in.

Breadth: 36 ft. 7 in.

Depth: 9 ft.

Speed: 19 knots. Twin reciprocating steam engines.

Armament: Two 4-in. guns for'rd.; one 12-pdr. aft.; four 20-mm cannon, hedgehog and depth charges.

Crew: 8 officers, 133 enlisted men.

She now lies on the bottom, off the Cuban coast, having foundered in 1953 after having been converted to civilian use.

Reference: *The Ships of Canada's Naval Forces 1910–1993*.
Ken Macpherson, John Burgess. ISBN 0-20277-91-8

CHAPTER 15

The Sand Runs Out

*Piloting requires the greatest
experience and the nicest judgement
of any form of navigation.*
— DUTTON, CAPTAIN USN

Ocean Falls, May, 1949. Footsteps thumping hollowly on the decking of the float, the squeak of rubber fenders rubbing against hull planking and a swaying as someone came aboard pried painfully into my consciousness. I opened one eye, cautiously. Sunlight peeking into the cabin through gaps in the curtains stabbed at it. Morning already? Seemed I'd just gone to bed. Actually, I hadn't been in it that long. The sky had begun to brighten when I had staggered aboard and fallen into the bunk. I let my eye flop closed, better to concentrate on all the unpleasant things going on in my head, such as little men picking away at the insides of my skull. My mouth tasted foul. My tongue felt thick and gooey, like a piece of soiled carpet.

Fragments of last night began to shuffle together, like a scattered deck of cards or a jigsaw puzzle, one piece at a time. But the picture that evolved was distorted, some of the pieces had to be missing. I remembered finding my way aboard. Yeah, I remembered that. No small accomplishment, a measure of lucidity must have taken hold and coerced some semblance of coordination into my weaving body, enough at least to pilot it through the sleeping town to the wharf, but I had only a dim recollection of the passage.

The tide had been out and the companionway leading down to the float had been almost straight up and down. I remembered talking to myself. "Now, take it easy. Don't want to fall in, do we? Water's gonna be cold." My finger marks were probably still etched into the handrails where I had frantically clutched them while lowering myself down the cleated walkway to the float. Obviously I'd made it all in one piece, but I had no idea of time.

There was more bumping in the rear cockpit and low voices. It sounded like Olwyn and Pete. I pried my eye open again.

"I wonder if he's in there," I heard Olwyn say.

"Dunno. Better look." Pete's mumbling monotone.

The door slid open. Olwyn stuck her head in.

"Yeah. He's in here. Whew! Smells awful...booze." Then, louder and cheerful, "Hey Paul. Come on lazybones. Get up. It's a beautiful day."

"Oh yeah," was all I had the will to say.

"Yeah. Not a cloud anywhere. The weather report is good. It's going to be great. A little fog further south, but that's all."

I pulled the blanket over my head. "Come back in a couple of hours and tell me again," I said.

"Why? What's the matter? What were you up to last night?"

"Not much. Visiting. That's all."

"Some visit. You smell like you fell into something...maybe like a vat of scotch."

"Could be. Not a vat, not quite, but some..."

"Who were you with?"

"George. Just George. We were saying goodbye."

"Well. I hope you got it said. It's almost time to go. Do you feel alright? You don't sound so good."

"I probably don't. And no, I don't feel so good. I'll be okay, though... maybe." I pushed the blanket back and sat up. The little men with the jackhammers picked up the tempo. "Yeah. At least I think so. Uh...Pete's about ready to go, 'eh?"

"Yes. I guess so. He's got everything on board, anyway. Can I get you anything? I brought a thermos of coffee. I'll get it. Maybe it'll give you a kick start." She backed out.

I looked out the cabin window. Olwyn was right; it had the makings of a lovely day. If it lasted, it might turn out to be one of those glorious up-coast days of which there were all too few. I had, however, little faith in its lasting power. Right now though, the water alongside the float was a black mirror, not a breath of wind ruffling it. Sunlight was winking on the glass and metal of the boats moored next to us. Seagulls lined the wharf and the garbage scow on the other side, standing and preening in the sunlight.

I watched Olwyn pour coffee into the cup from the top of the thermos. Even at this time of the morning and with a day off, she had herself properly put together. Her makeup was in place and impeccable as usual. She had on dark jeans—a little tight around the rear, testimony to advancing maturity and having born a child—a flowered jacket and a bright scarf over her hair from which a few strands escaped in front. Why, at this moment, I would notice that there were a few gray ones mixed with the dark auburn I had always known, I don't know.

"Here," she handed me the cup, "take a slug of this. I made it pretty strong. Might blow some of the soot out of your chimney."

A tremor went down my arm and my hand wandered as I reached hungrily for it.

"I'll get out of here and let you get some clothes on. Don't go back to sleep, now." She patted my hand comfortingly and smiled. A small gesture but one I could rely on, had relied on, ever since I was old enough to toddle around after her and needed reassurance and understanding. She slid the door closed.

I took a slug of the coffee, decided I could keep it down, eased off the bunk and located my pants in the heap of clothing on the floor. I pulled them on.

Outside it was cool, but the air was like silk. The sun was warm on my naked upper half. Pete had the engine compartment hatch-covers open and was down inside tinkering. I climbed over the side and bare-footed across the rough planking to the freshwater hose hanging down from the wharf. I let it run over my head and neck. I gasped as its icy needles pierced my skin. As I straightened, shuddering and shaking water from my hair, a towel hit me in the face. "Here," Olwyn said, "you look like a water spaniel. Feel better?"

Pete rose up out of the engine compartment, like a gopher out of its hole. "You ready to go?" he asked. His horse face was solemn, the expression of a man being led to the gallows or worse.

He'd got his mind worked around until he thoroughly believed that nothing good could come of going to sea on this sunny May morning, even though it was his idea. I'm sure he was convinced that all the perils that had beset the North Atlantic convoys a few short years ago were still out there lying in wait for him or anyone foolhardy enough to leave the safety of the wharf.

"Sure, I'm ready. Any time," I said. "Just tell me when and I'll fire her up."

"Yeah, okay." He ducked back down and grabbed the handle of the bilge pump. Whenever he couldn't think of anything else to do, he pumped. He could pump for hours, a task that needed little thought. Right now he was just putting off the inevitable.

"Much water?" I asked.

"Naw, maybe about the same."

I climbed back aboard and into the rest of my clothes, had another slug of coffee and went forward to the wheel. "Okay to start up? You in the clear?" I hollered. He left off pumping and nodded. I punched the starter button. The four-cylinder Kermath caught and settled down to a steady rhythm, the exhaust burbling at the waterline astern.

I let it idle and went back onto the wharf. I boosted my old dingy into the water and tied its towrope to the stern cleat. It wasn't much of a boat, but it was better than nothing. Of unknown ancestry and heavy as lead, it wasn't the best choice of rowboat, but it was the only thing I could find in a hurry. I had bought it for $5 from a fisherman when I found out Pete didn't have one. I wasn't about to go to sea without some kind of lifeboat. I figured once we got going, I would pull it up on the stern deck.

Olwyn handed me a picnic basket with a blue and white checkered tea towel tucked under the handles. "Here," she said, "I made a bunch of sandwiches. You won't have to cook until suppertime. Eat the egg ones first; they have mayonnaise in them. They won't keep." She looked closely at me. "And Paul, you're all right are you? Feel okay?"

"Yeah. I'll live." I didn't feel particularly robust, but I knew the malady I was suffering would eventually dissipate—it always had, anyway.

She put her arms around me and gave me a hug. "I feel a lot

better with you going with him," meaning Pete. "Look after him, won't you? He's not very good in boats." I hugged her back. She smelled fresh and clean. I had never been closer to anyone than I was to Olwyn. She had always been more than just a sister; she had mothered me as well.

"I thought Owen would show up to see you off," she said. "He's probably still in bed...somebody's bed anyway." She made a wry face. "He could have at least roused himself long enough to say goodbye."

"He had to go to work," I said. "I saw him last night. He's okay."

I gave her an extra hug and went aboard.

"You can let her go," I hollered at Pete. "If you're all set...."

Through the cabin window, I could see him on the wharf. Olwyn had her arms around him and was looking up into his face. I felt a twinge, not of jealousy more of annoyance or almost disgust. How could she, with a cold, sour-dispositioned guy like that? How could a warm lively person like Olwyn... I just couldn't figure. He said something and then disengaged himself. He went to the stern cleat, undid the line and threw it inboard. He slouched forward, cast off our last tie to the float and clambered awkwardly into the cockpit. I'd never seen anyone as awkward around boats as he was. I engaged the clutch and with a swirl at the stern *Monad* moved away from the float. I eased the throttle open a notch.

I pointed her head at the gap where the mountains on the right slid in behind those on the left leaving a dogleg entrance to the harbor and effectively screening the town from the outside world. The sun was slicing through the gap and painting a big patch of gold on the water. I headed for it. I glanced back at the wharf. Olwyn was making her way slowly up the companionway. Her head was turned, watching us. I stuck my arm out and waved. She waved back.

The Kermath responded, picking up the beat as I cracked the throttle a little more. I scanned the water ahead. Trapped in this circular bowl of the harbor where the tides couldn't get at them to flush them out, were dead-heads, lots of them, basking on the surface—great chunks of logs, byproducts of the booming grounds, lying awash, some barely breaking the oily sheen, waiting in

197

ambush for an inattentive skipper. Many a voyage had come to an untimely end by barging headlong into one. I had navigated this bay often enough that it had become second nature to keep an eye out and the speed down until clear of the entrance.

I set a course a few degrees to starboard of Pecker Point, that aptly named rocky finger running down from the height of Sawmill Mountain into the inlet from the left. On the right, the huge mass of a Davis raft, newly arrived from the Queen Charlotte's, waited to be relieved of its bindings. Most of it was under water, like an iceberg and just as solid. Broken into its parts, its logs would join those in the booms lining the shoreline all the way down to Twin Lakes and beyond.

Ocean Falls, looking past the booming grounds to the harbor exit. Pecker Point is on the left.

A towboat rounded the point and came plowing toward us with its diesels grumbling and its foaming moustache streaming away on either side. As it passed to port, I saw the white lettering on her bows. It was the *John M.* I felt an attachment to that squat, muscular vessel aboard which I had arrived ten years earlier. From her deck, I had first glimpsed the cluster of white houses terraced across the mountain side, and the soaring stack growing out the sprawling mass of vapor-spewing buildings of the paper mill, the industry that was the sole reason for every last person and dwelling being there, huddled at the end of Cousin's Inlet. Strange the *John M.* would be the last boat I would see as I left.

I glanced back. The sun was warming Old Baldy, the mountain that, depending on the weather and individual feelings, was thought to be either frowning or smiling down on this isolated hole-in-the-wall community. This morning, with the light glancing off its snowy cap and reflecting into the gloom of the forest at its feet, it seemed to be smiling. In the distance, the face of the hydroelectric dam glistened wetly behind the antlike figures of the day shift trickling across the bridge separating the mill from the townsite. Even as short a time ago as yesterday, I had been part of that parade.

Pete still had the engine-compartment hatch-covers open and was standing down in beside the engine. He had an oilcan in his hand. An untidy home-rolled cigarette hung from his lip. He still looked solemn, but that was his normal expression.

I cut in close to the point. The water was deep, even within a few yards of the sea-polished granite. As we slid in behind the point, its shadow closed like a great curtain, cutting off the view, first of the mill and then the homes. Within a few boat-lengths, Ocean Falls, the place that had nurtured me for almost a third of my life, become my home, the place that all through the war years I had said I was from, was totally concealed.

And then, for the last time, I heard the great sonorous organ-pipe drone of the eight o'clock whistle. Like a muezzin calling the faithful to prayer, it was bidding the day shift begin and releasing the graveyard shift to go home to bed.

I gave the throttle another notch and glanced back through the open cabin door to see Pete's reaction. His frown had deepened, as I expected it would. I left the wheel and walked back.

"I want to open it up a bit. Were not going to get anywhere fast if I don't," I shouted over the roar.

He shook his head. "Better not. Not until I see how these universals hold up. They're okay so far, but..." He looked dubious.

"And I'd like to pull the dingy up on deck," I said. "It's not very efficient towing it. It doesn't pull all that easily."

He gave me his annoying lopsided smile—the one that, whenever he was inclined to bestow it on me, indicated he didn't think I was very bright. He shook his head and said, "What the hell? It doesn't matter, this engine can handle it. We got a hundred horse-power here." He looked down at it, admiringly. Then, "I'd have to close the hatch-covers and I wouldn't be able to see what's going on."

I shrugged. I wondered how long he was going to ride like that. It can't have been very comfortable. I skirted around the gaping hatch to the stern cleat and adjusted the rope so that the dingy rode the following waves a little easier, then went back to the wheel. I poured a cup of coffee from the thermos. Maybe I would survive last night's overindulgence after all. But sleep, that's what I need-ed, just another few hours.

I sipped the warm brew as on the rock-bound shore a clutch of gray, dilapidated buildings went drifting past. They had once housed the cottage industry from which the name Pecker Point had been coined. On this isolated Alcatrazlike setting, a house of pleas-ure had flourished from the 1920s until sometime during the war when it was shut down by some department or agency of govern-ment that had deemed it hazardous to the national well being, much to the relief of some and the dismay of others. The elements: snow with the consistency of volcanic magma and rain like the outpour-ing of a sluice box, had worked on them until now only the weath-ered broken-backed shells and a rotting float remained. This enter-prise, like the larger one at the end of the inlet, had seen a stream of practitioners come and go over the years. The *Myrtle R.*, the scruffy one-lung ferry that freighted the paying customers to and from town, was no more nor was Judd Parker her skipper.

I had never visited there in its heyday. A puritanical streak instilled in me by a mother whose lips, I'm sure, had never uttered the word prostitute, forbade me experimenting along those lines.

My evening with George had become protracted. We had walked out of the mill together after my last shift and I had suggest-ed we while away the evening over a few beers. "No can do," he said. "I promised to babysit. Chris has gotta go out tonight."

"Maybe I should drop around by your house and keep you com-pany, then," I said.

"Sure, why not? Come about seven-thirty."

Not wanting to show up empty-handed, I had lugged a mint-fresh flagon of Johnny Walker's red label with me. We had chewed on it while we went over some of the salient points of our friendship that had spanned the last ten years. When Chris came home, the level in the square glass bottle had ebbed to somewhere below the halfway mark, but there was much yet to discuss. She took one look at us, shook her head and went off to bed. Our final goodbye was a little maudlin, as I remember, sometime deep into the wee hours.

I scanned the cottage ringing Wallace Bay. There had been some good days there—and nights. This whole area, right down into Fisher Channel was as familiar as it gets. I knew it as well as I knew any piece of the coast. I had never owned a saltwater boat, but I had plenty of friends who did and aboard these boats I had trolled for salmon, jigged for ground fish and hauled crabs by the bushel from the bottoms of quiet little coves. It was good water, far enough out that the byproducts of papermaking, most of it being pretty noxious stuff, that were continually spewed into the inlet were pretty well diluted.

I lounged at the wheel, squinting against the sunlight bouncing off the glassy calm, the drone of the Kermath running at half speed drumming in my skull.

I had arrived on a day such as this, but between then and now I had seen a lot of rainwater. That and the remoteness, I guess, is what had got to me and was finally driving me out. There were a couple of other reasons, both female, one I wanted to think about and the other I didn't, but I kept my mind away from both of them. In my hungover condition it was better not to chafe at old sore spots.

We were into Dean Channel, with the bulk of King Island on the left, when it hit me. "Hey, what am I doing?" I nearly shouted it. "What in hell am I doing!?" The realization that I had deliberately cut myself adrift, quit, divorced myself from the only steady paying job I had ever had, came almost as a physical blow. I had to fight a powerful urge to swing the wheel over and head back. Too late, the die was cast. I had better get my head around reality. My panic subsided. I would be alright, I assured myself, as I had for the umpteenth time in the last few weeks. Yeah, I would be alright.

No single event stood out as being the one that finally dislodged me, persuaded me to get out. It was more a combination of things—the depression I knew I was sinking into, the erosion of enthusiasm for living in isolation with no foreseeable improvement to my lifestyle, and finally, discovering sufficient courage to make the break, to overcome my natural inertia to change. At the same time, there was a growing confidence in my ability to compete in the workplace elsewhere. Those things, occurring more or less simultaneously, were what probably provided the final impetus. I knew I could make it somewhere else.

There were other things, of course, a whole bunch of them, that singularly were not greatly significant, but taken together added, measurably, to my burden of restlessness and dissatisfaction. However, in the main, it was the depression I was in that had become so obvious that friends had started remarking on it, thus straining the bonds of friendship. The fact that I had sunk that far was alarming. I was also becoming almost paranoid about the lack of sunshine. I was taking as a personal affront the perversity of a climate that could offer naught but weeks and months of clouds hanging over the rooftops and rain sluicing down day after day. Even to me, it was sure sign I was reaching some sort of crisis. Piled on top, was the boring sameness of shift work, of seeing the years sliding by with little likelihood of being more than I was. And lately I had lost the will to strive, all incentive gone. There was the singular lack of someone to prove myself to, and it seemed that as long as I stayed, there wouldn't be. The only plus side was that I had got a foothold in the electrical trade, something I knew I could build on. I had something to offer, and in the postwar climate, there were places to offer it.

I wasn't sure of what I wanted or where I wanted to go. But I knew I wanted more, and that I had to seek it somewhere else. "The break has to come sometime," an inner voice kept harping at me, "so why not now?" My bankbook was showing a substantial balance and there was little more to be had from this one-industry town. I had pretty well plumbed its limits. There was money to be made in other facets of the industry, if that's all I wanted, sweating in the steamy heat of machine room with the roar of newsprint machines in my ears and the stink of sulfite in my nose. Money was nice, but light and clear sky is what I craved—a place in the sun.

Ocean Falls, electrical crew. Photo taken in the powerhouse, circa 1948.

And there were the ghosts of failed relationships that needed exorcizing, and only in a different environment could I hope to lay them finally to rest.

Pete and his boat had been the catalyst. He'd wanted to get it to Vancouver, to sell it, but hadn't the slightest idea how to accomplish it. Olwyn had prevailed on me.

"Why don't you go with Pete?" She suggested it right out of clear blue sky one evening. However, I knew her too well. This was no spur of the moment thought. She'd been figuring for a while. "You know how to run a boat and navigate. You want to leave anyway. This would be ideal for you, kill two birds. Pete would never make it by himself. He'd never get across Queen Charlotte Sound." Then she threw in the clincher. "You wouldn't want to feel responsible if he drowned, would you?"

She was right on one score. I did want to leave.

I hadn't quite made up my mind when, but I knew the sand had

Olwyn and Owen, circa 1948.   Olwyn and Pete, circa 1948.

finally run out of the glass. I was marking time, going through the motions. Why not? A leisurely trip down the coast in the spring could be nice. There were, however, a couple of flies in the seagoing ointment—Pete and his boat. I had no faith in either of them. It was a thing to consider.

Olwyn had prevailed and, notwithstanding my natural caution, I agreed.

So here I was, slightly hung over, having committed myself to seeing Pete and *Monad* safely to Vancouver through some of the trickiest water to be found anywhere in the world. Beyond that, I hadn't really thought. Something would turn up. On that score I had rooted out most of my misgivings.

Ten years had made a difference. Whereas I had arrived with next to nothing, my few threadbare possessions floating around in a scuffed cardboard suitcase and no money in my pocket, with a will to succeed but no real knowledge of anything, I was leaving comparatively wealthy. I had a healthy bank account, three trunks of clothing following on the next CPR boat and above all I had a trade.

I had also spent the best part of four years in the Navy and seen a lot of the world. Now I was putting to use some of the skills I had learned aboard ship to safely pilot *Monad* past rock and shoal for the next 300 miles—that was the plan anyway.

Things were different now, I kept telling myself, far different to those dark days before the war. Confident though I felt at the moment, a whole family of dark misgivings still tugged at my coat tails. I remembered all too vividly the deprivation of the late 1930s, of roaming the streets of Vancouver almost begging for menial tasks that paid next to nothing. Things couldn't be that bad now, not with the economic climate of the whole country on the upswing.

I would be on my own from here on with no one of my own to turn to. I no longer had a home, not in Vancouver, not anywhere. I had left Owen and Olwyn behind me in Ocean Falls, for how long, I had no idea, but I was sure it wouldn't be for very long. Mother had passed on during the war in 1943, a young woman, only fifty-four, who had been ill almost half of her life. Father? Well, I'd have to see about him. Perhaps rescue him, if that was possible. But, by God, I would make it. Something would turn up.

CHAPTER 16

Boat Building

The boat on which I had cast my lot was *Monad*, an awkward, unseaworthy, graceless craft. Despite what I knew about her, I had agreed to pilot her down the Inside Passage to Vancouver. Most of the trip would be through waters I had no intimate knowledge of. Sure, I had traveled them dozens of times in all kinds of weather and in the dark of night, but always with the solid reassuring bulk of a coastal steamer under me, with impeccable linens on the bunks and snowy cloths, glistening silver and crystal gracing the tables. Navigating the tricky passages was something with which I had not had to concern myself. This trip would be different.

There was nothing sumptuous about *Monad*, and getting her through narrows famous for their seething tides, across broad expanses of unsheltered water and through rock-strewn channels was not a task I could leave to someone else. This time it was up to me. Confident though I was, it was confidence born, to some extent, of ignorance. It was also tempered with the knowledge that my navigating skills had never really been tested. I could read a chart, I had spent time in boats and had a familiarity with the sea from being in the navy, but there was a lot of unknown water between the cloud-filled end of Cousins Inlet and Vancouver. Had the soundness of *Monad* not been in question and had Pete been more of a congenial, even if inept, companion, I could have faced the challenge with fewer nagging misgivings.

Some say that boats take on the character of the builder, and indeed it seemed that many of Pete's less endearing qualities were embedded in *Monad*'s timbers. I had no love for her, in fact, more the opposite; I distrusted her and she was offensive to my eye. But I was determined to fulfill my commitment and get her safely into Burrard Inlet without her sinking under me.

Her name was one that Pete had thought long and hard on, and then with a router he incised it deeply into a pair of mahogany boards that he mounted either side of the cabin. To my way of thinking, it was the best piece of woodworking he had done on the entire boat. Its meaning was probably lost on all but a very few. But, of course, it was doubtful that anyone really gave much thought to what her name was or if they did, they might have confused it with "Nomad," a name appropriate to boats. Or maybe, knowing Pete, they just figured he had misspelled it. Anyway, I seldom heard anyone use it. "Pete's boat," was what it was referred to and usually with a wry smile and a shake of the head.

The name had some deep meaning for Pete, though. He explained it to me once, patiently, like a long-suffering tutor to a not-too-bright schoolboy, but I never did get the connection between a badly built boat and the *Oxford Dictionary*'s definition: "any ultimate unit of being, a soul, a person, God." However, regardless of name and meaning, fate and my own soft-headedness had seduced me into getting her and Pete safely past rock and shoal to a berth at the government wharf in Port Moody.

I first met Pete Fast about a year after the war and shortly after Olwyn took up with him. Olwyn had left her husband and moved to the Falls after the war. He had arrived at Ocean Falls, one of the faceless many that the tri-weekly coast boats regularly offloaded to fill the gaps in the work force that, like tidal sand, was constantly on the move. Whether he discovered her or she him, I don't know, but it was a relationship that, from the outset, I doubted was likely to succeed. What she saw in him I couldn't fathom. To my mind, they had little in common, other than, perhaps, a physical attraction, and even that was hard to rationalize. I could understand his interest, but I certainly couldn't see hers.

He was tall, raw-boned and with thinning hair and a melancholy countenance that reflected his dull, humorless outlook on life. There was nothing vigorous about him. He slouched along as though he alone supported the weight of the world and was charged with solving all its problems. He was something over twelve years older than Olwyn, a fact that in most cases would be of little significance, but beside her he seemed almost fatherly. His favorite topic of conversation was himself, and particularly how he had bummed around during the depression years, ridden the tops of boxcars from coast to coast and lived mainly on handouts. He seemed proud of these accomplishments. It was a way of life that was no novelty to our generation, but few would honestly say they wanted to return to. However, at any mention of that period a wistfulness would creep over and soften his lugubrious expression. To him, these were the "good old days." I could find nothing engaging about him and it was a mystery how Olwyn could. He had few social graces and at times was downright rude. He wasn't a snappy dresser, he didn't beguile her with flowers or presents, take her to dinner or to the one local movie; he just spent the evenings sprawled on the bed in her room freeloading the coffee she made in her plug-in perk and the cake and cookies she bought at the bakery.

I tried not to show active dislike for him or wage a campaign against him, but there was much about him I couldn't stomach. It was close enough to the end of the war, with memory of that unpleasantness still pretty raw in everyone else's minds and mine, that I just put it down to his being German. *What could you expect from a German*—even though I knew he had been born in Saskatchewan and served in the Canadian Army.

Among all the other things that rubbed me the wrong way was his never-ending prattle on politics. Of that topic he never tired. He would chew on it at the drop of the hat, on and on *ad nauseam*. Admittedly, my interest in politics was underdeveloped, it being far from a consuming passion with me. And when he got off on his half-baked theories, my boredom threshold was soon breached. Most times I managed to remember some piece of business elsewhere that needed my attention. He espoused a homegrown version of the Technocrat doctrine and considered anybody who he couldn't convert a fool—I guess that labeled me. I was hard pressed to contain a desire to holler "hogwash" when he began expounding his beliefs, but I held my tongue. I didn't want an open split with him for Olwyn's sake, but all in all, I found him pretty hard to digest. On top of all else, he had an inflated ego. He really thought he was an intellectual cut above the average. Why Olwyn couldn't see through him was a mystery.

I'm sure Olwyn sensed how I felt, but we stayed clear of talking about it. It made little difference to me whom she went with, but I could see a reoccurring pattern. She had made bad guesses about men in the past and, although I hated to think she had made another one, I wouldn't bet on the mileage she would get out of a relationship with Pete.

He worked, I'll give him that, on the townsite gang in the rain. Miserable work it was, but a job that gave him the title of carpenter and the union scale that went with it.

Ocean Falls had not been built to last. Its lifespan, like dozens of other one-industry towns, had been foreseen as finite. It would serve the purpose for as long as it was needed, then it would be abandoned to the weather to gradually rot away. First appearances to the contrary, there was nothing of substance about it, nothing of brick or stone underlay its façade. Everything was on the surface. Wood, the entire town was made of wood, wood that was in a perpetual state of decay, and that was constantly in need of replacement. All of the streets and sidewalks connecting the dwellings were of wooden planks nailed together, on edge, with spaces between to let the rainwater through. They rotted or broke, their lifespan no more than a year or two. Pete was part of the crew that dug them out and replaced them, a labor that, to my mind, just barely qualified as carpentry. I guess he was good enough at what he did, the kind of wood butchery that called for more brawn than brains, but it was a far cry from boat building, a task that required meticulous joinery skills.

Why he wanted a boat in the first place, I couldn't figure. He had no love of the sea, had no knowledge of it or a desire to sail on it. He just plain disliked being in boats. He was a landlubber, pure and simple. The few times that he and Olwyn went off down the inlet on somebody else's boat, he had come back a bundle of nerves.

"Pete's not a sailor. Some people are some people aren't. Pete isn't one." Olwyn was quick to defend him when I queried her about his nervousness. "It's all right for you, Paul. You were in the navy. You think everybody can just take to the water like a duck.

You can't expect everybody to be like that."

"Okay, okay, I was just asking. If he doesn't like being on boats, he doesn't have to go on them." I let the matter drop.

Anyway, for whatever motive, whether he thought he could make money at it or to show his superiority, he started the job of building for which his temperament wasn't right. For him, it was just a job, a task empty of creative need. He didn't understand about boats and their personalities; he had no desire to breath life and a soul into one, it was just a carpentry job. It could have been a wood-shed, for all the feeling he had about it.

Ocean Falls was a boat town. People didn't own real estate. They didn't build houses or garages or fences or the like; they rent-ed something from Mother Company who owned every last stick and stone, so they didn't use up their spare time on their homes. And because of the northern latitude and the rain that pelted down day after day, growing flowers and vegetables in the acid soil between the rocks was not a popular pastime. What grew best were devil's club and salmonberries, lush native flora that needed no encouragement. The ornamental shrubs and flowers that added color for a few brief weeks in summer were coaxed into being by the town gardener, a professional hired for the job. So gardening was not a time consumer, except for a few dedicated green thumbs who strove to outwit the hostile environment. And there were no automobiles to tinker with and no highways to drive them on had there been. People had boats. Boats were their lifeblood, their trans-portation, their recreation and the subject of their conversations. They worked on their boats and they talked boats.

Building one was a way to put in time when the weather pre-vented doing anything else outside, like fishing or hiking in the mountains, and a way to satisfy a need to create something substan-tial. And to some, who really wanted to own a boat for the first time or wanted better than the one they had, it was the most economical way of acquiring one, provided they had the skills and the patience to carry it through. In most cases, building a boat of any size was a lengthy undertaking; some spent three or four years at it. To most, it was a labor of love.

About a mile out of town, at the end of the only road, lies the Martin Valley, a gloomy conduit for the Martin River that drains meltwater from a tangle of lonely canyons and rugged peaks, in a vast unpopulated area larger than some European countries. There, at the river's mouth, the steep sides of the valley give way and ease into sloping beaches and open foreshores. The amateur boat-building industry took root and flourished there. Sheds made from scrap lumber and tarpaper, some with closed in rooms and wood-burning heaters, huddled together, tattered and leaning at odd angles, just clear of the high-water line. At any time of any year, from within these ragged confines, the rump of a newly painted boat could be seen protruding and glistening against the dull black shards of tarpaper.

In this dark, ramshackle, clustered, shantytown, where the sharp sulfite of the mill was almost overridden by the smell of freshly cut yellow cedar, linseed oil, oakum and paint, some fine boats had been built. Matt Williamson, a thoughtful, soft-spoken bachelor, for one, had built several boats there over a period of some twenty-odd years. Charley Hallam, an old-time sailor who had rounded Cape Horn on sailing ships, built a blue-water sailboat there. He designed it as he went and carved marvelous pieces out of whole tree trunks with an adz.

The sheds changed hands, were shored up and improved and, defying all laws of gravity and building construction, withstood the heavy wet snows and torrential rains of winter on their skeletal underpinnings and fragile sheathing. It was not the handiest place in the world to build a boat; everything had to be carted there by wheelbarrow or, if too cumbersome, delivered by the one company truck. There was no electric power so all woodworking had to be done with hand tools. By necessity, metalworking was done in the mill shops, of which there was a full range—machine shop, pipe shop, tin shop, welding shop, blacksmith shop and foundry. Most of the work was done with the blessing of the company and charged out at an affordable rate. There were a few, though, who believed that anything belonging to the company, time or material, was fair game, and night shift in the shops was the time for "government work" as it was fondly labeled. Wonderful schemes for transporting illicit mechanical parts past the night attendant at the gate were devised, some, unbelievably complex and daring.

I got into boat building not because I wanted to own a boat, but because of a need to do something creative with my spare time. For more than a year I had frequented the boat sheds, they being at the end of the road that was really the only place to walk and get out of sight of town. And having watched the process, I became intrigued with the fashioning of wood into a boat. There was something about the carving and shaping of the massive keel timbers, assembling the graceful bones of the stem and sternposts, and the seemingly fragile skeleton of the ribs and chines that fascinated me. Gluing everything and sucking it all together with bolts and screws into a unit that would flex but not break, and then bending cleverly shaped clear cedar planks to compound curves over it, was an art form that struck a chord within me. Without consciously thinking about it, I came to the conclusion that one of the most beautiful and practical products of man's ingenuity was the boat, and the absolute pinnacle of that, the sailing boat. Therefore, when an opportunity arose for me to build one, with someone to guide me, I had to make the attempt. My woodworking skills were at best amateurish, but unlike Pete, I knew it. And, even had I wanted to, I wouldn't have been able to kid anybody otherwise. My venture, simple though it was, may actually have been the catapult that propelled Pete into building.

In the ups and downs of Olwyn's troubled liaisons, I was the one she looked to for strength whenever she found her life being derailed. We had grown closer through the war years and whenever she needed a shoulder, remote though mine was most of the time, to cry on or a sounding board for a decision, I was the one she turned to. I wasn't around all that much during the war, only on leave, but we had kept up a correspondence of sorts. We remained close, and when the war was finally over—by that time, her marriage, that had been badly flawed in the first place, had run its course—she packed up and, taking her daughter, left Vancouver. She left Ralph, her husband, and the few possessions they had accumulated and sought sanctuary with me at Ocean Falls. So, buried in the rainforest and the sulfurous smog at the end of an isolated fjord, we, Owen included, saw each other almost daily.

Ridiculous though it seemed, I think Pete saw me as the Alpha male in her life and felt a need to oust me. To do so, he had to show himself superior. Ergo, anything I could do, he could do better. If I could build a boat, he could build a better one. It was small thinking, but I'm convinced that's what was in his mind. Anyway, at the time, I never gave it a thought. I just went ahead, suddenly full of enthusiasm.

Maj (short for Major) Bennett was a big man with an infinite capacity for kindness, at least to me. His Irish ancestry had bestowed on him a shock of curly midnight hair and the bluest eyes I have ever seen. They actually seemed to glow from below bushy eyebrows. He had huge thick-fingered hands that could, amazingly, dismantle and reassemble the most intricate piece of electrical equipment in the shop where he earned his living, and then, in his boat shed on weekends, they could effortlessly grapple great chunks of steamed oak and bend them as though they were spaghetti. They hung like clubs at the end of simianlike arms. His rumpled, down-at-the-heel appearance, largely because of tattered sweaters that he seemed to have an inexhaustible supply of and that he wore day in and day out and flatly refused to throw away until they were mere shreds, belied his talent. He had an analytical mind for anything mechanical and a curiosity about just about everything else. For him there was no bulling things through hoping for the best; every move he made was carefully thought out well in advance. He was a man committed to the pursuit of excellence. His vast knowledge was not something he hoarded; it was a well from which the lesser informed, like me, could draw from. Help was supplied with almost missionary zeal.

In his late twenties or early thirties when I first knew him, he and his family—parents, a brother and two sisters—had lived at the Falls for a decade or more. From whence or by what route they came, I don't know. Seems it never came up in conversation. He never spoke of having lived anywhere else. It wasn't my affair so I never probed deeply.

When I transferred from the finishing room to the electric shop, just about the time that things in Europe were getting really nasty, I gravitated to him and he became my electrical mentor. Only a few months later, I joined up and went off to war.

In those first hesitant searching months when I returned to civilian life and was trying to pick up where I had left off, he again took me under his wing. Almost four years of being away at war

213

had changed me, altered my way of thinking and my entire approach to things. Harking back to where I had begun was no easy task. Through those troubled years I had given little thought to the electrical trade, being more occupied with the intricacies of guns, depth charges and seafaring in general.

Maj hadn't been to war, and I didn't ask why. He was certainly big enough and seemed healthy enough, but I just let it lie. I was heartsick of the whole business of even talking about war and how people behaved during it—whether in the forces or not. I wanted to get on with my life. At twenty-five, I could finally see that I might actually have one.

Maj was constructing a biggish boat, something on the order of forty feet, out at the mouth of the river. He had itched to build one all through the war, but metal parts and high quality wood were just too hard to come by. Clear spruce and cedar went to build war planes, the fast mosquito bombers, and it went into the sleek motor torpedo boats that harried German shipping in the English Channel. Every scrap of metal went to make parts for some engine of destruction. And besides, everybody was working around the clock, making money. There was no time for boat building. Maj, like others with mechanical skills, had set up a metalworking lathe in his spare room and had got himself a contract to make small parts for some unnamed war machine.

Now with the most of Europe, the Pacific Islands and Japan lying in smoking ruins, vast stockpiles of arms and machinery were being dismantled. There were now plenty of materials available for boat building and other peaceful pursuits. Maj and those others whose dreams of big seaworthy boats had festered through the years and whose bank accounts had fattened during the same period to the point they could afford their dreams were off and running. Their sheds rose like mushrooms on a shingle at the mouth of the river.

Apart from work and the lackadaisical study of the electrical trade, my mind was footloose. I had nothing to occupy my thinking in the off hours. I had a room in a private home, an apartment with an old couple who wanted little of me other than the rent, in which I lay on the bed and read and when the reception was good, usually late at night, listened to the radio. I hung around the coffee shop or the beer parlor and rubbed shoulders with the veterans who congregated there, and whose minds had not fully returned from far off battlefields. But I had no direction, and as the second winter pushed its way into the inlets with its incessant rain and low-hanging clouds, depression seeped into me.

Whether deliberate or not, Maj rescued me.

The chain of events started with, "Hey Paul. Why don't you come to supper tonight? I think Vi has a fish she wants to cook." It was an early autumn afternoon, a Sunday, and the mill had been down for the weekend. We had worked through, doing electrical maintenance and were both dog tired.

"You're sure?" I asked.

"Course I'm sure."

I didn't hesitate. Violet Bennett could do marvelous things in the kitchen. And there was another reason.

"I'll be there. What time do you want me?"

"Oh...about six or seven. I don't know. If you're too early we'll drink something until its ready. If you're too late we'll drink something anyway."

"Okay, I've got to peel off a few layers of grime first. See you about six-thirty." I punched the clock and headed for my room. The rain was pelting down. I climbed tiredly up the plank stairs to the apartment block, avoiding stepping on the fat slugs oozing their way across the steps, their slime coating the wood and glistening in the weak light of the street lamps. God! I hated the gloom and the rain...and the slugs.

I thought about dinner, relieved I wouldn't have to walk back down and eat in the cafe. I should take something, though, something to drink. My scotch bottle, I knew, was running on empty and the liquor store was closed.

I shook the rain from my coat, hung it in the closet and then burrowed into the junk in the bottom where I had a few bottles of Calona Red cellared—a vile brew, and inappropriate with fish but it would have to do. It was one of the few wines available in the spartanly stocked local liquor store. In those immediate postwar days when the dispensing of any alcoholic beverage was governed by narrow puritan thinking, wine still hadn't caught on as a Canadian beverage, it being, in most cases, considered elitist. I selected a couple I'd aged for a week, showered and stretched out on the bed for a few minutes. I thought about Violet Bennett, thoughts I had an uneasy feeling were going to get me into hot water one of these days, unless balanced by sufficient guilt to keep things safely in check.

Violet had come to Ocean Falls sometime prior to the beginning of the war. How she and Maj had met had never come to light, but somewhere in that early war period she and Maj had married. And whereas he was a great bear of a man, she was a slight bird of a woman, a woman only a couple of years older than me, slim and attractive with a way of crinkling her eyes at me that created havoc with my libido. I was infatuated with her.

I thumped my way into the back porch. She opened the door to my rap.

"Hi, Paul." She came close and looked up at me. I could smell her perfume. Her voice was low and throaty. "It's so nice to see you. Come in, but hang your coat out here where it can drip."

There it was again, the crinkling eyes looking directly into mine…and the smile, well, it did things to me.

"Hi, Vi, hope I'm not too early." Looking at her made my throat constrict and made me trip over my tongue. "Here. It's the best I could come up with at short notice." I handed her the sodden brown bag with the Calona Red. She pulled a bottle out half way and inspected it as though it was a fine vintage.

"Oh good. I'm cooking a salmon you know, and I never thought to buy wine. I'm glad you remembered. It was thoughtful of you."

"It's red. You think it will go with salmon?"

"We'll make it go." She smiled up at me again, hitting me with the full glow of it. "Go on in the livingroom. Maj's got his feet up, but he'll put them down long enough to get you a drink." She held her ground in the doorway, and as I pushed past her, I was sure I felt her move against me. My imagination? Maybe.

Maj's chair was buttressed on all sides by books, rolled up blueprints and stacks of boating magazines. A glass of scotch teetered on top of the right-hand pile. He pointed at the sideboard.

"Fix yourself something. I'll play host some other time." He leaned back into the leather depth. I poured myself a substantial libation and then slumped into a corner of the sofa where I could see into the kitchen and keep an eye on Violet's trim figure as it moved between the stove and table. He handed me a detailed drawing of a spoked steering wheel. I sipped the scotch and studied it.

"That's what I'm building now. After supper I'll show it to you. It's out back. It's black walnut. The metal will be brass. If I get around to it I might electroplate it, chrome might look nice. I'll have to see."

I couldn't imagine even attempting such a complex piece of joinery.

I said, "How'n hell does anybody learn to put together something like this? It's marvelous, but so bloody involved...its got to be so precise. How can you do it?"

"Hell, Paul. Anybody with five cents of brains and a little mechanical know-how can do it. It just takes time and, I guess, mostly desire...and patience, yeah, patience and being careful. That's all. Anybody can do it."

"Yeah, but I wouldn't know where to even start, not on something like this, or any part of a boat for that matter. A wheel like this is a project in itself."

"Oh, it takes a little doing alright, but it's not like it was brain surgery. If you make a little mistake, the patient won't die." He laughed. "You can fix it." He sipped his scotch. "Haven't you ever tried building anything?"

"Not much. I haven't really got a place to muck around and make a mess in. Sometimes, though, I think I might like to take a shot at making something, but it would have to be something simple like a square box or a breadboard. Right now, I'm pretty sick of doing nothing. I've thought about woodworking, and I've watched these guys working on their boats, you know...out there. Maybe I could make something out of wood, something useful and maybe artistic. I've never worked much with wood, though. I envy guys like you, ."

He laughed. "Paul. Go to it. If you want to build something go ahead. All you gotta do is start. Anybody can learn." He paused. "Tell you what. If you're sure you want to fiddle around with woodworking, I'll give you a hand. I'll even give you a set of plans for a boat, a small sailboat. You could build it as a rowboat. It's a ten-footer, but it has all the elements, and it has a bit of class to it.

It's a pretty simple design, but artistic. It's a nice little boat. I built one back a few years ago. I learned a lot from it."

It was an exciting thought, but formidable. A boat to start with, I didn't know… "Yeah, but where. I'd have to build a shed. And suppose it didn't work out."

"You wouldn't have to build a shed. There's a lean-to on mine. All you have to do is add a little tarpaper to it. Plug up the holes a bit. Rent free too." He chuckled. "I'll help you, and when I need an extra body to push on something, you'll be handy. Okay?"

"It's a deal." He reached from the depth of his chair and we shook. The seed was sown.

The salmon was good, even washed down with my astringent contribution. And sitting next to Violet and feeling her brush against me, anything would have tasted good. Finally clutching a rolled up tube of boat plans, I staggered off to bed, determined to give it my best effort. Just to keep Maj's respect, if nothing else.

I had one thing going for me—a natural ability with tools. I hadn't any woodworking tools, though, and had to buy them, forking out the money in the hardware store as each one became a dire necessity. Learning to use them came naturally. And with Maj there to take me step by step through the drawing out of the plans full size and the setting up of the frames, I began to see that what had seemed impossible was not. As Maj had said, what it took was desire, care and patience. It took money too, but on a project as small as mine, the cost was not anything I couldn't afford.

It seemed the more I thought about Violet, the more advice I needed from Maj. Even small unimportant problems that I should have been able to work out on my own, had I applied my mind to them, I used as excuses to drop around to Bennett's house. Then one day something clicked. I was acting like an idiot. The bearing I was on could only set me into shoal water. I had better start listening to the voice of guilt that was growing louder by the moment. I did an abrupt course change and stayed away. Only if I was invited did I go. If I wanted to keep Maj as a friend, and I did, it was the only way.

I worked along side Maj in the mill shop, and then in the boat shed, spasmodically, through the winter, when it wasn't too desperately cold. I had the framing done to the point I could see a boat emerging from the lattice of spruce and cedar when spring rolled around. Sure, I measured wrong and cut things when I shouldn't have. I wasted lumber, but I learned the hard way. Over time, my measuring became more accurate and I learned patience. At some point it dawned on me that the actual building was what was important to me. Like the classic idea of the game, it was not the winning or the final score but how it was played. I guess that's what I was seeking in the first place. Acquiring a finished boat was a secondary consideration. I began to take pride in my ability to shape pieces of wood and make them fit. The fact that the project was slow to advance became unimportant. As time went on I became almost overly fussy.

One rare sunny day, Olwyn, with Pete slouching along beside her, out for a walk, came by.

Ocean Falls. My boat under construction, circa 1947.

"So, this is the boat you've been bragging about," Pete said, looking it over. "Heh, heh," he whickered, horselike, through his nose. "Its sure not much of a boat, is it? The way you talked about it I thought it was away bigger, like a real boat. Why didn't you build a proper boat? You can't go anywhere in a thing like this. Just a toy." He shook his head.

"Suits me," I said, bristling.

"You know," he continued unabated, insensitive to my hostility, "I could build a boat, not a tea cup like this, but a real boat. There's really not much to it, just carpentry."

I knew different, but I didn't want to argue the point. In fact, I didn't want to talk to him about it at all.

Olwyn stepped into the breach.

"I think it's a nice little boat. It's not a big motorboat, but I think it's nice. Don't you think it's nice, Pete?"

"Oh yeah. I suppose. Heh, heh. But then it's not a real boat is it—just a toy."

I was rapidly losing my cool, when they wandered off.

A few weeks later, my feathers still ruffled, but smoothed to the point I could almost be civil, Owen, Pete and I were congregated in Olwyn's room engaged in the ritual of 'happy hour,' when Olwyn, practically bursting at the seams, announced "Pete's going to build a boat." She blurted it out as though it was the one piece of news the world had been waiting for. She looked at Pete, seeking approval for having divulged it. He sat there with a silly self-satisfied grin on his face, nodding assent.

"Yep, that's right. I'm going to build a boat." There, the great secret was out.

"Oh, yeah? What kind of a boat?" Owen asked.

"I haven't decided yet, but it's going to be bigger than anything being built out there right now. It will make that thing of yours, Paul, look pretty amateurish."

He sure had it in for my rowboat. I couldn't understand why at the time, but I should have twigged. He was grandstanding, belittling me in Olwyn's eyes. What hadn't dawned on him was that we weren't competing for her affection. I was her brother, not a suitor. I didn't give a damn what he did, as long as he treated Olwyn decently. He could have built the *Queen Mary* for all I cared. I was enjoying what I was doing and nothing he could say or do would change that.

From then on, that's all he talked about, to anyone and everyone who would listen. He bought a couple of books on boat building and regaled me at every turn with his newfound knowledge. He started coming out regularly to inspect my project and point out various things I was doing wrong: I was using the wrong glue or the screws weren't right or whatever. I got to the point where I dreaded seeing him come.

He also began hanging around other boat sheds and giving unsolicited advice. On a couple of occasions, builders got a little short with him.

"You've been talking a lot about building a boat," I overheard one of them say. "Why don't you get on with it? We'll damn soon see whether you know what you are talking about or not."

"Oh, I'm going to build a boat all right, as soon as I can find the right set of plans," said Pete, unabashed. "Come next spring, you just watch."

He reached the point where it was either fish or cut bait. He sent for a set of plans. At that time, most of the builders were getting their plans from Edwin Monk, a naval architect in Seattle, so that's where he sent.

The design was not what I expected. It was hard to know why he chose that particular one. Perhaps because he didn't really know what he was looking at. I had thought he would choose something more splendid. There was nothing unique about it. In fact, for the time, it was pretty standard—thirty-six feet overall, kind of beamy and with a trunk cabin. It was pretty big for one person to build, even for a competent boat builder, which Pete wasn't. One aspect of it, though, was different and would give him, and anyone else who became associated with it, a lot of trouble. It had a V drive.

There weren't too many V drives around. In fact, they were rather a novelty to many. On most designs, the engine was mounted close to amidships, the drive shaft pointing to the rear, down through the packing gland in the keel and out to the propeller. In the V drives, the engine was located in the rear, under the rear cockpit. The drive shaft pointed forward to a gearbox from which a second shaft, at an angle to and underneath the main one, extended rearwards through the keel to the propeller. The two shafts forming a V configuration, hence the name V drive. The main benefit of this arrangement was that the engine compartment was out of the main cabin, thereby freeing up space and cutting down on noise. The big problem with them was that they were a devilish thing to line up, unless a great deal of care and attention went in to the mountings.

For the next few months, V drives were all Pete talked about. Anyone who didn't have a V drive in his boat was lagging away behind the current trend in boat building. He got the plans drawn out, full size, and put an order in at the sawmill for the materials— yellow cedar for the frames and red cedar for the planking, which was standard for the day.

Despite whatever else I felt about him, I had to admit he wasn't exactly dumb. He just thought what he was doing was better than what anyone else was capable of. Not only that, he wouldn't listen; good advice rolled off him without much of it sinking in.

He built himself a shed among the others out at Martin Valley. Olwyn prevailed on me to give him a hand. It was only a few steps from Maj's shed where I was working, so I agreed. The trouble was, it didn't end with the building of the shed. Whenever he had anything he couldn't handle by himself, starting with laying the keel blocks, he would holler for help and expect me to come running. It got to the point that I only worked on my boat when I knew he wasn't working on his.

It went like that through the two-something years it took him to finish the job. My boat was, to all intents and purposes, finished within the first year, but I hung on, sanding rough spots and giving it extra coats of varnish. I actually hated to admit it was finished*. I thought about starting another one, but I was feeling the first twinges of itchy feet and I was loath to begin something that would pin me down. I wasn't out there as much anymore, but he would get Olwyn to ask me to go out with him on my days off, to help with something too big for one person. None of the other builders, notwithstanding they were pretty easy-going helpful types, wanted anything to do with him. I spent a lot of time, more than I wanted, helping him.

Owen, being more outspoken and who felt as I did about Pete,

*I never actually launched my boat. I sold it to a yachtsman shortly after it was finished.

left no doubt in anyone's mind that he wanted no part of him or his boat. So Pete didn't pester him.

For a while, during his early building stages, it happened that he and I were rooming in the same place, a fairly large house up on the side of the mountain. I had moved from the apartment where I had stayed with the old couple when they began talking about leaving. My room was on the main floor and Pete had the upstairs, a room that was most of the attic. He was forever accumulating things up there, things like bolts, screws, glue, buckets of paint and bits of hardware. He even bought a band saw, a pretty big machine that was driven by a one-horsepower motor, assembled it and set it up in the end of the attic. Our landlady, Mrs. Linkhart, was not too ecstatic about this. She was, I thought, a bit too fussy anyway, but Pete was pushing things.

One day when she was out, he opened the end window and hoisted all his yellow cedar framing lumber into his room. There was quite a bit of it, two inches thick and of varying lengths. She could smell it, I guess, when she came home and went storming up there and gave it to Pete. Somehow he managed to pacify her, but it was only a matter of time until something really hit the fan.

It happened one Sunday morning when she was in church. Pete fired up his saw and started cutting frames. I had changed jobs. I was now in the powerhouse and was on night shift. I had gone to bed sometime about nine in the morning. The whine of the saw, as it bit into the yellow cedar, woke me, and the oily smell that had permeated the house for days, became more pungent.

I lay in bed, unable to sleep because of the noise and knowing that battle was soon to be joined. Mrs. Linkhart came home about noon. By this time, there was yellow cedar sawdust sifting down the staircase and throughout the house.

"MY HOME! WHAT ARE YOU DOING TO MY HOME?!"

"I'm not hurting anything," said Pete, "just sawing a few frames. You're always complaining about something."

"Look at the mess; there's sawdust all over everything."

"Heh, heh," laughed Pete. His laugh always infuriated me, so I knew what it must be doing to her. "It's just cedar. People pay good money for cedar sawdust, it makes the house smell nice."

"You stupid, insensitive man," she said, almost in tears. "You

223

get this mess cleaned up and I want you and all of your junk out of here, the sooner the better."

The shouting went on for a while longer. I couldn't sleep so I got up and put my robe on.

I went upstairs to Pete's room. Mrs. Linkhart had plenty to complain about. Yellow sawdust was cascading down the stairs and out into the hallway. Pete's room was practically awash in the stuff, yet he wasn't making any attempt to clean it up. In fact, he started up his saw again and continued cutting frames. I guess I looked a little aghast. He just laughed and made signs in the direction of Mrs. Linkhart, as much as to say, "she's nuts." I heard her coming and I knew a return bout was in the offing. I got out of there and went downtown.

Pete was gone by the end of the week, but he had all of his frames sawn out.

"Silly woman," he remarked to me, next time I saw him, "I was going to give her a couple of bucks for her trouble, but since she was so unreasonable, I gave her nothing."

The *Monad*'s blueprints, like all Edwin Monk plans, were pretty detailed and if Pete followed them, there wasn't too much he could do wrong. He got the keel laid, the stempost attached and the transom bolted on. He set the frames in place and fastened them to the keelson according to the dimensions on the plans.

Pete had been told by several boat builders not to fasten them securely until he had them lined up. Lining them up involved bending a baton around the framework and moving the individual frames slightly until there was a smooth line from stem to stern at every point. There is always some variation, due to inexact lumber dimension, warping and assembly give-and-take, that needs to be corrected. It is an exacting job and takes time, but unless done properly, every hump and hollow will show up once the hull is planked. Pete didn't believe it or maybe he didn't want to.

"It's no different to a wall," he said, when I queried him about it. "You just put up the studs and when the sheathing goes on, everything pulls into place. You won't see small variations. Don't tell me about building."

He began planking, down along the keel, laying in the garboard strakes. He asked me to help him. And really, on that size of a boat,

Ocean Falls. *Monad's* keel, circa 1947.

it was a two-man job, even then it was awkward and hard to get at and hold things. They were a pretty sloppy fit.

"Aren't you going to fit them better than that?" I asked.

"Heh, heh," he laughed, as though I was some kind of idiot, "you don't have to worry about things like that, the lumber swells up when it gets wet and tightens. As soon as it's in the water, it'll be fine. You don't need to tell me about fitting things. I might put in a little caulking, but it'll be okay."

I wasn't convinced that gaps that wide would soak up enough, but it was his boat. And so it went.

Curiosity was rife among the boat-building fraternity; builders kept a constant eye on how things were progressing on everyone else's boats. They were always wandering over to each other's sheds to have a look.

"Those planks don't fit too well; they'll give you trouble," some were heard to remark while hunkering down and peering at the bottom.

"They'll soak up," was Pete's standard reply.

As the planking advanced up the sides, humps and hollows, that had been foretold, began to make their appearance. It was not unusual to see one of the builders standing, eyeing the lines and shaking his head.

"Why would a guy deliberately build hollows like that into his boat?" one builder remarked to me.

Most of them, by this time, had written it off as an expensive joke. Pete pushed on. He didn't have much choice; he had a lot invested and couldn't just walk away from it. His best option was to finish it and sell it, that is, if he could find a buyer—an unlikely scenario. Everyone in town, knowing how it was built, would shy away from it. The biggest hurdle he still had to face was whether it would float, and, if not, would he have to rip off some of the planking and redo it. He wouldn't know until he launched it.

He spent a lot of time trying to plane and scrape the aberrations out of it. Some of the small ones became less apparent, but several big ones defied remedy.

"Once it's painted and in the water, no one will notice," he said. I think he actually believed that that would be the case. The thing was that boats were the lifeblood of the community. Most people, even the kids, had educated eyes and could spot any abnormality in a boat a couple of city blocks away.

He decked it in, through the second winter. He was getting pretty sick of the whole project by now and Olwyn was complaining of inattention. He was spending all of his spare time on the boat and not enough of it with her. Trouble was, he had started building for all the wrong reasons. He wanted a boat to point to and say, "See what I built." He wasn't getting any enjoyment out of building and he wasn't thirsting to go sailing in it. He began taking shortcuts.

He decided to launch in the spring and finish building the cabin while moored at a float in town. He wouldn't have so far to go and could take advantage of power tools. He would also be close to the company marine-ways and shops when it came time to install the engine. By this time I was fed up with going out to help him. I have to admit, I had learned a lot—not all of it good.

Perhaps I was too hung up on appearances. As long as a boat was sound, what the hell. But looking out along *Monad*'s foredeck, where the canvas was improperly glued and had wrinkled, I couldn't help but retrace in my mind all of the things I knew were wrong with her. To my mind, art and craftsmanship went hand in hand. If one was neglected, then it followed that the other was bound to be. Even in those dark days before the war when in my desperate quest for livelihood I ranged the streets of Vancouver, my untrained eye was naturally drawn to the artistic. Art was synonymous with quality, or so I came to believe. And nothing that had transpired in the last ten years had made me think otherwise.

Author, Olwyn and Owen on the verandah of the Old Hotel, circa 1946

CHAPTER 17

Keeping Afloat

The first chart, the one that showed every bulge and indent of the coast down to Cape Calvert, was rolled tightly with the rest in a fat cardboard tube hanging from the deckhead in a metal rack. I dug it out, unrolled it and laid it on the settee table, pinned down at each corner with sardine cans to keep it from rerolling. We were still in familiar waters, but they were getting less familiar all the time. Soon I would have to start paying attention.

Our progress was agonizingly slow. Half speed wasn't getting us as far down channel as I would have liked or, for that matter, where I had calculated we needed to be. But there wasn't much I could do about it. At any suggestion of my cracking the throttle another notch, Pete's reaction was to look more dour and shake his head. He was firmly convinced that any malfunction, imagined or real, that could possibly infect an engine would surely come to pass if I did. I didn't know what was going on in his head, whether he knew something I didn't or whether it was his natural pessimism, but I thought he was being a good deal more cautious than was called for. In the back of my mind though, enough nagging doubts were eddying around that I didn't want to push him too hard. God knows, he could be right. Trouble was, I had much too intimate a knowledge of this tub that was plodding tiredly along under me to have much faith in it. A little more speed would have seemed more purposeful, but I wasn't in all that much of a hurry to get to Vancouver that I wanted to argue with Pete, not at this stage any-way. What were a few more revs if there really was a chance of

Monad disabling herself? Time enough to put her to the test, play captain and say how things were going to be if the going got dicey, and I had an uneasy feeling it would.

My stomach had stabilized in the last hour to the point that a few hunger pangs had begun gnawing at my middle. I burrowed into basket of sandwiches Olwyn had brought and sat at the wheel munching. I hollered at Pete and motioned at the sandwiches. He hauled himself out of the engine compartment, came forward and grabbed most of the egg ones that were left. He picked up the thermos and shook it.

"Not much coffee left."

"You could make a pot on the Coleman stove there. It wouldn't take long," I said.

"You better make it." He nodded at the engineroom. "I should keep an eye on things." He scurried back and lowered himself into the compartment, like a fussy guilt-ridden hen that had been away too long from the nest. He settled himself back, munched his sandwiches and gazed morosely at the sea around him. He was not enjoying this trip one little bit.

I stopped the wheel and dug out the naphtha stove. I guessed if I wanted coffee, I would have to make it.

There hadn't been much fanfare or flag waving at *Monad*'s launching. Not a single whistle or horn acknowledged her taking to the sea. There was no champagne bottle shattered across her bows either. She had been set afloat in the dreary half-light of a cold, rainy spring morning with only a handful of dog-tired witnesses to take note—not one of whom raised a cheer.

Hundreds of tides had come and gone while she was being fabricated. A good many months had passed as she rose from keel timbers to foredeck there at the extreme upper limit of a gently sloping tide-washed beach. Her leaving of it, her vacating of the tarpaper womb where she had been gestated, was not without a struggle. But it was we, the midwives, who had felt the pain. Her launching was an exercise I would not look back on with nostalgia. Had she been on slipways, where the simple act of knocking holding blocks out from under her would have set her free to slide down greased skids into the water, it might have been different. But she had to be hauled, literally, across barnacle-encrusted cobbles far enough for the rising tide to hoist her free of her cradle. There were no power assists; there was nothing like a truck with a winch that could be borrowed. It was hard-slogging hand power, nothing more.

Builders, those with boats of any size, usually launched when the high spring tides came lapping up the beach almost to the doors of the sheds. When they occurred, a boat could be floated with the least amount of dragging. Pete said it really didn't matter that much, any tide would do. Thankfully, he came around and listened to wiser heads. He opted to launch on a tide that would occur the second week of April. It would crest, according to the tide table, early on a Sunday morning. He scheduled himself a couple of weeks of vacation from the townsite carpentry gang.

Owen, who was a machinist and had to this point kept at arm's length from Pete and his boat, allowed himself to be dragooned into helping but not without reluctance and a few snide remarks on the side. I was actually surprised that he let himself get talked into it at all. Olwyn, of course, had recruited him over a lunch at the coffee shop. She gave him the same earnest look that she used on me.

"You could, just this once, give him a hand. It wouldn't hurt you. Paul's is going to help, aren't you Paul?

"Yeah. I guess so," I said. My lack of enthusiasm didn't add much in the way of persuasion to Olwyn's plea.

She kept wheedling, anyway. "Without you two, he won't be able to do it. There's nobody else, and it's just too much to expect of one person to launch a big boat like that."

"Oh, all right," Owen capitulated, as I knew he would. Neither of us was a match for Olwyn when she wanted something. "I just hope he's got everything figured out. I don't want to spend the next couple of weeks fooling around out there. Maybe someday he'll get the bloody thing finished and that will be the end of it. I just hope she floats, that's all."

We walked out of the coffee shop together, leaving Olwyn to go back upstairs to work.

"I hope he's got a bunch of oakum and a couple of good pumps," Owen said. He shook his head and a wry grin crept over his angularly handsome face. "I wouldn't be surprise if old Pete there hasn't built himself a submarine. Want to bet?"

"You could be right." I knew he was thinking, as I was, that

Pete just hadn't paid close enough attention to detail. His boat was congenitally flawed. He was going to have a lot of trouble keeping her afloat.

We asked for enough time off from work to get the job done, not an unusual request, figuring a couple of days tacked on to a weekend would be more than enough. One never knew, of course. We had seen other boats launched and knew that it was a task fraught with unforeseen problems and that once started, it had to be kept going. We also had to figure that Pete had probably not thought of everything. Now that we were committed, however, we would see it through, no matter what. We assured Pete of that.

The launching scheme had evolved over time and had been well tested. Many a good boat had been successfully set afloat over the years by using it. There was, in fact, no other way. Granted, most were not as big as *Monad*, but some were pretty substantial. At extreme low tide, anchors—the bigger the better and all that could be laid hands on—were set at the waterline, attached to which were cables leading up the beach. Chain hoists, again, whatever could be found, were attached to the cables on one end and to the boat cradle on the other end. Between tides we hauled on the chains, inching boat and cradle toward the water.

It took a lot of pulling across a flat, muddy beach from which we had spent half a day unearthing the biggest boulders and rolling them to one side. The anchors had to be drawn a long way into the mud before they gained enough purchase to be effective, and the travel of the chain-hoists was only a few feet before they had to be unhooked and extended again. The blocks were designed to be hung from overhead and to hoist things vertically. We had them lying horizontally on the beach where they became fouled with sand, seaweed, shells, driftwood and miscellaneous junk. Every few minutes, they jammed and had to be cleaned. As the incoming tides advanced, we had to vacate, leaving everything lying there. When they receded, all the stuff that had floated in had to be got rid of before we could recommence pulling.

There was only one really high tide, and if we missed it, we would have that much further to haul to catch the next one that would be significantly lower. We had calculated that highest tide would occur close on to six in the morning. By that time we had to have her down the beach, right to the water's edge, and hope she would lift off by high slack.

We worked all that day, hauling on the chains, resetting them and hauling some more. The cradle, creaking and groaning and threatening to upset, inched ever so slowly down the shingle. Olwyn brought lunch to be eaten while we waited for the tide to recede, huddled in a corner of the shed. It had been raining for days without let up and it was cold. I was drenched with sweat under my raingear and as soon as I stopped working the chill set in. My hands were raw from the sand on the chains; I had worn through my gloves in the first few hours. Owen and Pete were pretty much the same.

We worked frantically following the tide as it ebbed. It was hard to maintain enthusiasm. It started to wear thin as the afternoon wore away and the gloom of evening descended. We couldn't let up though. All through the night by the light of a few coal-oil lanterns we worked. The rain never even paused. By the final low-slack, we had given that last effort and she was in position, as close to the anchors as we could get her. We piled rocks on the cradle to keep it down while the incoming tide lifted the hull free of it. All we could do now was wait and hope she floated. Pete had arranged for a small towboat to hook on and tow her around to the townsite dock. It was standing by as a watery daylight crept slowly up the channel.

As the tide advanced, first tasting the keel and then licking its way up to the chines, Owen stood on a ladder, looked down inside and noted that water was starting to pour rather freely through the bottom—not entirely surprising.

"Man the pumps," he hollered, "she's coming in like a river!" Fortunately, Pete had not been so hard headed that he had not foreseen that this might happen—even though he'd sworn it wouldn't—and had borrowed a couple of hand pumps. He, Owen and I manned them, pumping furiously, spelling each other off.

She floated free, just barely, on the last few inches of tide. We had to decide then and there whether to chance trying to keep her afloat with the pumps while she was towed the mile to town or let her settle back onto her cradle and frantically try to jamb more caulking into her before the tide came in again. The thought of working and waiting for another tide was too formidable; we opted to pump like hell and get her to town.

We got her towed around and tied against the pilings of the townsite wharf. In the depth of water next to the wharf, even at high tide, she would go aground before she could sink all the way. Pete was still confident that what he had assured us all along would happen—she would soak up and the leaking would lessen. We were all pretty well exhausted by this time and I couldn't have cared less if she sank all the way to China. Owen and I went home to bed.

Tides came and went. Pete had borrowed an electric pump, one that could stay ahead of the leaks. She would settle until she grounded and then lift off when the pump emptied her. It was impossible to keep her dry unless someone was there to start the pump regularly. Owen and I stood pump watches with Pete, but our time ran out and we had to go to work.

The leaking slowed as the planking soaked up, but we knew that some of the seams would never swell enough, and we told Pete so. We were all there together. "Pete, you're going to have to pull her," Owen said, in no uncertain terms. "This is crazy. You can pump from now until doomsday and you still won't keep her afloat. You've got to fix her."

"Oh, I don't know. She's soaking up pretty good." Pete wasn't one to give in easily.

"Come on Pete, get her into the marine shop and caulk her," I said. "You're going to have to eventually. Why not save yourself a lot of time and trouble and do it now? We'll give you a hand."

"I'll see," was all he said.

Whether we had provided the impetus or whether he had arrived at the same conclusion on his own, I don't know, but next day he had her pulled on the marine shop ways without telling us. With the help of the professionals, he went to work on the bottom. They did what they could. However, without considerable work, work that Pete wasn't in a position to pay for, she would always leak...but she was better.

There were no end of suggestions—some pretty far out and delivered with wry humor.

One suggestion that Pete tried was to mix a bunch of dry cement and fine sawdust together and throw it over the side. Apparently, some of the mixture would get sucked into the leaks and gradually harden. It worked, a little at a time, and almost imperceptibly the leaking slowed.

I had to hand it to him, he did try to fix things. He got to the point where he only had to pump every six hours, so he was able to get most of a night's sleep. Eventually, he got it down to about eight hours. By this time, he had used several bags of cement, a lot of sawdust and all of his scheduled time off.

Monad sat there bobbing at the townsite float, not a very prepossessing sight. Pete continued working on her, under tarpaulins rigged on a spindly scaffolding, building the cabin and the interior furnishings—bunks, a settee and cupboards. We noticed a difference in him. He was morose and didn't want to talk about what he was doing. I guessed that he had been proven wrong so decisively that he was going to be a lot more cautious from here on with his comments about boat building. The starch had really gone out of him.

The day came when he had to buy an engine. By whatever reasoning, he settled on a Kermath 100-horsepower, four-cylinder marine type—a good enough choice. He couldn't just go and buy an engine though; he had to be clever. Somehow, he talked the Kermath people into granting him the exclusive agency for Ocean Falls. That meant that for every Kermath engine sold in the community he got a commission on it. He snickered when he told me. "These people around here don't know that it doesn't matter where they buy their engines, if they're Kermaths I make money on them."

The word must have got around. To the best of my knowledge, no other Kermath engine was ever sold in Ocean Falls from then until we left—almost a year.

Pete was fed up with boat building; all he wanted was to get *Monad* finished the easiest and quickest way possible and get rid of it. He had long ago decided to sell it.

The cabin was finished by fall. He had abandoned the Monk drawings as being too meticulous and had gone ahead with a cracker-box style of building, anything to get finished. It looked like a pretty amateurish job. He just had no eye for the clean flowing lines that separate boats from boxcars; the cabin stuck up like a doghouse. He built a wooden steering wheel during the following winter. It was no Maj Bennett wheel. It was a pentagon with five spokes sticking out of the flats. It was a pretty odd-looking wheel and trying to steer with it was something else, too.

Owen agreed to line up the engine and the V drive, a decision he regretted almost immediately. Pete had figured wrong and the engine bed was in the wrong place and at the wrong angle necessitating using two universal joints, one in each shaft. He bought Blood Bros., good quality universals, but even of them it was asking a lot because things were that far out of alignment. The universals were working at the outer limits of their capability. At low speeds they were okay, but as soon as the revolutions increased, they heated. Owen worked on them for long hours and then threw up his hands.

"You'll have to move the engine bed, that's all there is to it. I can't make it any better. It's either that or always run at half speed or slower. Do you want that?"

"I'm going to sell it anyway. We'll just take it easy, run slow. There's no need to go fast anyway. It should be alright just sailing it to Vancouver. Nobody will know the difference down there."

"Don't bet on it," said Owen, "but I can't do anything more with it."

"I'm not going to spend any more money. They'll be alright until we get to Vancouver. After I sell it, it won't matter. Let somebody else worry about it."

We took her out for a few trial runs—Pete wouldn't leave the wharf without me going along—never very far and always keeping the speed down. The hull design and an engine of that size swinging the specified propeller should have pushed her along in the neighborhood of twelve knots, but we were seldom able to log more than six. It wasn't much fun. Pete always explained, even when nobody asked, that our snail's pace was a gas-saving measure. I doubt he fooled anyone.

The interior outfitting was pretty spartan. Pete was out of money, so he put in only the essentials—a small sink with a pump from the fresh-water tank, an oil stove to cook on and heat the cabin and a couple of foam pads on the bunks. He did buy a compass, not a very good one but adequate. He didn't want to buy an anchor, he figured we wouldn't need one.

"We'll tie up at night, there's lots of wharves along the coast. We won't need to anchor."

"You get an anchor from somewhere or I don't go," I said.

He found one—I think he borrowed it—but there was no chain, just a length of rope maybe twenty-five or thirty feet. He was adamant that's all we needed.

He didn't have a dinghy either. He wasn't about to buy one, so I did. I found one, a sorry-looking thing, seemingly abandoned and lying on the end of the wharf. I asked a Native fisherman lounging nearby if he knew who owned it. He said, squinting at me through a curl of cigarette smoke drifting up past his eye, "That's my boat." The foxy look that suddenly appeared on his swarthy face made me kind of doubt it, but I had no way of knowing whether it was his or not. "I need a dinghy," I said, "one that I can get cheap and in a hurry. This one looks like it should be cheap. You want to sell it? I'll give you a couple of bucks for it."

"Couple of bucks ain't much money. Boat, any kind of boat, gotta be worth more than a couple of bucks."

"Three. How about three then?"

"Five's gotta be better than three, 'eh. Gimme five and she's yours, and I'll throw in the oars. Them is pretty good oars."

I gave him the five. He chuckled. "You better get that boat out of here in a hurry, 'eh." He headed up town, in the general direction of the pub. I wondered who actually owned the boat I'd just bought. It sure wasn't much of a boat, but at five bucks...

For the next couple of days I worked on it and got it to the point where I figured it would do in an emergency.

"We'll share expenses," said Pete, seriously. He'd obviously been thinking about it. "After all, I'm giving you a ride to Vancouver. There's gas, food and charts to buy, so we'll just split it down the middle."

"Forget it," I said. "I can ride in style on the *Cardena* for less than half the cost of the gas. I'll tell you what I will do though, I'll buy the food. You look after the rest, and I'll pilot you to Vancouver."

He finally agreed. He had to, I was the guy with the leverage.

We made it up to leave in early May. I gave my notice at the office. Pete had decided quite a while ago to quit. Olwyn and Lynda would follow in a few weeks, after we had got safely to Vancouver and sold the boat. Where they would go after that, I don't think either one of them had thought through. They had talked lately about going farming somewhere, but whether it had solidified into a firm plan, I had no idea. Somehow, I couldn't see Olwyn on a farm.

It would take us at least a week to make the trip, if we maintained the modest speed that Pete insisted was all *Monad* was capable of. I made a list of the groceries we would need, working out menus for each day. I intended to eat well, so it was a fairly long list.

I had been seeing a girl named Wendy, blonde, nice figure and smart, who worked in the company store—nothing serious, just someone to go to the show or have a beer with. She was a nice girl, easy-going, comfortable to be with, from somewhere up around Fernie. She'd traded the one mountain-ringed town where you could at least see the sky for this one where you couldn't. She'd been at the Falls for a year or more. For most of that time she had played house with a guy named Ed, figuring they would get married one day. Seemed, though, that Ed had got weary of the climate, his job and Wendy, all at about the same time. Seemed he'd also entered into some sort of arrangement with a waitress from the coffee shop. They'd bought themselves a pair of tickets on the *Charlotte*, packed their stuff and left. Wendy was left high and dry and smarting a bit. She wasn't ready to get into another relationship, but both of us being at loose ends we had drifted together and she had cried on my shoulder for a while. That was about all there was between us. A few nights before I was to leave, we were sitting in the pub going over my list. She suggested a few changes and additions.

"Come in first thing in the morning," she said, "when it isn't busy. I'll help you get it all together."

I showed up just after the store opened. We went around, list in hand, gathering up the various items, mostly nonperishable foodstuffs. We wouldn't have any refrigeration, so we would rely heavily on canned goods.

She installed herself at the cash register and started checking me through. She was an artist with that register. Her fingers flew, punching keys with one hand and sliding the cans and packages through with the other. I was getting a little uneasy at the amount of stuff I had. I began wondering if I had enough money in my pocket to pay for everything. Turned out there was no problem.

"Six dollars and fifteen cents," she announced, deadpan, her expression that typical of a bored checkout clerk, smoothing the smile-wrinkles at the corners of her mouth and turning down the lights in her eyes, but then I noticed an almost imperceptible wink.

I had trouble keeping my jaw from dropping. I paid her and carted my stuff out of the store, suffused with guilt. I borrowed a hand-truck and wheeled my boxes to the wharf. I then stopped by the liquor store and laid in a goodly supply of potions guaranteed to ward off chills and other maladies associated with traveling in small boats.

The next evening, Wendy and I had a couple more beers and then she came up to my room to help me pack. Among other things, we talked about living in small, isolated towns, about infidelity and abandonment. We didn't discuss the price of groceries.

I hollered at Pete. "Coffee's ready." He spat the but end of a home-roll over the side, clambered out of the engine compartment and came forward into the cabin.

"How're the universals behaving?" I asked.

He shrugged. "So far, they're alright. I gotta keep an eye on them though." He rummaged around, located a mug and poured from the bubbling pot. He didn't offer to pour any for me.

I thought again, while I worked my way through fresh coffee and a couple more sandwiches, about what I would do when this voyage ended. So far, I had been more concerned with getting out of Ocean Falls than what lay in the future. I had nothing planned beyond getting to Vancouver. Having a fairly substantial bank account had made me complacent, probably more so than was healthy. Money had a way of slipping through my fingers.

I had nothing lined up in the way of a job. I knew a few people, but they were not the kind of people who would be much help to me. They were people whom I had known briefly during the war, mainly people of the female gender whom I'd met while on leave and partied with. Yeah, some whose husbands had been overseas getting shot at while we partied. It was a different time then and different people. They were people I had forgotten about until now. The husbands, if they had survived, were sure to be back by now. The past was better left undisturbed.

But then there was Gunnar. I wondered what ever became of Gunnar and Gus. They could both be dead for all I knew. I hadn't heard of them since back in 1939, before I left for up coast. It might be worthwhile seeing if they were still around.

Oceans Falls. Pete's boat, *Monad*, 1949.

CHAPTER 18

Out of Ocean Falls

I crowded over to starboard, clear of the main channel, keeping close inshore on Hunter Island. Not that there was a lot of shipping, it was just that I didn't want to be bothered avoiding anything that was there. On our port side was King Island, a huge mountainous mass, where I had hunted deer. And where I had once got lost, the only time in my life, in its dense underbrush and meandering canyons. The sun was shining in the cabin windows and I sat, half asleep, slumped on the pilot stool with my back against the cabin bulkhead, giving the wheel a kick every once in a while to keep us from straying too far off course. My mind was not on the voyage ahead, instead it was scanning across the panorama of the previous ten years and mulling over the events of my leave-taking.

Pete was still standing down in the engine compartment, clutching his oil can like a weapon. Every once in a while he'd lean down and squirt some of its contents onto something I couldn't quite see, but suspected it was the universal joints. So far he had resisted any suggestion of a speed increase. His tobacco can was open, nestled in the corner of the hatch combing. He was chain-smoking hand-rolled cigarettes and looking unhappy.

The shoreline of gray rock and trees, almost vertical and dropping into deep water, ran straight for miles, unrelieved by indents or bulges. All I had to do was keep parallel and watch for deadheads. The engine snored along, running at no more than half speed. The traffic going in the opposite direction was sparse—one fisherman, the "pow, pow" of his one-lunger audible over the roar of our Kermath, and a single pleasure boat that had materialized out of an inlet and passed to port, hugging the far shore and moving slowly, most likely trolling. A towboat came foaming up the center of the channel passing well clear of us, too far to read her nameplate. I knew this had to be the easy part.

By afternoon we were abeam of Walker Point where Burke Channel broke the monotony of the green and gray port shoreline, running east-by-north along the southern reaches of King Island. Ahead, to starboard, was Kiltik Cove. Pete left the engine long enough to come into the cabin to eat a sandwich and drink a cup of coffee. He looked as though any good feelings he may have harbored about this trip had curdled, and he didn't say much. I knew his nerves were probably fiddle-string tight. I have never known anyone, before or since, who was so completely out of his element on the water. He didn't inquire about our course or where we were or anything like that; he had dumped the responsibility for getting us to Vancouver squarely on my shoulders. I had a pretty good idea that if we got into any kind of a bind, he wouldn't be a lot of help. Until now, I don't think he had fully appreciated the magnitude of the task he had set for himself, and me, and that there were real dangers involved. As soon as he was finished eating, he scurried aft, pumped the bilges, climbed down into the engine compartment and grabbed for tobacco and papers. Somehow, he seemed to feel more secure there.

The sky stayed clear. It was one of those perfect up-coast days of which there never seemed to be enough. My latent hangover was dissipating, but now I was suffering from lack of sleep and had trouble keeping my eyes open. I had thought that Pete and I would share the helm, switching over every couple of hours, and I would be able to catch forty winks. It was not to be; he wouldn't touch the wheel. I did get him to fire up the Coleman stove and brew some coffee after the first pot ran out. Without it, I would have been dead to the world just sitting there.

As Hakai Passage opened up to starboard, the swells, running in obliquely from the west, were abeam and we rolled a bit, not much, but enough to make Pete look more worried than ever.

"The waves are getting awfully big," he hollered, over the roar of the engine.

"These aren't waves," I said. "Wait and see what they're like in Queen Charlotte Sound." I guess that didn't reassure him much,

241

just made him a little more nervous knowing there were bigger ones ahead.

By four o'clock we were well into Fitzhugh Sound, running close to Hecate Island. The afternoon wasn't waning any faster than I was. I was ready to quit for the day. I had planned to anchor for the night in Safety Cove on Calvert Island. It was the only logical safe anchorage, without detouring across into the maze of inlets that laced the mainland coast. Whether I was half asleep and not keeping a close enough watch, I don't know, but somehow I missed the entrance. The mountain sides were folded, one over the other, giving the appearance of a solid wall of green; I suspect that, due to the events of the previous evening, my perception wasn't as sharp as it should have been. I just didn't see the opening. I guess I really didn't expect it quite so soon either. We had gone another few miles before I realized we were nearing the southern tip of Calvert Island and the open water of Queen Charlotte Sound. There was nothing for it, but to come about and backtrack. I finally found the narrow passage as dusk was settling in.

There were a couple of gill-netters anchored to one side of the small, well-protected basin; we dropped anchor away from them as far inside as we could get. There were some old, rotting boom-sticks, but nothing we could get hold of to tie to. Fortunately, the water was only about three fathoms deep, so we had enough anchor rope to reach bottom.

What Pete didn't realize when he was finding us an anchor, was that any anchor needs the weight of its cable to keep its shank flat to the bottom and its flukes biting into the mud. We didn't have any chain, just the rope, so we were dependent on the weight of the anchor alone to keep us in one place. It would take a pretty heavy anchor to hold a boat the size of *Monad*; ours wasn't heavy enough—not by far. The weather was calm, though, so I figured we would be all right for the night. I didn't have much alternative. It was the only anchor we had.

We opened a few cans and made coffee. By this time it was dark, and we turned on the cabin light while we ate and cleaned up—a convenience we would regret having used. We turned in about nine o'clock. I set the alarm clock for midnight and took a couple of bearings on the shore so I would know whether we were dragging or not. I must have gone dead to the world as soon as my head hit the pillow. I came awake, as though ascending out of a long tunnel, with the alarm clock ringing its head off. It took a few moments to sort out where I was and what was making the noise. I looked out through the side window at the shoreline. The sky was clear overhead, and there was enough reflected light to see that we were not where we had been when I went to sleep. We were dragging, and the ebbing tide was taking us toward the mouth of the cove.

"Hey Pete," I hollered, "we're dragging anchor."

"Yeah, yeah...okay, it'll be all right. There's lots of room," said Pete, mumbling from the forward cabin.

"We won't be all right if we land up on the shore," I said. "We had better move further back inside." I went on deck and pulled up our next-to-useless anchor. I hit the starter button, with the intent of running back to our original anchorage. Nothing happened. The engine gave a grunt and that was all. I figured out what was wrong. The luxury of light, while we ate supper, had drained the battery to the point that it wouldn't turn the engine over. There wasn't a whole lot I could do in the dark, so I found the oars from the dinghy and paddled. *Monad* was a heavy boat and it took awhile to get us back to where we had been. Pete didn't stir. I dropped the anchor and went back to bed. This time, I set the alarm for three o'clock. When it went off and I looked out, we hadn't moved.

Pete, banging hatch covers and working the hand pump, at about eight o'clock, woke me. We still hadn't moved from where I had last dropped the anchor so we made breakfast and took our time eating it.

"You know the battery is down and wouldn't start the engine last night," I said.

Pete just shrugged. "It'll be okay. It's probably just a loose connection or something."

"I don't think so," I said. "I think we ran it down last night with the cabin light. We had it on quite awhile and it's a pretty big bulb."

He looked dubious. "I doubt using that little bit of light would drain the battery. It's probably a loose connection. I'll check everything over."

"I hope you're right," I said, unconvinced. "Whenever you are ready to go, let me know." I relaxed against the cabin bulkhead with a cup of coffee. Pete opened the engine hatch and disappeared

243

down under the deck. I could hear him grunting around and cursing as he bumped into things in the confined space.

It was nice sitting there in the cockpit drinking coffee. There was no wind and the sun was shining. The other boats had departed sometime in the early morning and it was quiet, except for the usual squawking of seagulls and the music of ripples slapping the planking. My ailments of the previous day had cured themselves; a night's sleep, broken though it was, had worked wonders. I was almost looking forward to the trip ahead.

"Well, I've been over all the connections and tightened them; it should start all right now," said Pete, emerging like an inquisitive groundhog.

"Okay, let's go," I said.

I depressed the starter button. Same result as in the night—a grunt, no more.

Pete didn't usually swear much, but he did now. He called on all the gods of engines, batteries and boats in general, exhorting them to give him a break. I tended to sympathize with him. We were a long way from a shop or a jumpstart.

"Have you ever started it by hand cranking?" I asked.

"No, I haven't, but I guess there's no other way right now, so we might as well give it a try."

There wasn't a whole lot of room to turn a crank, but by kneeling, crouched under the rear decking, it was possible. We took turns. For a while it seemed hopeless—not a sign of life. Then there was a puff of smoke at the exhaust pipe. A couple more turns and it caught, faltered and then settled down to a lusty rumbling. It was a relief. I had visions of imploring some fisherman to tow us back to Ocean Falls. I cringed at *that* thought; the loss of time I could live with, the loss of face was something else. I think scuttling *Monad* and going down with her would have been preferable.

I went forward to pull up the anchor. Oddly enough, it now seemed to weigh a ton. It got heavier and heavier the more I pulled. I realized it had fouled something, likely the reason we hadn't dragged anymore during the night. I engaged the clutch and moved cautiously ahead, trying to pull at a different angle—same result. By the feel of it, it had snagged an old cable lying on the bottom. It took a while, but eventually, by pulling it up as far as our combined strength was capable of and then suddenly letting it go, it came loose.

I pointed our head at the opening and threaded our way back into Fitzhugh Sound. It was just after ten o'clock.

To the south hung a bank of clouds, suspended no more than the height of a tall spruce above the water. Had I been seeing it as a shore dweller, its beauty would have entranced me. The fog, a gossamer curtain, was diffusing the sunlight and imparting a dreamlike quality to the seascape ahead. It was the kind of illusive scene that artists are compelled to try to capture with paint and canvas, but, invariably, fail. Having dabbled at art, I was intrigued, but as the not-too-confident pilot of an unsound boat, I was nervous. I would have been a good deal happier had it not been there. I could see a long way underneath it, and as long as it remained stationary we would be alright, but if it settled, we would be in trouble; we wouldn't see anything.

By 11:30, we were clear of the southern tip of Calvert Island and into the open water of Queen Charlotte Sound. The fog was still hanging, but underneath, in the distance, I could see Egg Island. I took a compass bearing that would ensure that we would pass well to starboard of it, plotting a straight-line course for Hope Island and Bull Harbour, our destination for the night.

We were rolling a bit in the beam swell and Pete's face was showing increased consternation.

"If we could close the engine hatches, we could pull the rowboat up on deck and make better time," I suggested.

"Yeah, but I wouldn't be able to see what was going on, and if those universal joints started to heat up I wouldn't know, and then maybe they would seize up," he replied.

"At least, let me speed up a bit. It'll ride a lot smoother if we can make a few more knots."

"No, I don't think we had better. We're doing fine. It's not as if we were in a hurry." He twisted another cigarette and lit it.

He can't have been comfortable standing there, hour after hour, half in and half out of the hatch. As we rolled, he had to continually push against the hatch covers to keep them from flopping closed. From what I could tell, the universals had not heated at all, and increasing speed beyond our snail's pace probably wouldn't do anything drastic. There was not much I could do to convince him to try it though.

Egg Island passed abeam, and then we were off Cape Caution.

I got another compass bearing. We would pass to starboard of Storm Islands and Pine Island, staying close enough to see the lighthouse beam if the fog thickened—a condition I had noticed happening for the last hour—but far enough off that we wouldn't be set onto them by the westerly swell. The port shoreline was not as distinct as it had been, and the ceiling was lowering, but as long as I held the course I had set, I was confident we would find Bull Harbour. I estimated it was still three hours away, but I could no longer see the low outline of Hope Island.

The beam swell was picking up and we were rolling more. Pete was having trouble with the engine hatches. With every roll they tried to fall shut, and he had to fight them. The rowboat had water in it and it was dragging along like a sea anchor. Between us we pulled it up over the stern and dumped most of it, but even empty it pulled pretty hard.

"How are we doing for fuel?" I asked.

"Okay, I think. I had it figured that we would have plenty to take us to Bull Harbour, but maybe I should dip the tanks and find out."

He came forward into the cabin in a little while. He looked puzzled.

"I think were out of gas," he said. "I don't know how we could be, but the tanks are almost empty."

"How can we be out of gas?" I almost shouted. "Were the tanks full when we left?"

"Yeah, they were, plumb full, right up to the top. I don't understand how we could have used so much."

"The rowboat...dragging that bloody rowboat, that is what's done it. If we had got that thing up on deck where it belongs we wouldn't have used so much gas."

Pete's face, normally long and mournful, was now more so. I knew how he felt. A big knot was forming in the middle of my stomach. This was not in the script. Running out of fuel had never crossed my mind.

"Maybe we should just cut it loose and leave it. It'll sink pretty soon. We don't need it anyway," said Pete.

"We can't do that. If the engine quits and we start drifting up onto the rocks, we might be damn glad to have it. And besides, we can't just leave it drifting for someone to run into. It's made of wood and it won't sink, not for a long time," I said.

"Well, what're we going to do?"

"We are going to close those hatches, we are going to pull it up on deck and we are going to keep going until we run out of gas—unless, of course, you have a better idea," I said.

He went aft, mumbling, and closed the hatches. We pulled the dinghy up and laid it crosswise. It would only take a moment to boost it back into the water if the need arose.

That we had run headlong into the thorny edges of a predicament, there was little doubt in my mind. The fog was becoming thicker and the water and sky were a uniform gray making it difficult to tell where one left off and the other began. Gone was the translucent beauty of the morning.

The engine continued to rumble along, but for how long I didn't want to guess.

The only thing to do was to hold to the bearing I had plotted and, if the gas held out, we would eventually find Hope Island. I estimated the visibility at about a half a mile, enough that we wouldn't run right up on it.

Pete, unable to get down inside the engine hatch, now paced the cabin or stood peering ahead, smoking one cigarette after another.

"Why are we turning?" he asked, alarmed.

I looked at him, trying to understand what he meant.

"We're not," I said. "Why? What do you mean turning? We're steering a straight course. Look at the compass. Look at the wake."

"It looks like we're turning clockwise. Are you sure we're not turning?"

"I'm sure," I said.

Then I guessed what was happening. I said, "It's one of the oldest tricks in the book, an optical illusion. In fog, if you gaze at quartering swells long enough you'll swear that your boat is turning. You have to have implicit faith in the compass. Ignore all else. Steer by the compass. If you don't, you'll wind up going in circles."

"I never would have believed it. It still looks like were turning, but we're going straight. It's hard to believe," said Pete.

"Do you want to try steering for a few minutes," I asked.

"No. No, I don't think so." He shied away from the wheel as if it was evil. He looked horrified.

"Help me keep a lookout then, there could be boats around and we won't see them until were right onto them, especially if they are big and moving fast."

I concentrated on the landward side where there were things to run into if we were being set eastward by the swell. I caught the first suggestion of surf breaking at the farthest limit of visibility on the port bow. It had to be Storm Island. I kept an eye on it, trying not to lose it in the gray, flat light. As we got closer, I could see the low black outline of rock, and I was sure. It was the only thing there that it could be. We were still on course.

"There's a boat!" shouted Pete, pointing over to starboard.

A dark bulk was angling in on us at an alarming rate. I put the wheel hard over, and as *Monad* swung, I got ready close the throttle and disengage the clutch, or do whatever else was called for in the way of evasive action. We rolled in the swell as what turned out to be a big seiner bore down on us.

Pete was out of the cabin like a shot and standing on the deck waving both arms frantically. They must have been keeping a pretty good lookout; they saw us almost immediately. They swung in close and cut their diesel. The name on the bow said she was the *Pacific Ranger* out of Vancouver. They stayed a half a cable's length off, and we rolled together, mushing in the small sea. Three figures appeared and stood looking curiously at us. The person I took to be the skipper, a young slim guy wearing a baseball cap, came out of the wheelhouse.

"Hey, are you all right?" he hollered.

I left the wheel and went out on deck just as Pete replied, "No we're not, we're out of gas, we don't know where we are and the waves are awful big."

"That's not quite right," I called, nettled, "I know where we are, but we are short of gas. We intend making Bull Harbour tonight. How far away are we, do you know? We're making about six knots."

"At that rate, you're about an hour and a half away. Do you have enough gas to get there?" I looked at Pete. He shrugged.

"We don't really know," I said. "It'll be tight."

"Look, we're going to anchor in the lee of Pine Island for the night. This fog should lift again by morning. Why don't you anchor there with us and see what it's like then? You could get lost in it right now and if you don't have a lot of gas, it could be bad. It's getting thicker and thicker all the time."

Pete was nodding wholehearted assent, so I said, "That's probably a real good idea. If you know where it is, we'll follow you."

He waved and went back into the pilothouse. The thrum of his diesel picked up and he swung away from us. I engaged the clutch, opened the throttle and took after him. He was moving a lot faster than we had been and I had to keep inching the throttle open to keep up to him.

"Hey, slow down," said Pete.

"If we are going to follow this guy we have to be able to keep up to him. We'll lose him in the fog, if we aren't careful."

Then suddenly, we were running up on him. He had stopped and was waving at us from the wheelhouse window. I slammed the throttle closed. A massive, dark shape loomed ahead, moving at an unbelievable speed across our path. It resolved itself into a big ocean-going tug, towing a string of empty barges. It must have been making twenty knots. I could hear the low drumbeat of its engines coming up through our hull. The fog enveloped it again within a few seconds. I was relieved. Had the fisherman not been ahead of us, we just may not have seen it. We were crossing right through the north-south shipping lane—not a very safe place to be in fog.

The foghorn was blaring from the top of Pine Island and we homed in on it. The seiner let go his anchor as we came up along side of him.

"How much water under us?" I called.

"About fifty fathoms," replied the deckhand, who was making the anchor cable fast on the foredeck.

"Fifty fathoms, did you say?"

"Yeah, fifty fathoms. Why?"

"We don't have that much cable." I didn't tell him how much we had.

"Well, why don't you just tie on to us for the night?" suggested the skipper, emerging from the wheelhouse.

"That would be great," I said. "In fact, it's about all we can do."

"Yeah, that would be great," echoed Pete.

We made fast, fore and aft. In the lee of the island, there was little swell. There was no wind and the fog settled in thick and woolly. Tonight, though, I wouldn't have to stand an anchor watch; the people on the *Pacific Ranger* would look after that detail. There were five of them and they stood watches.

Rather than take a chance on using the cabin light and depleting the battery again, I dug out a Coleman gas lantern. By its yellow glow, I went to work in the galley. It had suddenly dawned on me that the miserable feeling in my middle was hunger. What with the tension of the day I had forgotten to eat, so I went to some effort to cook a proper meal, even if it did come out of cans.

While I was cooking, Pete went visiting next door. When I called him to come and eat, he seemed a lot more jovial than he had been all day. He was also lugging a five-gallon can of gas that he had made a deal for.

We ate and cleaned up. With food in me and a feeling of security, at least for the night, I relaxed. I crawled into my berth and lay there listening to the sounds of the moored boats: the squeak as they rubbed together and the slap of water on the hulls. Rising above these normal night noises was the mournful wail of the Pine Island foghorn. The next thing I knew it was six in the morning, light was easing into the cabin and the seiner was getting ready to up anchor.

The fog had risen to masthead height but, unlike yesterday, it was dark and solid looking. However, the outline of Hope Island, the land beyond and the port shoreline was crisp and clean. Bull Harbour seemed almost close enough to touch. My spirits rose.

Pete poured the five gallons of gas into our tanks and returned the gas can to the deck of the seiner. With my fingers crossed, I punched the starter button. The engine sprang to life. At least something had gone right; the battery had recharged.

We thanked the skipper and crew of the seiner, let go our mooring lines and drifted clear of them. I set a course for Shadwell Pass, the narrow corridor we would thread to circle Hope Island and find Bull Harbour on the southwest side—an indent off Goletas Channel. We were nestled alongside the wharf by ten o'clock.

CHAPTER 19

Away from the Sea

A bone-hard westerly wind got up shortly after we left Bull Harbour, scouring out the fog and letting in the sun. It chased us down Goletas Channel and into Queen Charlotte Strait. Had I been able to crank a few more revs out of the Kermath, *Monad* could have made good use of it, but Pete wouldn't let me. Instead, she mushed along making me steer her all the way. I had played captain and told Pete in no uncertain terms that the dinghy was going to ride rather than be towed. I didn't want it yawing all over the place and acting like it had a mind of its own. He didn't accept gracefully. He stayed outside, coming in only to pour himself a cup of coffee. He didn't speak, so I didn't. By four o'clock we were off Alert Bay. I'd had enough, so I eased in behind the breakwater, tied *Monad* between a couple pleasure boats and called it a day. I wouldn't have to stand an anchor watch.

The business of anchoring was a concern I knew I was going to have to do something about, but I had been letting it slide. What we would have done last night in behind Pine Island, had we not been able to tie to *Pacific Ranger*, I had no idea. But I was sure that sooner or later we were going have to anchor in more than a fifteen or twenty feet of water—something we just weren't equipped to do. Still mulling it over, I climbed up the companionway to the dock. I needed to stretch my legs on solid ground.

"I'm going for a walk," I hollered down to Pete, who was tinkering, as usual, down inside the engine compartment.

"How long're you going to be gone?" He looked alarmed.

I had a devilish urge to tell him I wasn't coming back, that I was going to wait and catch the next CPR boat, but instead I said, "Just long enough to get my land legs back."

"If there's a store up there, get me a can of tobacco and a package of cigarette papers."

"What kind?"

"McDonalds, if they've got it...any kind of papers."

"Anything else?"

He shook his head.

In the general store, a place with a blend of odors that said it sold everything, my eye fell on a coil of brand new half-inch Manila rope. I debated. I hated to spend the money, but gut feel told me that buying a length of it would be buying good insurance. If I needed it, I would need it real bad. So what the hell... The price wasn't going to break me, so I forked out for a hundred feet. It wasn't going to work as well as chain, but I couldn't see buying chain. At least it would get to the bottom of most of the places we might have to anchor. I carted it back, debating whether to splice it or just knot it to the piece attached to the anchor. Pete was standing in the cockpit, one foot on the rail, smoking and gazing out across the harbor. I guess he didn't hear me coming. He jumped like somebody had goosed him when I threw the coil onto the foredeck.

"What the hell're you gonna do with the rope?"

"I'm going to tie it to that tag end piece that's on the anchor," I said.

"What for?" He snorted, "We won't need it. We'll just tie up like we are here. What's wrong with just tying up, eh? Why're you so worried about that bloody anchor?"

I handed him the tobacco and papers. "You owe me $2.55."

He made no motion toward his wallet. He just pried the lid off the can and started to roll a cigarette. I let it go. I didn't want to argue over a couple of bucks. And no matter what I said, I wouldn't get through to him about having a proper anchor.

Next morning, the westerly picked up again blowing harder as the day advanced; it followed us down Johnstone Strait. Running at little more than half speed, *Monad* wallowed. Pete paced, baffled by the dinghy that wouldn't let him into his beloved engine compartment. I let him stew. Running at this speed, I was pretty sure nothing was going to happen to the universals. One thing he could do was keep the bilges dry. He worked out some of his frustration on the pump handle. Working the way *Monad* was, she was taking more water than usual.

We'd gassed up at Alert Bay, so I wasn't worried about fuel. I only wanted to make Shoal Bay on East Thurlow Island by nightfall anyhow. We could fuel-up there before attempting the narrows.

Had I a better boat under me and a more boat-smart and congenial partner, it would have been nice to have explored this section of the coast. I'd sort of had that in the back of my mind when I was contemplating this junket, but the idea had withered. Now, in the light of the way things were going, Pete would have had a fit had I even suggested it. However, I still thought that it would be a nice thing to do sometime.

On the mainland side was a dogtooth row of snow-capped mountains running down into a vast network of inlets and channels that, according to the chart, wandered inland for miles. There would be fishing camps, hand-logging operations and just quiet water where we could have crab fished or lazed around looking at the scenery. I remembered back to my first sight of this coast from the *Catala*. I hadn't changed my opinion; it had a grandeur unmatched anywhere. And since that day ten years ago I'd seen a lot of real-estate—with or without ocean frontage.

I unrolled the chart that I would need to pilot us through Chancellor and Cordero Channels. I had to give Pete his due, he had bought a complete set of charts. I liked charts and maps—always had. And I was grateful to those in the navy who had shown me how to use them to pilot a ship in coastal waters.

Lieutenant Porter, a watch officer aboard *Bellchasse*, had given me the basics. A big man with a broad face, he could have passed for Mussolini had the shadows on his jowls been black instead of red. The resemblance, however, was superficial; there was nothing of strut and swagger about him. He was a mild-mannered, kindly man who had been a schoolteacher in civilian life. And he saw no reason to suppress his instinctive desire to impart knowledge just because he'd joined the service. With him, the barrier between commissioned and noncommissioned ranks was all but transparent. We'd stood countless bridge watches together, he as watch officer and me as messenger, steersman or lookout. As messenger, I usually had little to do. Lounging against the chart table, I'd watch him plot our course, using parallel rules and dividers, my curiosity drawing me closer and closer until I was practically hanging over the chart. My obvious interest was enough. He began showing me. Thereafter whenever an opportunity presented itself, I'd asked questions—not just of Porter, but of others on *Bellchasse* and, later, on *Capilano*. Most times they were answered civilly, other times I'd wished I'd kept my curiosity to myself. Over time I had pieced together a working knowledge of charts and piloting.

Those I had talked to who had navigated these waters before, Matt Williamson for one, were unanimous in the opinion that the Ucaltas Rapids was by far the more friendly route than Seymour Narrows, even though longer. Both were known for their strong tidal currents, but Seymour was considered more dangerous, Ripple Rock being the main hazard. Both could be traversed safely if done so at slack tides, but the slacks didn't last long and if we missed Seymour by even a few minutes we could be in trouble. I had mulled it over and then opted for prudence; we would take the slightly longer route, since we weren't in a hurry anyway. I toyed with the idea of visiting Kelsey Bay, but then decided instead to stay to port of Helmecken Island, the more direct route into Chancellor Channel. The wind dropped and the sea smoothed as we got under the lee of Hardwicke Island, so I suggested to Pete he could boost the dinghy over the stern and tow it, that is if he thought he needed to get into the engine compartment. He jumped at the chance. We snored along for the rest of the afternoon.

Shoal Bay was not much. A wharf and a few buildings, one of which had a sign on it that said it was a hotel. There was a corrugated sheet metal shed on the end of the wharf with a clutch of red drums by the door that suggested boat fuel. We probably had enough to get us to Powell River, but why take a chance and wind up like we did in Queen Charlotte Sound. This time, Pete and I were thinking along the same lines.

A thickset man in spattered overalls was painting an old rowboat that had become a planter and was full of geraniums. He left off this chore to fill up some five-gallon cans. While he worked the pump we found out he also ran the hotel and just about everything else in this little isolated bay.

When Pete came back from returning the cans, he told me he was going to spend the night in the hotel. I was a little surprised, but if that's what he wanted to do...

"Have a good meal for a change and sleep in a proper bed," is the way he explained it.

It didn't say a lot for my cooking, but the bed, yes. He was sleeping in a bunk under the foredeck, his choice, which was cramped for a man of his length.

The idea had its good points. However, I was a little uneasy about leaving *Monad* unattended. My bunk in the main cabin was pretty comfortable and I was looking forward to what I had figured out for supper, even though it would come out of cans, so I told Pete to go ahead and enjoy. I would stay aboard and look after things.

I had pumped the bilges and was lounging in the cockpit when my eye fell on something that for a moment didn't register. Then it did. It was a length of chain lying among the grapefruit-sized cobbles on the beach. Only a couple of feet of it were out of the water. It looked like it might be a boom chain, or part of one. I clambered over the side and gave it a tug. It was heavy, but it came free. It was a boom chain, at least it had been, but somewhere it had lost its towing ring and toggle. It was about six feet long, well rusted and barnacle encrusted, but sound. I doubted anyone would it miss it.

I hauled it inboard and sat in the cockpit splicing it between the original piece of anchor rope and the new piece I had bought in Alert Bay. By the time darkness dropped down I had it done and stowed.

The tide tables said low slack tide would occur close on eight in the morning. I had that firm in my mind as I put my head down. We would be down to the narrows in plenty of time if we got away about seven. It was quiet, only the slap of small ripples against the hull and the creak of wood against rubber bumpers. I drifted off thinking that once we'd passed the narrows there wasn't a great deal to contend with until we got to the Lions Gate Bridge and Burrard Inlet.

I awoke with a start, glanced at the clock that said seven-thirty. I had slept in. This morning of all mornings I would sleep late. Pete must have slept late too. I scrambled into my clothes and headed for the hotel. Pete was sitting in the small diningroom. He'd had his breakfast, and was dawdling over coffee and talking to the manager, who was sitting at the table cradling a huge mug with "Dad" inscribed on it.

"Pete, we've got to get moving. We're going to miss the tide, if we haven't already," I said, feeling guilty. "It's my fault; I slept in. We have to leave right away."

He brushed aside my intrusion, barely giving me a glance. "We should be all right," he said, seeming unconcerned. He went on talking.

The manager looked at the wall clock. "Yeah, I don't know how many knots you make, but, yeah...you'd better get started." He got up from the table, prompting Pete to do the same.

By the time we got away, it was pushing eight o'clock.

I could feel the current as we crossed Nodales Channel and headed on down to Big Bay. Things got busier as we approached Stuart Island. The currents were violent and were setting us one way and then the other. The tide was bent on filling Bute Inlet and every nook and cranny in that coastline in the shortest time possible. Seemed we were going uphill against it. The shore was barely crawling past, so I cracked the throttle a notch or two. This brought Pete into the wheelhouse looking worried.

"Hey, you better watch it. Take it easy, 'eh."

"I've got to, we'll be going backwards if I don't," I said. "And we'll be up on shore if I can't maintain steerage way."

I kept moving the throttle forward until I had the Kermath wide open. We barged through whirlpools, rips and cross currents bucking a tide that was now running full bore. There were a couple of tense moments as we were set toward the rocky shore.

Once past the Narrows and Stuart Island, the writhing quieted down a bit. We were still running against a river of tidewater, but at least it was going more or less in one direction. I relaxed a bit. My only anxiety now—and I was sure it was Pete's—was how were the universals holding up at full throttle. They may not have been quite as ready to self-destruct as he would have had me believe, but I knew they weren't 100 percent either. I didn't voice my concern; I figured he was worried enough.

Abeam of Rendezvous Islands, I was able to throttle back and still maintain a respectable steerageway. We were through the worst and the tide was slowing. We boosted the dinghy into the water and Pete dove into the engine compartment. I don't know what he expected, but everything was fine—no bits and pieces laying around, no roasted universal joints. I pumped the Coleman stove and set the coffee pot on it.

The run on down to Powell River was uneventful. I parked *Monad* in behind the big solid breakwater that was crowded with fishing boats and all manner of pleasure craft. Pete had to mention that these tie-up places were arranged pretty handily down the coast. "Person really doesn't need to anchor at all." I agreed that it was nice that things had panned out that way so far—except for Pine Island, of course.

While Pete topped up the fuel tanks, I laid out the chart for what I hoped was our last leg. It would probably be a full day from Powell River right through to Port Moody. There were a couple of logical stopping places, but we were getting close enough that if we could go the distance, it would be preferable to spending one more night just for the sake of stopping. I decided to let the weather dictate. The westerly was still blowing, but not too violently.

It was still blowing next morning, and with a tad more muscle I thought. However the sky was mostly clear, just a few long streamers of white stretched across it. I made breakfast and cleaned up. I set my third cup of coffee on the shelf above the wheel, hit the starter button and, when the engine settled down, I eased *Monad* out from behind the breakwater.

I was right. The westerly had more muscle. There was a good chop running between Texada Island and the mainland. Knowing how our powerplant had behaved yesterday, I ran with a little more throttle, confident nothing was going to fly apart. Even so, we were getting a bumpy ride.

As we cleared the end of Texada Island the full force of the wind hit us; it had built considerably. *Monad* began pitching and yawing in earnest. Pete, braced in a corner of the cockpit looked a little green. He wasn't smoking—a sure sign all was not well.

I had a couple of choices—keep going or pull in somewhere and wait until the westerly abated. How long that might be, was anybody's guess. There was Half Moon Bay or Sechelt. I didn't know anything about either of them, but from the chart, they both looked pretty open to the weather.

"What do you think, Pete. Do you want to keep her going, or should we try to get in to some kind of shelter and wait it out?"

He didn't answer for a moment. He was watching the other boat traffic, most of which was commercial: big fishermen and tow-boats. The only pleasure craft were under sail and were substantial boats.

"Maybe we should tie up someplace until things quiet down a bit," he said. "These waves are awful big." He looked pretty scared. I had to sympathize with him. Anyone who "goes down to the sea in ships," at sometime or another gets scared.

"Trouble is," I said. "If we don't pull in to Sechelt, there's really nowhere else, and we might as well keep going."

"Why don't we go into Sechelt then?" We can tie up there. Why don't we? Maybe the wind will go down."

Sechelt turned out to be pretty exposed. A small indent in the coastline, it offered a little protection, but there was nothing to really get behind...no breakwater or docks. We'd have to anchor if we were going to stay there. I eased in as far as possible to the beach, which was mostly sand, and dropped anchor. If we were over good ground it just might hold us. I paid out most of the line I had bought and I could feel the weight of that old boom chain hit bottom. It would act as a shock absorber and give the anchor flukes a chance to haul into the bottom. I saw Pete watching me, so I said, I just had to, "An anchor's a pretty handy thing to have when you can't tie up anywhere." He just grunted.

It seemed to be holding. After half an hour we hadn't moved. Now, if the wind didn't get any worse...

It didn't get any worse, but it didn't get any better, either. It blew all night and all the next day. Just sitting there doing nothing was pretty boring. We read and slept. We didn't talk much. There was time to do a lot of thinking.

I wondered if I would ever see Ocean Falls again. I had left before and gone back. Two years ago I had actually gone job seeking while I was on holidays, testing the waters so to speak. I had found one as a mechanic with Brown and McDade, a mining company. "Must have knowledge of diesel and electricity," the ad said. They had hired me without knowing I hadn't yet quit Pacific Mills. They gave me a ticket on the Kettle Valley Railway and sent me to Beaverdell in the Okanagan. Before I left Vancouver I purchased a second-hand book on diesel and read it on the train. When I arrived, that's what I knew about diesel.

The job was up on a mountainside at a silver mine—the Highland Bell. The master mechanic, an unshaven corpulent man, looked at me with a jaundiced eye. I got the impression he didn't like what he saw. I had been told in the hiring office that he wasn't the easiest man to get along with, and within the first few hours I could understand why.

He pointed at a pile of carefully milled lumber and said, "That there is a 15,000-gallon water tank; it has to be assembled, over there, on that flat spot. Do you think you can manage that?" His look and tone told me he didn't think I could.

I was something of an electrician and I could operate a hydro-electric powerhouse, skills that didn't really qualify me for the job at hand. But by God, if he wanted a tank put together, that's what he would get.

And put it together I did.

I labored in the hot sun, high above the valley, for three days, fitting the curved boards together like a jigsaw puzzle. At night I slept in the bunkhouse (I couldn't help but think I had slipped back in time about ten years} with the dozen or so others, mostly miners who worked underground. I had little interest in them, and their only interest in me was limited to whether I could play baseball. Seemed that baseball was the only recreation around, and the Highland Bell team needed another outfielder. They had a big game coming up against their main competition, the team from Carmi. I wondered what they did in winter.

I would lie on my bunk thinking of my comfortable room at Ocean Falls, my friends and the civilized lifestyle I had enjoyed there. It was such a solid, if not exciting, way of life, one I could continue until retirement if I wanted to endure the rain and isolation. I thought deeply. Then with the tank finished and full of water that wasn't leaking out, I told the master mechanic I was leaving. He didn't seem shattered. He paid me and wished me well. I think he was a little surprised I had succeeded.

The Kettle Valley Railway delivered me back to Vancouver, and when my holiday was up, I went back to Ocean Falls. Although in some ways I was glad to be back, I couldn't help but taste the sour ashes of defeat. I hadn't had the courage to persist and make a place for myself somewhere else. I, like dozens of others who had made the attempt, had come scurrying back to the security and benevolence of Mother Company.

My bunk on *Monad* was also a good place to lie awake and think. Funny thing about Pete, awake he was a worrier, but as soon as he crawled into his berth under the foredeck, he died. *Monad* could have sunk under him and he'd never have known the difference. I lay there listening to him snore and staring at the deckhead in the dim reflected light, trying to get a grip on my future. This time I had burned my bridges; I couldn't go back. I had quit. I had quit with this voyage uppermost in my mind and crowding out thoughts of what lay beyond. Now it was just a day away from being over. So, what now? Even though Beaverdell hadn't panned out, the country it was in had hung in my mind. Its arid beauty, that at the time I hadn't paid that much attention to, kept coming back. The more I thought, the more I became determined that my search for a place to settle and earn a living would take me into big blue sky country, like that of the Okanagan. I wanted to walk outside without a raincoat or a hat. I wanted a place where tools didn't rust and silver didn't turn black overnight. I would leave the coast and dry out, for a while anyway.

Could I leave the sea behind for good? I didn't know. And could I leave behind the friendships I had come to depend on? I had no idea whether I would ever again see Dick Green and his sister, Kay, and brother-in-law Cecil Morrow; George Lee and his wife, Chris, and their two children, Ken and Linda, and of course, their parents and grandparents Dwight and Daisy Lee; or Hank Adams and his sister, Nita—all people who had become more family than friends. I had corresponded with Arline during the remainder of the war and for a couple of years afterwards. She had left Ocean Falls and was working in Vancouver. I had seen her when she came home for holidays, and when I was in Vancouver we had gone out, usually with a group. I wouldn't see her again; that I knew. That part of my life was over. And although I would cherish the years I had known her, I knew our relationship had passed from realism into memory.

The wind had abated. It still had some punch, but it was dropping. We up anchored and set a course for the Lions Gate Bridge. This was heavy traffic country.

I had looked down on the Narrows from Stanley Park so often, I thought I knew that stretch of water by heart; we would just pass underneath the bridge and continue sightseeing up Burrard Inlet to Port Moody. How little I really knew of it, soon became apparent.

Again we were going uphill against the tide, a tide I hadn't taken into consideration. It was running full force. There was a lot of traffic, big and small, so I tried hugging the Stanley Park side as close to the rocky shore as I dared, but kept getting swept into midchannel. Again, I had the engine wide open and we were crawling along being set one way and then the other. The West Vancouver ferry came barreling toward us hooting for room. I put the wheel over but our progress was so sluggish I was convinced he would cut us in two. He went growling by with only yards to spare. I could see the passengers staring blankly at us from inside. Once through the gap the tide was not so muscular, but there was a lot of water traffic to look out for.

I watched the docks and the railroad yards drift by. I knew them intimately from the shore side, but it was the first time I had really seen them from the water. At the Second Narrows, I again had to go full throttle, but that was the last. From there to the government wharf in Port Moody was easy.

As we snugged *Monad* home to the floats my mind, for no apparent reason, went harking back a few years, back to the wheelhouse aboard *Capilano*. I remembered back to the familiar brass handles of the engineroom telegraph that stuck up like ears over the big round dial just to the right of the steering wheel, and with which "finished with engines" would have been rung down. Ours had not been an epic journey, but it would be one I would remember.

Down at the dock, I lived aboard for three weeks while Pete wooed prospective buyers. Since I hadn't anything pressing, I had agreed to look after *Monad*. until she was sold or for a couple of weeks, whichever came first. Pete had moved in with his mother, who lived in Port Moody, and when Olwyn arrived, about a week later, she moved in with them.

I kept the bilges pumped, slept late (so late one morning the water was up over the floorboards), read, dug clams from the tidal flats, jigged for ground fish and, whenever Pete brought a customer around, I fired up the Kermath and demonstrated *Monad*'s capabilities. One of them—I never found out which—bought her for an undisclosed sum. I moved to a hotel.

The pickup truck is old—1936 vintage. It was once dark blue, but the paint has oxidized to a pale powdery multihue. It has a dented righthand-side door and a starred windshield. The tires have only the remnants of tread. It is not a great truck, but it had two things that said "Buy me." Its six-cylinder engine had been recently overhauled and the price was right. At least it was within my means. I probably paid more than I should have, but I had never before bought a vehicle or even contemplated buying one, so I had nothing to go on and no one to advise me. However, it is doing what I want it to do and at the moment, that is what matters. In the back, covered with a tarp, are my tool box and three trunks.

It is hot. I have the windows rolled down, but the sun reflecting off the rocks of the Fraser Canyon is frying my unprotected left elbow that is protruding out the window. The heat is good. They say it is even hotter in the Okanagan. So that is where we are going— my truck and I.

Epilogue

My fear of abandoning Ocean Falls and re-entering a depressed outside world proved groundless. The atmosphere of the country had changed dramatically. The postwar boom was in full swing, driven by a hunger for consumer goods and the reconstruction going on in much of Europe. It was actually a very good time to cut loose from the rain-washed safe haven I had called home for ten years.

My truck—that, in my ignorance, was probably the worst vehicle I could have purchased—ground its way up the Fraser Canyon and, only by dint of sheer mechanical willpower, persevered through Ashcroft and Savona, and finally to the parking lot of the Leland Hotel in Kamloops. There it stalled with steam gushing from under its hood and oil dripping from its underparts to the pavement below.

"Where now?" I asked myself. It was a question to which I had no ready answer. Somewhere in the back of my mind, however, I recalled that Stan Lapham, a friend from Ocean Falls whom I had roomed with before the war, was now living in Kamloops and working for B.C. Power Commission. The following day I tracked him down at his workplace in the Kamloops Steam Plant, the major supplier of power for the region, where he was rebuilding an electrical substation.

"Say, they're looking for a hydroelectric powerhouse operator for the Barriere plant up on the North Thompson river, a summer relief operator," he said, after we had caught up on each other's activities. "Why don't you go and see Spencer Cox at the district office."

That was the best suggestion I've ever received.

The following day I was hired for the summer. I headed up the dusty North Thompson Highway in my truck that had received some hasty first-aid from a mechanic who had shaken his head and inquired if I had been drunk when I bought it.

I wore out the summer in Barriere and then, having traded my truck for an almost equally bad car, I headed north along Highway 16. I headed to where Stan, who had completed his work at the Kamloops steamplant, had gone to build small diesel generating stations, part of B.C. Power Commission's rural electrification program. I worked alongside Stan as a construction electrician for the winter in the communities of Vanderhoof, Burns Lake, Smithers and Hazelton. Then, in late spring, I was called back to Barriere to replace one of the operators who had quit.

In the meantime, Olwyn and Pete had established themselves on a farm in the Upper Louis Creek Valley, a distance of some twenty miles from Barriere. I visited them occasionally during the summer. After September my visits increased in frequency; I discovered that they were boarding a schoolteacher, Doreen Kozub—a young, green-eyed, blonde from Vernon, B.C., in her first year of teaching. She had come to open the rural school at Cahilty Creek.

The following spring, the word went out that the Barriere hydro plant was to be shut down. A new and substantially bigger plant had been constructed on the shores of the Arrow Lakes, at Needles, and the operators at Barriere were given first option to move there. It would be a permanent job, so I jumped at the chance. Being single and unencumbered, I was the first to be transferred. I was flown in to start up the plant (at that time the Monashee portion of Highway 6 was closed in winter and didn't reopen until May when the snow went off).

In September, 1951, Doreen transferred from Cahilty Creek to Fauquier, another one-room school, across the lake from Needles and the powerplant where I was working. That Christmas, when the school closed for the holiday, we drove to Vernon—by this time I had upgraded to a new 1950 model Chev Sedan—via Nakusp, Trail, Rossland, Washington State, Grand Forks, Penticton and

Kelowna. We were married on December 24, 1951, in the United Church on 27th Street, Reverend Payne officiating.

Our son, Stephen, was born the following October in Nakusp. Five years later, our daughter, Sydney, was born in August at the Red Cross outpost hospital at Edgewood.

During the period of 1951–58, I honed my skills as a hydro-electric powerhouse operator and took correspondence courses in electronics. Also in that period, I narrowly escaped being killed when successive mud and rock landslides that came roaring down the side of the mountain one week apart buried the powerhouse. I was on duty both times but was unscathed. The plant was rebuilt in a matter of months.

In the fall of 1958 I was moved to Vernon to become a communications technician. B.C. Power Commission had newly acquired a mobile radio system and needed someone to maintain it.

Our first years in Vernon were sometimes hectic. I was learning on the job, a job that took me as far as Ft. St. John, Kamloops, Merritt and into the Kootenays to Golden and Kimberly. At the same time we were building a house and raising a family; the latter task was left pretty much to Doreen, since I was away for weeks at a time. She handled it well.

B.C. Power Commission eventually became B.C. Hydro and continued to grow. I grew with it. I moved up from technician to foreman and then to supervisor. I was handed additional tasks not related to electronics. It was work I enjoyed immensely.

I retired in 1982 to travel, paint, write and become involved in community projects. These latter years have been some of my the most rewarding. Our roots have extended deeply into the fabric of the Vernon community and there is no thought of living elsewhere.

Father lived out his days in the Patricia Hotel on Vancouver's east side. He moved there after the war when George Mellors, his landlady's husband, came home from the army. His room, over-looking the alley, was furnished with a brown iron bed, a brown varnished dresser, a free-standing closet, a bedside table and a scrap of threadbare carpet on the floor. There was a washbasin but no toilet. The toilet and bath were down the hall. The light came from a single bulb in the middle of the ceiling and a small lamp by his bed, with a shade like an inverted flowerpot.

He visited me while I was living at Barriere, north of Kamloops, and again at Needles but only for a few weeks and in summer. As soon as winter threatened, he went back to Vancouver and the Patricia Hotel. He seemed more at home there than anywhere.

Later, he lived with Olwyn for a few months one summer, but where she and Pete were farming was remote and he soon tired of it. After that he refused to leave Vancouver. Owen, who was living in Langley, kept an eye on him.

He spent his days in the lower east side pubs, hotel lobbies and coffee shops, socialising with his cronies, elderly single men who dwelt in the same area and pursued the same lifestyle. He died, Christmas Day 1952 in Vancouver General Hospital at age sixty-six.

Olwyn and Pete married and went farming in the Upper Louis Creek Valley, north of Kamloops—a venture doomed from the outset.

They moved to Kamloops where Olwyn worked in retail stores: Wodlingers, Beatons and Woodwards. Pete worked as a school janitor.

They moved to Lantzville on Vancouver Island in1972, where Olwyn opened a small gift store that became so successful she opened two others, one in the Coast Bastion Hotel in Nanaimo, the other at Silva Bay on Gabriola Island. She died September 8, 1988, at age sixty-nine, having outlived Pete by eight years.

Owen left Ocean Falls in the summer of 1949. His eyesight, that had never been good and had kept him out of the forces during the war, had deteriorated to the point that he was unable to continue as a machinist—the trade he had learned in Ocean Falls. Instead, he went to work as a car salesman in New Westminster.

In 1953, he married Jean Perrin and moved to Langley where their four children were born. Later they moved to Penticton. Owen continued as a car salesman until his death in 1972; age forty-nine.

Mother, author, Father, Olwyn and Lynda,
Olwyn's daughter, Vancouver, 1942.

Index of People

Hancock House Publishers

Afloat in Time
James Sirois
ISBN: 0-88839-455-1
SC, 8.5" x 5.5", 288 pp.

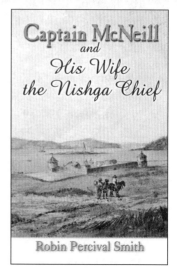

**Captain McNeill and His Wife
the Nishga Chief**
Robin Percival Smith
ISBN: 0-88839-472-1
SC , 8.5" x 5.5", 256 pp.

Dowager Queen
William A. Hagelund
ISBN: 0-88839-486-1
SC, 8.5" x 5.5", 168 pp.

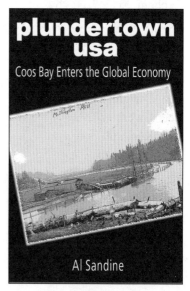

Plundertown USA
Al Sandine
ISBN: 0-88839-525-6
SC, 8.5" x 5.5", 176 pp.

The Best in the Northwest

hancock
house

Logging
Ed Gould
ISBN: 0-919654-44-4
HC, 11" x 8.5", 224 pp.

Big Timber Big Men
Carol Lind
ISBN: 0-88839-020-3
HC, 11" x 8.5", 160 pages

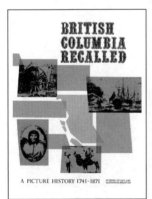

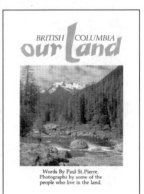

B.C. Recalled
Derek Pethick,
Susan Im Baumgarten
ISBN: 0-919654-12-6
SC, 11" x 8.5", 96 pp.

B.C.'s Own Railroad
Lorraine Harris
ISBN: 0-88839-125-0
SC, 8.5" x 5.5", 64 pp.

B.C. Our Land
Paul St. Pierre
ISBN: 0-919654-96-7
HC, 14" x 10", 160 pp.

Tlingit: Their Art and Culture
David Hancock
ISBN: 0-88839-530-2
SC, 8.5" X 5.5", 96 pp.

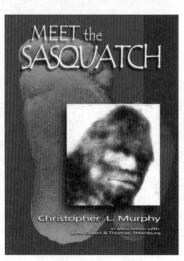

Meet the Sasquatch
Chris Murphy, John Green, Thomas Steenburg
ISBN: 0-88839-573-6
SC, 11" X 8.5", 256 pp.

The Best of Chief Dan George
Chief Dan George, Helmut Hirnschall
ISBN: 0-88839-544-2
SC, 8.5" X 5.5", 128 pp.

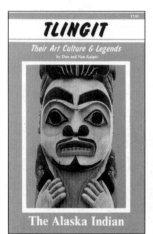

Tlingit: Their Art, Culture & Legends
Dan and Nan Kaiper
ISBN: 0-88839-010-6
SC, 8.5" X 5.5", 96 pp.

Raincoast Sasquatch
J. Robert Alley
ISBN: 0-88839-508-6
SC, 8.5" X 5.5", 360 pp.

Bald Eagle of Alaska, BC and Washington
David Hancock
ISBN: 0-88839-536-1
SC, 8.5" X 5.5", 96 pp.